REPPIN'

REPPIN'

Pacific Islander Youth and Native Justice

EDITED BY KEITH L. CAMACHO

UNIVERSITY OF WASHINGTON PRESS
Seattle

Composed in Minion Pro, typeface designed by Robert Slimbach

25 24 23 22 21   5 4 3 2 1

Printed and bound in the United States of America

UNIVERSITY OF WASHINGTON PRESS
uwapress.uw.edu

LIBRARY OF CONGRESS CATALOGING-IN-PUBLICATION DATA
Names: Camacho, Keith L., editor.
Title: Reppin' : Pacific Islander youth and native justice / edited by Keith L. Camacho.
Description: Seattle : University of Washington Press, [2021] | Includes bibliographical
    references and index.
Identifiers: LCCN 2020045481 (print) | LCCN 2020045482 (ebook) | ISBN 9780295748573
    (hardcover) | ISBN 9780295748580 (paperback) | ISBN 9780295748597 (ebook)
Subjects: LCSH: Youth—Oceania—Social conditions. | Pacific Islanders—Social conditions. |
    Internet and youth—Oceania. | Mass media and youth—Oceania. | Social justice—Oceania.
Classification: LCC HQ799.O24 R46 2021 (print) | LCC HQ799.O24 (ebook) |
    DDC 305.2350995—dc23
LC record available at https://lccn.loc.gov/2020045481
LC ebook record available at https://lccn.loc.gov/2020045482

The paper used in this publication is acid free and meets the minimum requirements of American National Standard for Information Sciences—Permanence of Paper for Printed Library Materials, ANSI Z39.48–1984.∞

CONTENTS

ACKNOWLEDGMENTS

This book is the product of labor, love, and laughter. Many people and programs supported the making of this anthology, including the Luskin Endowment for Thought Leadership. This foundation generously funded the Youth Studies in Oceania conference held on April 13, 2019, at the University of California, Los Angeles. In particular, Laura E. Gómez of the UCLA School of Law and the Social Sciences Division played a vital role in securing the Luskin award. Josephine Ong, a PhD student in gender studies, successfully co-organized the symposium. Additionally, the Institute of American Cultures; the Asian American Studies Center; the Asian American Studies Department; the Office for Equity, Diversity, and Inclusion; the International Institute; the Department of Musicology; and the Pacific Islands' Student Association co-sponsored the program. The University of Southern California's Department of American Studies and Ethnicity, the USC Pacific Islander Student Association, and the Pacific Island Ethnic Art Museum also promoted the gathering. Their guidance and participation partly served as the basis for this volume. Overall, though, this collection is largely informed by the Indigenous youth activists of Oceania. It is my modest attempt to feature some of their incredibly talented artists, educators, and organizers.

I also extend a heartfelt *si yu'us ma'åse* and thank you to Audrey Aofia Kawaiopua Alo, Cheyenne Aoelua, Ronia Auelua, Victor Bascara, Diane Bernardo, Alfred Bordallo, Melany de la Cruz-Viesca, Sandra Carbonell-Kiamtia, Keith Castro, Calvin Chang, Mei-Mei Chun-Moy, Tina DeLisle, Elizabeth DeLoughrey, Vicente Diaz, Kristine Espinoza, Vaka Faletau, Cindy Fan, Alfred Peredo Flores, Wendy Fujinami, Carol Fujino, Cindy Gagle, Mishuana Goeman, Heather Heleloa, Kristopher Kaupalolo, Lono Kollars, Annie Le, Betty Leung, Fran Lujan, Nancy Lutkehaus, Magele Vernon Mackenzie, Kyle T. Mays, Krista Mercado, Alex Muñoz, Tam Nguyen, Arnold Pan, Lenn Pereira, Heidi Quenga, Joey Quenga, Barbra Ramos, John Carlos Rowe, Kirisitina Sailiata, Kylin Sakamoto, Tavae Samuelu, Kelani Silk, Irene Soriano, Patricia Soung, Duc Ta, Ty Tengan, Christopher Tenorio, Karla Thomas, Victor Thompson, Meg Thornton, 'Alisi Tulua, Karen Umemoto, Chris Vaimili, Victor Viesca, Judy Wu, and David Yoo. I especially thank Nitasha Sharma for reviewing an earlier version of this manuscript and Josephine Ong for preparing the volume for publication. I thank, as well, the authors for their insights and inspiration. The students of the seminar AAS 222: Colonialism and Law in the Pacific deserve a shout-out too. I thank Megan Baker, Sarah Beggs, Kenneth Chan, Kapua Chandler, Christian Gella, Lauren Higa, Daniel Iwama, Elyse Izumi, Paul Mendoza, Edward Nadurata, Nicole Ngaosi, Jeronimo Ortega, Sarah Saokai, and Jessea Young.

In February and March 2020, my colleagues at Fulbright New Zealand and the University of Auckland provided me with the resources to complete this volume. I thank Melani Anae, Jesi Bennett, Betty Bernard, Penelope Borland, Pip Climo, Michelle Erai, Melissa Favreault, Jarrod Gilbert, Jack Gray, April Henderson, Jennifer Lee, Taylor Lee, Marcia Leenen-Young, Therese Lloyd, Sarita Magan, Malcom McKinnon, Denis O'Rourke, Sushila Pinto, Steven Ratuva, Albert Refiti, Jamie Robertson, David G. Schmale III, Tamasailau Suaalii-Sauni, Rory Taylor, Patrick Thomsen, Jemaima Tiatia-Seath, Yvonne Underhill-Sem, Julie Williams, and Magnolia Wilson. And how can I forget Jo and Maihi Diamond, Maryann Heather, Lou Pangelinan, Damon Salesa, Lisa Uperesa, and Tea Vadiga. They often fed and teased me during my time in Aotearoa. One day I will say more about Damon's shirtless cousin and entrepreneur, Jo's friendly neighbor with a flashy car, and Tea's role as the prime minister of all Pacific countries south of the equator.

Lastly, my biggest thanks go to my editor, Mike Baccam, of the University of Washington Press. He also has a great sense of humor and an even better eye for details. In fact, I have worked with many editors over the years, and Mike is one of the very best. At the University of Washington Press, I also want to thank the tri-campus press committee, Mellon Diversity Fellow Hanni Jalil, Julie Van Pelt, Alja Kooistra, the two anonymous reviewers, and other members of the editorial team for bringing everything together. Jason Pereira, a Sāmoan artist from Long Beach, California, designed the cover art, and David Martinez, a fellow football enthusiast like Jason and me, indexed the book. I thank them both. Of course, I cannot thank my 'aiga and familia enough for their support. Juliann Anesi, my partner, has likewise been very patient and understanding and is now writing her own book and more.

I wish everybody good health during the era of COVID-19. May we abolish, as well, the racism that has exasperated the growth of this pandemic in Oceania and globally. And may we continue to advance the many goals and contributions of Pacific Islander youth.

REPPIN'

REPPIN', ISLAND STYLE

KEITH L. CAMACHO

WHAT IS THE STATE OF YOUTH STUDIES IN OCEANIA? NOT SINCE the 1998 publication of Gilbert Herdt and Stephen C. Leavitt's volume *Adolescence in Pacific Island Societies* have there been substantial efforts to evaluate the study of Pacific Islander children, teenagers, and young adults.[1] Only Helen Lee's anthology, *Pacific Youth: Local and Global Futures*, released in 2019, has taken stock of this vital matter within the frameworks of anthropology and development studies.[2] Otherwise, a few articles, ethnographies, and memoirs have emerged, most of which remain pathological in their orientation.[3] That is to say, academics and government officials seldom question the colonial origins and politics of behavioral and developmental categories in Oceania. As their recent publications and public policies reveal, they increasingly define Pacific Islander youth in ways that strip them of their dignity and integrity. Spun in racial, spatial, and temporal terms, this pathology often racializes the youth as Black and Brown "criminals," spatially tethers them to the "blight" of cities, and temporally restricts them to the agency of "children."[4]

Moreover, the lack of robust debates across academic fields and national governments has led to the reification of youth as a diverse people not capable of producing intelligent thoughts. Pacific Islander youth now pose "risks" to themselves and "problems" to society, a modern phenomenon that arose from European forms of industrialization that made laborers out of children.[5] As a result, colonial and postcolonial countries across Oceania often mobilize this one-sided story of youth to morally justify, legally sanction, and economically profit from the criminalization and militarization of their bodies.⁶ If we wish to address these challenges, we must cultivate cross-regional, interdisciplinary, and trans-Indigenous approaches in our study of youth. Over the past twenty-five years, I have co-facilitated such conversations with Pacific Islander youth in Aotearoa New Zealand, Australia, California, Fiji, Guam, Hawaiʻi, Pohnpei, Saipan, Utah, and Washington. These discussions have emphasized academic advancement, ethnic representation, health education, and Indigenous self-determination.

In keeping with that focus, *Reppin': Pacific Islander Youth and Native Justice* features scholars who work closely with and for Pacific Islander youth. The contributors represent disciplines as many and varied as anthropology, education, ethnic studies, history, law, media studies, musicology, nursing, social work, and sociology. This interdisciplinarity allows us to examine our methodological and political stakes while stressing the unique and shared contributions of the Pacific Islander youth in our scholarship, as is shown in the volume's three parts. In part 1, Governance, Law, and Education, the contributors examine Māori youth courts in Auckland, Tongan storytelling in Salt Lake City, and homework study sessions in Melbourne. The chapters in part 2, Popular Culture, Social Media, and Hip Hop, examine ni-Vanuatu multimedia in Port Vila, Tongan social media and transnational identity, and Marshallese hip hop and spoken word poetry in Arkansas and internationally. In part 3, Indigenous Masculinities, authors explore Native Hawaiian beachboys in Honolulu, Sāmoan gang members in Auckland, Tongan *faikava* circles in Auckland and Salt Lake City, and Chuukese and Filipino bicycle organizers in Kalihi. Each of these ten chapters reveals how Pacific Islander youth continue to define and redefine themselves in white cities that would otherwise render them as deviant and disposable. Along these lines, we heed the education scholar Awad Ibrahim's expansive definition of youth "as action; as a performative category; as an identity that is both produced through and is producing our bodies and sense of self; as an agentive, ambiguous, fluid, shifting, multiple, complex, stylized, and forever becoming category."⁷

From this vantage point, the anthology makes two interventions. The foremost intervention concerns *Native youth* as a critical category of analysis in Oceania. Given the tremendous cultural, linguistic, and political diversity of the region, however, I do not presume to offer a comprehensive genealogy of Pacific Islander youth. I instead pursue a more modest endeavor here by briefly contextualizing how European missionaries naturalized Pacific Islander "children" as a label of control and conversion. I then analyze the subsequent behavioral and developmental category of *adolescence* that now distinguishes "youth" from "adults" in the region. But unlike other studies that polarize youth as either a deviant group or a liberated community, I foreground "critical" to underscore the radical systems of representation employed by the youth. As the contributors illustrate, neither the prevailing scholarship nor the Indigenous societies of Oceania take seriously the power and politics of the youth. Yet Pacific Islander youth have been creating new ideas, languages, and technologies as much as they have been appropriating, resisting, and transforming older ones. As the activist Angela Davis has astutely observed, "Those of us who are older have a great deal to learn from our younger sisters and brothers, who are in a better position than we are to develop the political vocabulary, the theory, and the strategies that can potentially move us forward."[8] To be clear, though, the qualifier *radical* does not simply include social movements for freedom, as suggested by Davis and other theorists.[9] By radical systems of representation, I also mean the ways in which Pacific Islander individuals, pan-ethnic communities, transnational collectives, and virtual identities present and re-present themselves as "youth" who variously resist and survive colonialism, gentrification, incarceration, militarism, and postcolonial governance in and beyond Oceania.

The youth understand these circumstances because they—and not us—radically fashion the concepts, signs, and things that lie at the heart of their production of meaning.[10] Toward this effect, I selected *Reppin'* as the volume's title to represent the vital roles that Pacific Islander youth have played in shaping the cities of Oceania and the diaspora. As the scholar Halifu Osumare eloquently put it, representing entails "the process of taking on the mantle from the past in the present moment. It also connotes responsibility to one's present context—crew, family, and community."[11] This responsibility likewise applies to the contributors of this volume, many of whom acknowledge the profound influence of Black English and other Black cultural expressions among Pacific Islander youth. After all, reppin' signals the youth's appropriation of the visceral bodily appeal, aesthetics, and urban proximity of Black hip hop, a major theme in these chapters.[12] Herein lies the second intervention of this volume: namely, the manner by which *Native cities* serve as critical sites of analysis in Oceania. Given that second-, third-, and fourth-generation Pacific Islander communities now reside in cities, the contributors call our attention to their participation in the cultural, educational, legal, political, religious, and social spaces of Aotearoa New Zealand, Australia, Hawai'i, the Kingdom of Tonga, the Marshall Islands, Sāmoa, Vanuatu, and the United States.

At the same time, the contributors advise against drawing hard distinctions between the false binary of urban and rural landscapes. Nevertheless, they recognize that Pacific Islander youth often perceive style and swagger as uniquely urban phenomena even though the youth traverse the multiple physical and virtual worlds of Oceania and the diaspora. In the second part of this introduction, I survey the making of cities in the region and examine how their colonial governments racialized Pacific Islander youth as "problems" of society. I then show how the city of Los Angeles has projected urban fantasies about fashion, media, and music that have attracted young audiences since the mid-twentieth century. As in Los Angeles, colonial officials, pastors, and traders carved cities out of Pacific Islander landscapes, established Christian missions, indentured Asian and Indigenous laborers, built railroads and roads, and excluded nonwhites altogether. For these reasons, several of the contributors problematize the taken-for-granted nature of cities as white, urban, and cosmopolitan by foregrounding the Native peoples upon whose lands these cities have been violently built and touted as civilized and modern.

This Native-to-Native acknowledgment in *Reppin'* not only emphasizes the dialectic of Native youth and Native cities but, above all, also seeks to advance social justice methodologies, programs, and theories across the region. With the continued colonization, incarceration, and militarization of Pacific Islander youth, the stakes could not be greater. Indeed, they often bear the brunt of corporate, familial, religious, and state violence in the Native cities of Oceania and the diaspora. On the surface, the youth appear as commodified athletes, dogmatic preachers, expendable sex workers, pubescent soldiers, or uninsured laborers. But, as the contributors here reveal, Pacific Islander youth contest these racial, spatial, and temporal classifications. This anthology thus features their incredibly rich perceptions about marginalization and oppression, on the one hand, and their impassioned calls for collective healing, individual rights, and social justice, on the other. I call this sensibility "island style," a critical framework that allows the contributors to *rep* youth-inspired narratives about identity, place, and power.

NATIVE YOUTH AS A CRITICAL CATEGORY OF ANALYSIS

In Oceania, the colonial category of youth originated with the rise of Christianity in the sixteenth century to the late nineteenth century. The island of Guam, also known as Guåhan in the indigenous Chamorro vernacular, recorded the first landfall of Catholic missionaries in the late sixteenth century. Shipwrecked priests and sailors then began to informally spread Catholicism to the Chamorros of Guam. But it would take another hundred years for the religion to become immersed in Chamorro views of the body, land, and spirit. As the primary proponents for Catholicism in Guam and the wider Marianas archipelago, the Jesuit missionaries identified "children" as potential converts because of their perceived innocence, impressionable personalities, and connections to older and more powerful relatives. Their principal missionary, Padre Diego Luis de San Vitores, set out to attract Chamorro children and make Catholics out of them. Of Padre San Vitores's penchant for youth, the Filipino-Pohnpeian critic Vicente M. Diaz had this to say: "No doubt because [San Vitores] always had little presents and sweets for them, the children also followed San Vitores from village to village, and in time San Vitores seized on the idea to organize contests among them involving the recitation of the doctrines."[13] In April 2, 1672, Padre San Vitores then baptized a newborn from the coastal village of Tomhom in Guam. It was one of his many baptisms. But San Vitores never received approval from the father, Matå'pang. Upon his arrival at the beach and upon his realization of what had taken place, Matå'pang and his friend, Hirao, attacked and killed San Vitores and his Filipino assistant, Pedro Calongsor. Matå'pang then disrobed San Vitores, placed him in a canoe, and cast his body into the sea.

In early-nineteenth-century Hawai'i, Protestant missionaries similarly targeted youth for conversion. Recognizing that Native Hawaiians or Kānaka Maoli collectively raised their children, the missionaries also found that childcare was not viewed as a concern for mothers and females.[14] Still, missionaries sought to impose their models for fathers, mothers, and children by way of schools and scriptures. Once again, they utilized children as a convenient proxy for exerting their patriarchy, domesticity, and discipline. As the anthropologists Margaret Jolly and Martha Macintyre explain, "Missions in all areas disapproved of the ways in which children were nurtured, seeing parental engagement with children as deficient or lacking in discipline."[15] In Sāmoa, the missionaries likewise demarcated the gendered and religious boundaries of the white nuclear family, with an emphasis on the subordination of wives and children. As Latu Latai notes, the "missionaries encouraged monogamous marriage and the idea of a nucleated family consisting exclusively of father, mother and their children." Latai continues, "Samoan women were taught to be proper Christian wives to their husbands and good mothers to their children. Special classes were conducted to teach how to best do domestic chores and how to bring up children."[16] Across the board, missionaries found in Pacific Islander children the moral, physical, and religious means by which they could advance Christianity and suppress Indigenous practices.

As citizens of their home countries in Europe and North America, the missionaries also brought their ideas about industrialization to the atolls, islands, and mountains of Oceania. As their churches and missions grew, so too did their capacity to influence Native leaders, colonize Native lands, and develop cities for American and European citizens, a matter I explain in greater detail below. Nevertheless, the missionaries frequently struggled to define "youth" in Oceania and elsewhere. As the sociologist Chris Brickell notes, Europeans often perceived "boys" as not having the strength and mental capacity to conduct physical labor.[17] Men only became adults at the age of twenty-one when they possessed these abilities; in the nineteenth century, everybody else that fell under this age bracket was considered a youth or a boy. As a result, missionaries and other Europeans rarely described girls as "youth," an "exclusion that reflected their ongoing domestic dependence on others, whether as daughters, wives or workers."[18] By the turn of the twentieth century, youth had clearly emerged as a colonial and social category for the missionaries and their industrialized countries of Europe and North America. Boys were youth, and girls were non-youth.

But as labor laws and educational reform sought to prohibit child employment, youth subsequently "became a policy question and a life stage that requires an age range, descriptors, and psychological attributes."[19] This arbitrary age division reflected a manipulation about and an intergenerational struggle over power in industrialized countries.[20] As Ibrahim discerns, "It is manipulation because 'adults' seem to talk about 'youth' as if it were a social unit, with common interests, strengths, and weaknesses at a biologically defined age. It is an intergenerational power struggle because the current negative media representation of young people as dangerous social beings and the resultant moral panic represent the side/site of more powerful and older generations."[21] Expanding upon this transition between "childhood" and "adulthood," the scholar Sunaina Marr Maira states that this "notion of in-betweenness and instability is at the heart of the ambivalence with which youth are often associated and the exceptionalism that sometimes overdetermines this category. Youth are assumed to fall between the cracks of 'innocent' childhood and 'stable' adulthood, dangerously outside of normative social structures and always teetering on the brink of revolt."[22] For the early missionaries of Oceania, youth invoked comparable structures of childhood and adulthood. Yet the missionaries lacked the global influence and reach of anthropologists who sought to study youth in "faraway" villages and who aimed to elevate their brand of empiricism about childhood behaviors in Oceania.

The idea of adolescence—otherwise understood as the childhood-to-adulthood transition as described by Ibrahim and Maira—proved especially appealing for a number of anthropologists. While they agreed that humans share common biological structures, such as the increase in hormones and the accompanying physical changes that come with puberty, they differed in how they determined the scales of "intelligence" and the types of adolescence among "civilized" and "primitive" cultures.[23] Many anthropologists already concurred that Pacific Islanders came from primitive societies. As such, the anthropologists' eugenic theories often represented Pacific Islanders as not having the intellectual abilities of whites. On the matter of adolescence, however, they debated the degree by which biological determinism and cultural relativism shaped the transitions between childhood and adulthood in Oceania. As the anthropologists Herdt and Leavitt note, "Early studies of adolescence in the Pacific took the relative influence of biology and culture as a central theme in understanding adolescence. Margaret Mead and Bronisław Malinowski had to argue against views that deemed biology decisive in defining adolescent experience."[24] More than any other work, Margaret Mead's 1928 publication of *Coming of Age in Samoa: A Psychological Study of Primitive Youth for Western Civilization* asserted the value of cultural relativism among the general public and became one of the most cited texts about Oceania.

In 1925, Mead questioned whether or not adolescence was a universal—that is to say, a biological—stage of life or if it was determined by culture and society. She asked, "What is there in Samoa which is absent in America, and what is there in America which is absent in Samoa, which will account for this difference [in adolescence]?"[25] In her ethnography of Sāmoan girls on the Sāmoan island of Taʻu, Mead answered this question by showing that adolescence did not exist as a "stage" for Sāmoan girls. She thus challenged the scientific truth of eugenic theories of race and racial development. By suggesting that Sāmoan girls participated in a wide range of heterosexual and homosexual activities, Mead provocatively represented Sāmoans as a society that possessed few sexual restraints. Unlike adolescents in the United States who frequently faced moral dilemmas, as with the independent character of "flappers" who sought to transgress gender norms, Mead argued that Sāmoan girls rarely encountered such behavioral predicaments. As she expressed, "The Samoan child faces no such dilemma. Sex is a natural, pleasurable thing; the freedom with which it may be indulged in is limited by just one consideration, social status."[26] With this thesis, Mead greatly shaped anthropology, psychology, and public policy in the twentieth century. But she not only focused on Sāmoan girls per se. Rather, Mead identified the girls of New York City, the Occident, and rural Indiana—that is, her spatially coded language for white girls—as maintaining the ability to experience sexually free lives and to pursue careers beyond the household. However, Mead also implied that the "primitive" Sāmoan girls simply experienced sex as "play." Their political horizon was limited to Sāmoa and not to the American and Atlantic worlds of white mobility from which Mead drew her authority and notoriety.

Given Mead's global prominence, one would assume that analyses of Pacific Islander youth would quickly emerge after Mead made her mark in the 1930s. However, very few anthropologists have studied Pacific Islander adolescence since that period. Herdt and Leavitt suggest that the topic "had been dormant, even nonexistent, except for occasional ethnographic pieces scattered in monographs" from the 1950s to the 1980s.[27] With the exception of adolescent psychology, they speculate that the relative absence of such studies stemmed from the "decline of developmental perspectives in anthropology following the demise of culture and personality studies, especially those anchored in the Freudian tradition."[28] For this reason, their book, *Adolescence in Pacific Island Societies*, treated Pacific Islander youth as a complex and liminal demographic influenced by cultural, psychological, and even historical factors, notably colonialism and postcolonialism. In these ways, they nodded toward the potential for articulating Native youth as a critical category of analysis in Oceania. Acknowledging the significance of youth formations, Herdt and Leavitt recognized that young people "have the most direct exposure to agents of social change, such as schools, technological innovations, and popular culture. It could be argued that they therefore play a disproportionately large role in defining how social changes will be constructed locally."[29] Following their lead, the contributors of Lee's anthology, *Pacific Youth*, align with these sentiments. As the volume's first chapter states, the study of youth can reveal how they "experience challenges of citizenship, civic engagement and personal development."[30] Yet these volumes do not flag a common structural parochialism in the humanities and social sciences, namely, the age bias in what constitutes normative subjects of study. This euphemism for "adults" endures today.

In this respect, the dearth of studies about adolescence in Oceania can be partly attributed to the age bias in the academy and to the trends in anthropology and psychology. Overall, though, studies about youth are generally few and far between. When they do surface, as with research about youth resistance, they tend to follow a masculinist thread. As the scholars Eve Tuck and K. Wayne Yang assert, research about "youth resistance is often masculinized, theorized through and onto the male body— when it is theorized through women's bodies, it is specific to their bodies, made un-universal."[31] Of the ten chapters in this volume, six explicitly focus on Pacific Islander masculinities, itself a vital contribution and understandable limitation in light of the broader research about youth. Four chapters offer more balance in terms of gender representation. New work by and about nonheteronormative youth should therefore inform critical youth studies.[32] At the same time, I cannot overstate the importance of examining Pacific Islander boys and other youth in the heavily militarized and policed areas of Oceania where they are lauded for their perceived athleticism and damned for their supposed criminality.[33] Of course, the contributors and I do not imply that the youth should not be held accountable for their actions, as with the harming of people. As Stella Black, Jacquie Kidd, and Katey Thom reveal in their analysis of ngā Kōti Rangatahi (Māori youth courts) in chapter 1, an increasing number of Māori youth utilize the ngā Kōti Rangatahi to reconnect with their relatives, address injuries, and seek justice. By drawing on the mana (power) of marae-based youth courts, they show how the Māori customs and protocols of the marae can help Māori youth compassionately restore their identities and genealogies.

Given this survey of youth as a colonial category in Oceania, coupled with the promising research of the Indigenous and non-Indigenous scholars presented in this volume, how, I ask, might we advance Native youth as a critical category of analysis? In the remaining parts of this section, I offer a methodology by which we can address this inquiry. The first move would acknowledge the plurality of Native youth identities and their ever-changing agencies, contributions, and performances. Presently, the United Nations defines youth as individuals between fifteen and twenty-four years old and estimates that youth make up 18 percent of the global population, or more than one billion people.[34] In Oceania, some countries classify youth as being fifteen to thirty-four years of age, as with the national policies of the Cook Islands, the Federated States of Micronesia, Nauru, Niue, and the Republic of Palau.[35] Overall, the ages for youth range from twelve to thirty-four across the region. Otherwise, most countries in Oceania define youth in conflict with the law as seventeen or eighteen years and older; anybody that falls under this age bracket is normally considered a "juvenile." In each case, Pacific Islander youth "may be individuals who are unmarried, financially dependent, not working or even those whose parents are still alive."[36] With this rubric, the age of youth can reach the forties, an age threshold that contradicts the canonical views of adolescence. In fact, the fluid definitions of youth in Oceania actually reflect their countries' efforts to meet the customs and obligations of locales and regions.

Nowhere is this sensibility more apparent than in the general expectation that Pacific Islander youth respect their elders. Across the region, many societies uphold their elders, knowing that they embody the chiefly, genealogical, material, sacred, and supernatural worlds of the lands, skies, and seas. In Sāmoa, for instance, the children acknowledge the prestige bestowed upon their elders. Very seldom, though, do the children receive such accolades and authority. As one Sāmoan put it, "Children are not heard, nor seen."[37] Moreover, children—like other members of a nuʻu, or a village—support the overall well-being and high status of the chiefs. As the sociologists Cluny Macpherson and Laʻavasa Macpherson explain, "Samoan culture prescribes for adolescents a period in which they are expected to serve (*tautua*), not challenge, those who hold power over them. Adolescents are told that service is the path to power: *o le ala ile pule ole tautua*."[38] In the Republic of Palau, the youth similarly extol their elders.[39] As the anthropologist Rachana Agarwal elaborates, "Unconditional deference toward elders is a hallmark of the social norm and it grants mature adults and the elderly unrestricted authority over the conduct of young Palauans."[40]

However, these hierarchies differ in their meaning and application, as in Aotearoa New Zealand, where, the legal scholars Alison Cleland and Khylee Quince argue, age does not play a significant determinant in the Māori social order. Specifically, Cleland and Quince note that the relationships between children and adults are "not linear or hierarchal in the sense of the Western notion of family. Hierarchy of status may be attributed to different levels of mana between persons or kinship groups, but this is not dependent on age."[41] As they observe, a child "born to a high-ranking lineage is senior to those of lower lineage, irrespective of age."[42] In their indirect critique of adolescence as a colonial category of youth, Cleland and

Quince also state, "While physical development will see a child mature into adulthood, the framework of relationships remains the same—a person is always a mokopuna (grandchild) and always a child of the whānau [family]. People do not 'grow out' of their childhood in the way that Western concepts imply."[43]

As these examples illustrate, Pacific Islander youth occupy a range of ages and subject positions within their societies. But I would be naïve to suggest that one's deference to an elder would guarantee a harmonious relationship between two or more individuals and groups. Given that many youth do not speak when they convene in private and public circles with their elders, practitioners and theorists of critical youth studies must learn how to navigate these spaces in order to highlight the marginalized perspectives of young people.[44] They should likewise discern what constitutes Native deference, obligation, and respect as well as possess the ability to recognize elderly abuse and familial violence more generally whenever they operate under the guise of such terms. For instance, in chapter 3, Vaoiva Ponton evaluates homework study groups in Melbourne, Australia. In her research, she followed Sāmoan cultural protocols, respectfully engaged the mothers of the girls featured, and ensured that the youth also met their obligations. In the process, the youth spoke candidly about the opportunities and challenges posed by fa'aSāmoa (Sāmoan customs) and high school education in Melbourne. As with other Pacific Islander youth in Australia, the Sāmoan teenagers also felt alienated from the latter's curricula. For our purposes, Ponton nicely shows how an educator like herself can adhere to the norms of fa'aSāmoa and still constructively analyze said customs without belittling or embarrassing the youth and their families.

The ways in which Ponton addressed the relative exclusion of Sāmoan students in the high schools of Melbourne also proves instructive for our criticisms of institutions writ large. Critical youth studies would thus encourage new research about the institutionalization of youth in Oceania as well as support youth-inspired policies across local and regional institutions. While this proposition resembles a paradox, the sheer diversity of the colonial and postcolonial Pacific would demand that research projects and public policies regarding youth follow site-specific and multi-sited approaches. Clearly, these initiatives would complement and contradict one another, an outcome that would be expected but nevertheless analyzed in light of the competing interests. With regard to funding schemes, governments, nongovernmental organizations, and universities must increase their annual allocations to the preexisting and already poorly funded programs. Although AusAID, the US Department of Interior, and the World Bank substantially subsidize agricultural, commercial, educational, and employment programs in Oceania, all of the countries in the region agree on one point: youth receive the least funding.[45] As one report in 2011 indicated, the national youth ministries of the Pacific are "notoriously under-funded."[46]

In terms of the research projects, academics could analyze the industrialization of young transient agricultural workers; the military recruitment of boys, girls, and transgender individuals; the psychiatric housing of foster children; the teaching of homophobic principles in churches; and the commodification of young football and rugby players, among other topics. Critiques of white supremacy and Indigenous hegemony should also figure prominently. Indeed, we know much about the criminalization of Aboriginal youth; the incarceration of disabled girls of color; and the older usage of eugenic theories in K–12 instruction in Canada, the United States, and elsewhere.[47] But we have yet to disaggregate data about the Pacific Islander populations of Australia and the United States; to date, this information remains obscure or altogether nonexistent.[48]

Nor have we developed extensive studies about comparable institutions in Oceania. In Hawai'i, for instance, Sāmoan youth, ages ten to seventeen, represented 12.5 percent to 100 percent of murder arrests for the years 1991 to 2000.[49] Native Hawaiian youth also disproportionately outnumber Sāmoan youth in such correctional facilities, demonstrating the punitive reach of the state among Native Hawaiians and Sāmoans alike.[50] Recognizing the colonial nature of these prisons, the scholars Katherine Irwin and Karen Umemoto assert that the "underlying institutional problem here is that we do not have a justice system that is, broadly speaking, restorative—one that helps to restore the well-being of the survivors of violence, the victim's loved ones, the perpetrators of harm, and the broken relationships resulting from such events."[51] In this respect, a critical youth studies approach would cultivate restorative ways to address the actions of Native youth while welcoming alternative solutions to the state-sanctioned violence of militaries, prisons, schools, and other institutions.[52]

In her ethnography of the Kalihi Valley Instructional Bicycle Exchange program (KVIBE) in chapter 10, Demiliza Saramosing explores one community alternative to the often hostile environments of schools in Hawai'i. With her focus on Chuukese and Filipino boys in Kalihi, a district of Honolulu, she shows how KVIBE's curriculum of bicycling and popular education has fostered a strong sense of belonging for the youth. In this regard, Saramosing demonstrates how the youth authored inspiring narratives about their bodies, connected to Native Hawaiian genealogies of Kalihi, and organized public policies about the making of safe streets in Honolulu. Above all, Native youth as a critical category of analysis in Oceania would be meaningless without the active participation, reflection, and contestation of Pacific Islander youth themselves.

Given that the contributors in this volume work closely with many Pacific Islander youth, appreciation of and compassion for young people appear in every chapter. But only chapter 2 by Kepa 'Ōkusitino Maumau, Moana 'Ulu'ave-Hafoka, and Lea Lani Kinikini features a young Pacific Islander lead author. As the principal investigator, Maumau represents a new generation of Tongan writers and illustrators who seek to abolish the mass incarceration of young Tongans and other young people of color and Indigenous youth in the United States. In their chapter, Maumau, 'Ulu'ave-Hafoka, and Kinikini offer Tongan forms of storytelling as a way to address the judicial murder of Siale Maveni Angilau, a young Tongan man who was murdered by a federal marshal during a trial in 2014. But rather than normalize Salt Lake City, the site of the case, as US property, they foreground indigenous Ute notions of the place, criticize the settler violence of US law, and provide new directions in the study of Tongan youth and in the advancement of justice, seen and unseen.

NATIVE CITIES AS CRITICAL SITES OF ANALYSIS

Given that the US government, news organizations, and sport teams regularly disavow American Indian communities, what factors compelled Maumau, 'Ulu'ave-Hafoka, and Kinikini to acknowledge the indigenous Ute in the settler United States? What motivated Tongans, as well, to migrate to Salt Lake City in the first place? Did they anticipate that its police and courts would racially profile their youth as criminals? Spatially place them in the low socioeconomic areas of the city? And temporally prosecute them as "adults" for offenses they committed (or did not commit) as "children"?

These questions can be explored by tracing the development of cities in Oceania and highlighting the migration patterns of Pacific Islanders after World War II. Pacific Islander youth increasingly became associated with urban landscapes, with Los Angeles, in particular, figuring in their popular imaginations. As the chapter by Maumau, 'Ulu'ave-Hafoka, and Kinikini illustrates, a growing number of Tongans and other Pacific Islanders recognize cities as Native sites from which to expose settler colonialism and cultivate Native-to-Native relations.[53] On the matter of settler colonialism, Patrick Wolfe has described this historically fraught structure as the "elimination of natives" for the purposes of resource extraction, labor exploitation, and monetary gain.[54] Expanding upon his definition, the historian Kelly Lytle Hernández argues that settler colonialism enables colonists to "envision building a new, permanent, reproductive, and racially exclusive society. To be clear, settlers harbor no intentions of merging with, submitting to, or even permanently lording over the Indigenous societies already established within the targeted land base."[55] "Rather," she continues, "settlers invade in order to stay and reproduce while working in order to remove, dominate, and, ultimately, replace the Indigenous populations."[56]

In the second intervention of this volume, several contributors peel off the veneer of settler colonialism and illuminate Native cities as vital locations from which to advance critical youth studies in Oceania. Although the authors do not closely analyze Pacific Islander perceptions of and relations with Aboriginal Australians, American Indians, and other Indigenous communities, they gesture toward more sustained conversations about these topics. In this regard, many of them approach, as I do, Native cities by way of trans-Indigenous acknowledgment and recognition. As Vicente M. Diaz explains, trans-indigeneity, broadly construed, means the "claims and conditions of aboriginal belonging to specific places."[57] In light of ongoing Indigenous struggles to assert their politics, reclaim their lands, and forge their futures, Diaz contends that trans-indigeneity reminds "us that where we stand is always on indigenous land, waters, and skyways. And that indigenous lands, waters, and skyways on and for which we stand are also never so separated, so compartmentalized from each other, as they have long been conceptualized and managed so in colonial discourse."[58] The making of cities in Oceania is a case in point.

As previously noted, missionaries proselytized "children" for a number of religious reasons, efforts that, in fact, had informed their colonization of space. The urban landscapes of the region now owe their existence to the presence of missionaries and colonial governments. For instance, the Chamorro leader, Maga'låhi Kepuha, gifted land from the village of Hagåtña, Guam, to Padre San Vitores in 1668. The priest died four years later, but his spatial creation, a church, grew into a city for subsequent American and Japanese colonial administrators who had a fondness for flying flags. Honolulu also became a city for churches, as did Apia in

Sāmoa. Reflecting on these spatial arrangements, the urban development scholar Paul Jones has examined how these missions and towns evolved into cities. He writes, "The spatial expression of Pacific towns was often led by a surveyor or governor, with town layouts based on variations of an underlying grid pattern imposed on the prevailing geographical landscape."[59] "Importantly," Jones argues, "the physical form of ports and the introduction of planning and building regulations based around promenades, open spaces, public buildings, and squares . . . had more to do with the needs and aspirations of foreign civilizations than with a sound understanding of the social and economic needs of the indigenous population."[60]

Colonial governments then imposed various land laws and policies to advance their economic, military, and political control and to displace Indigenous communities throughout the region. These governments likewise placed travel curfews and restrictions on Indigenous visitors and workers, thereby ensuring that these cities remained the exclusive domain of white elites.[61] As Frantz Fanon has compellingly shown, colonial cities in Africa, the Caribbean, and elsewhere have similarly cast out nonwhite bodies, if not subjected them to slavery or indentured labor. Reflecting on how Blacks have experienced the psychological, racial, and spatial violence of cities, he said, "In the white world, the man of color encounters difficulties in elaborating his body schema. The image of one's body is solely negating. It's an image in the third person. All around the body reigns an atmosphere of certain uncertainty."[62] Using the example of reaching for a pack of cigarettes on a table, Fanon then carefully calculated how he would reach for the cigarettes, move other parts of his body, and locate the matches in a nearby drawer. "And I make all these moves," he theorized, "not out of habit, but by implicit knowledge. A slow construction of my self as a body in a spatial and temporal world—such seems to be the schema. It is not imposed on me; it is rather a definitive structuring of my self and the world—definitive because it creates a genuine dialectic between my body and the world."[63]

In *Tahiti beyond the Postcard: Power, Place, and Everyday Life*, the anthropologist Miriam Kahn demonstrates how the French utilized comparable tactics to transform Pape'ete, Tahiti, into a city that resembled the racial codes, spatial dimensions, and visual perceptions of Paris. Originally a site for missionaries, French colonists reshaped Pape'ete into an area that suited its economic and military interests. As Kahn explains, "The French colonial administration inhabited and redefined space in

Pape'ete as part of its strategy of expansion and production of capital. It linked transportation networks, established sites of capital accumulation, invested in urbanization projects, and orchestrated everyday life.... Pape'ete, like most colonial cities, was a distinctly colonial phenomenon—a place where the *métropole* and colony intersected, and a site for the *métropole* to reproduce life in the colony."[64] As Kahn shows, French settlers later utilized Pape'ete to sexualize Tahitian bodies and militarize Tahitian lands. Youth and adults alike have contested these political and social matters; the *raerae*, or transgender individuals, for example, have been featured in debates about sodomy laws and in legislation about gay marriage.[65] Yet some Tahitian families stigmatize *raerae* who labor at nightclubs and engage in sex work in Pape'ete. Furthermore, they are not considered as "culturally authentic" and as community oriented as their counterparts, the *māhū*. The *raerae* also occupy marginal subjectivities because of their association with street activities and affinity for Western fashion.[66]

The *raerae* are not exceptional in their desire to live in French colonial cities like Pape'ete. According to a policy report funded by the United Nations Children's Fund, Pacific Islander youth frequently "equate urban life with 'freedom' and a release from the expectations of rural and island life."[67] As with Pape'ete, the urban space of Suva, the capital of Fiji, has attracted an increasing number of youth from the villages of the Fijian archipelago. Feeling less bound by cultural expectations, the youth pursue higher education and formal employment, including "hawking, setting up side street markets, shining shoes and pushing wheelbarrows."[68] At the same time, many youth often struggle with the limited spaces afforded by the adult-centric, colonial, and racially segregated areas of cities, as do some *raerae* who live in the bush or under bridges.[69] They are thus subjected to the spatial violence of cities and settler colonialism and generally lack the support and supervision of their extended familial networks.[70] A critical youth studies approach would thereby unpack the urbanization of cities as a historical and ongoing project of settler colonialism as well as consider youth formations as mutually constitutive of these processes. In chapter 7, the Kanaka Maoli historian Alika Bourgette shows how the US print media represented the spatial layout of early-twentieth-century Waikīkī as a beach exclusively made for heterosexual clients. However, by focusing on the oral histories of Native Hawaiian gangs and beachboys, he not only taps into the youths' profoundly Indigenous, playful, and mischievous world but also demonstrates that some young Native Hawaiian beachboys found in the Waikīkī tourist industry opportunities to resist racial prejudices, protect their beaches, and negotiate homosocial leisure.

Today, the Asian Development Bank (ADB) identifies twenty-two cities in Oceania based on their annual contributions to local and regional economies, such as with agriculture, fisheries, and remittances.[71] Specifically, they list Melanesia, Micronesia, and Polynesia, the colonial and postcolonial subregions that define Oceania as a geopolitical entity of the sea. In chapter 4, Thomas Dick and Sarah Doyle examine youth multimedia in Port Vila, Vanuatu. As do South Tarawa in Kiribati and Mata-Utu in Wallis and Futuna, Port Vila constitutes one of the region's postcolonial cities. With an emphasis on ni-Vanuatu youth involvement in Nesar Studio, a media production facility, Dick and Doyle examine how the youth negotiate various obligations while leveraging opportunities to produce multimedia. In this respect, they theorize "screen sovereignty" as the manner by which the youth generate films and photos about Port Vila. In doing so, they show how the youth develop new terms about the media in Bislama, the lingua franca of Vanuatu. As in other areas of Melanesia, the youth of Port Vila have been the trendsetters in communicating and mainstreaming novel ideas, stories, and technologies across diverse ethnolinguistic groups.[72]

But while Dick and Doyle address the movement of ni-Vanuatu youth in Port Vila and its neighboring areas, the ADB excludes the cities of Australia and New Zealand even though Pacific Islanders participate in their economies. To situate these countries in wider historical perspective would account, as well, for their colonization of Indigenous communities in Niue, Papua New Guinea, Sāmoa, and elsewhere. Contrary to popular opinions about Australia not counting as a "Pacific" country, Australia is very much tied to the region, as evidenced by the Māori, Sāmoans, and Tongans who reside in New South Wales, Queensland, and Victoria.[73] Earlier descendants of Melanesian indentured laborers have also established homes in these areas. As for New Zealand, the historian Damon Salesa has described it as "becoming more Pacific by the hour," a reference to its growing demographic of young Pacific Islanders.[74] As the contributors demonstrate, they, too, seek to redefine "Oceania" as encompassing more than the cities listed by the ADB. They subsequently examine settler colonialism in some way or offer new approaches for the study of youth identity and mobility in London, Tokyo, and further afar.[75]

While the migrations patterns of Oceania have ebbed and flowed for thousands of years, World War II played a fundamental role in shaping

Pacific Islander mobility from the mid- to late twentieth century. The sudden and rapid manufacturing of airplanes, cars, munitions, and weapons required the labor of new workers, including African Americans from southern states and women more generally, in cities across the western United States. Mass production of automobiles and planes also lowered the costs for travel, a luxury that before the war was limited to middle- and upper-class communities. Additionally, cities across the Americas, Australia, and Europe began to accommodate greater numbers of immigrant and refugee communities who were fleeing wartime persecution and violence. In Oceania, the fall of Japan's empire also led to the formal dissolution, realignment, or establishment of colonial governments. Following in the wake of the war's industrial growth in cities, its recalibration of political boundaries, and its democratization of mass travel, many Pacific Islanders subsequently migrated to cities in Aotearoa New Zealand and the United States. In the former, internal movement also occurred, as with the Māori communities of Panguru who found employment in Auckland in the 1950s.[76]

The New Zealand government inaugurated programs to "assimilate" the Māori as nuclear family units into the limited work opportunities afforded by the Pākehā (whites) of Auckland. Yet, as the Māori historian Melissa Matutina Williams argues in *Panguru and the City*, this postwar resettlement campaign actually extended earlier efforts by the Pākehā to "detribalize" the Māori and to sever their ties to their families and lands. The Māori migration to the predominately white city of Auckland was not new in this regard. But rather than focus on the pathology of its Māori residents as young, poor, and uneducated, Williams encourages us to appreciate and examine the body language, humor, and knowledge of Panguru migrants who redefined what it meant to be "home" and "backhome" in Auckland.[77] One redefinition concerned the meaning of *teenagers* as a postwar category associated with the individual autonomy of cities and the consumerism of American popular culture.[78] Although this term surfaced around the 1930s in the United States, its affiliation with adolescent individualism and materialism did not gain mainstream appeal in Aotearoa until World War II. As Brickell explains, the war brought American troops to the archipelago, many of whom transported their understandings of the jitterbug, the motorbike, the soda shop, and other forms of American popular culture.[79]

Of the many youth formations that coalesced as teenagers, gangs comprised a few of these new identities in Aotearoa. By the 1970s, Māori,

Polynesian, and white gangs had emerged in Auckland, Christchurch, and Wellington. Despite their different ethnic makeup and diverse political orientations, they commonly drew from American popular culture in crafting their respective notions of masculinity and rebellion. As the sociologist Jarrod Gilbert notes, "Inspired by American pop culture, New Zealand youth adopted the style of their international contemporaries—a trend that continues in the LA-style street gangs of the present."[80] In chapter 8, the Sāmoan social worker Moses Maʻalo Faleolo takes stock of one such gang in Auckland. By analyzing the Sāmoan Bloods, he not only examines why some Sāmoan boys and young men appropriate the "colors" and ethos of the Los Angeles–based African American Bloods but also shows how they address their unresolved grief as a result of losing their loved ones. In chapter 9, Arcia Tecun, Edmond Fehoko, and ʻInoke Hafoka similarly explore how young Tongan men cultivate belonging in their sharing and drinking of kava, a ceremonial drink. With their focus on *faikava* circles, they specifically show how the youth appreciate the healing properties of kava in Aotearoa and Utah. As with Dick and Doyle's analysis of ni-Vanuatu youth innovation in chapter 4, Tecun, Fehoko, and Hafoka comparably examine how Tongan youth merge "Hip Hop" (capitalized for its political significance) and kava as a cultural philosophy.

In chapters 8 and 9, these authors thus demonstrate how Sāmoan and Tongan youth, respectively, have come to treat Auckland as an integral "place of vibrancy, energy and diversity."[81] Moreover, the Black English that appears in their naming of the Sāmoan Bloods and in their claiming of hip hop derives, as well, from the equally complex but lesser known histories of African American and Black peoples in Oceania.[82] In Hawaiʻi alone, escaped and freed slaves settled in the archipelago at the turn of the nineteenth century. Reflecting on their lives, the anthropologist Nitasha Tamar Sharma states that "Blacks integrated themselves into island life without forming distinct communities by intermarrying with local and particularly Hawaiian women. Sailors and plantation workers who stayed after their contracts 'assimilated' to local culture by adopting local customs and sometimes learning Hawaiian."[83] During World War II, another watershed moment for Black political mobility, African American and West Indian sailors and soldiers also interacted with Aboriginal Australians and Papua New Guineans. While only a few studies of Blacks and Pacific Islanders exist, a growing number of scholars analyze how Black musical traditions shape Pacific Islander youth formations, as with hip hop.[84]

As the scholar April K. Henderson discerns, "Hip hop—music, dance, and visual art—is one of the many transplanted popular cultures that have taken root in Pacific Islander communities."[85] Stressing its widespread appeal among the youth, she adds, "Hip hop participation is particularly notable in both the urbanized communities of the Pacific Rim where Islanders have settled and, increasingly, in the islands closely connected to those communities by patterns of circular migration."[86] In chapter 5, for example, the anthropologist Mary K. Good analyzes the ways in which girls and boys utilized social media to convey the "coolness" of hip hop on the island of 'Eua in Tonga. With her emphasis on the platform Bebo, an early form of social media, she also shows how they engaged ideas about transnational citizenship and identity through this social network. As Good demonstrates, Bebo offered the youth opportunities to create their own unique profile pages, inclusive of personal messages, photos, song clips, and video. In doing so, they found ingenious ways to virtually navigate their many connections to Aotearoa, California, and Tonga.

In chapter 6, the musicologist Jessica A. Schwartz foregrounds the diasporic worlds of the Marshallese hip hop artists F.O.B, Flavah C, and Yasta-Man and the slam poet Kathy Jetñil-Kijiner. By highlighting their acoustic engagements, Schwartz shows how the youth mobilized their music in Arkansas, the United Nations, and elsewhere to challenge the "sounds" of US militarization, modernization, and religion that have sought to silence them. In light of these Pacific Islander appropriations of African American and Black dance and musical traditions, the Black and Saginaw Anishi-naabe scholar Kyle T. Mays has queried, "What is the link between blackness and indigeneity?"[87] As he explains, "It is time we find creative ways to reimagine black-Indigenous relationships, cultures, and histories in ways that bring to the fore new scholarship and new understandings not tied to stories of enslavement and dispossession, even as those things are a ubiquitous part of our presence. Hip hop helps us do that in one way."[88] The youth featured in the studies in this volume clearly identify with popular meanings of hip hop, as with ni-Vanuatu *rimix* and Tongan social media. Given that Pacific Islanders have also employed the oppositional theories of blackness in Aotearoa and Australia, as with the making of the Polynesian Panthers, some of the youth featured also follow these traditions.[89] But we can do more than simply examine Pacific Islander appropriations of blackness. As Mays rightly ascertains, Pacific Islanders should continue to creatively and critically engage African Americans and other Black diasporic communities in North America, Oceania, and elsewhere.

The popular imaginary of Los Angeles as a city of style and swagger, hip hop beats, Disneyland, the Lakers, and every A-list actor imaginable underscores these concerns. Since the 1960s, this city has informed the spatial geographies of Pacific Islander youth just as much as their respective cultural norms and obligations have defined them. The fantasy of Los Angeles is real, an oxymoron best captured by the sociologist Darnell Hunt's description of the city. As he notes, Los Angeles "has figured prominently in the popular American imagination. Often this imagery portrayed the West Coast, which Los Angeles has come to anchor, as a final frontier. This wide-open destination, teeming with possibilities, has at times symbolized the pursuit of the American Dream."[90] As with many immigrants, Pacific Islanders idealize the United States in these terms. Take, for instance, John Tunui, a Rarotongan poet from the Cook Islands, who moved from Aotearoa New Zealand to San Francisco in the 1980s. As he remarked, the United States represented an "apple-pie-in-the sky! It was easy to transition New Zealand into it, to transition England into it. They were all White. They spoke English. White and English equaled America."[91]

After World War II, many Pacific Islander communities from American Sāmoa, Guam, Hawai'i, and Tonga migrated to Los Angeles and other parts of the continental United States. Most of them worked for the US military and others found employment with the churches and shipyards. With regard to the Sāmoan community, the anthropologist Ilana Gershon notes that when they "first arrived in Los Angeles or San Francisco, the cities were experiencing a post-war boom. As a result, there were plenty of manual labor jobs available, and Samoans quickly fit into a particular socio-economic niche, the men working in factories or at the docks, and women often working as nurses."[92] Many thus acquired low-wage positions, and a few even pursued higher education. In California, most Pacific Islanders lived in the districts of Carson, Compton, and Long Beach in Los Angeles County. According to the 2010 census, 150,749 Pacific Islanders now dwell in California, with more than one-third residing in Los Angeles. And like the poet John Tunui, they often represent the cities of California along the black-white racial binary. But while many Pacific Islanders adhere to the fantasies of Los Angeles, the city can nevertheless help us analyze and understand the interface between urbanization, settler colonialism, and trans-indigeneity.[93]

After all, Los Angeles is home to the indigenous Gabrielino-Tongva people. Comprised as a collection of lineages, they have long connected to the sacred Kuruvungna Springs and the surrounding mountains and valleys of the present city. As the educator Angie Dorame Behrns explains, the Kuruvungna Springs are "sacred because they're life. You look at this area, everything has been destroyed. Here these beautiful springs bubble up. There wouldn't be plants, there wouldn't be animals, there wouldn't be you and I without water."[94] Reflecting on why she also supports the community, the Tongva scholar Desirée Martinez adds, "For the ancestors. It's always been about them—being treated with respect and being remembered for who they are, and what they did."[95] While many of the youth featured in this volume do not know the Gabrieliño-Tongva, most of the contributors understand the deep respect Pacific Islanders hold for their lands, skies, and seas. In fact, an increasing number of Pacific Islanders in Aotearoa New Zealand, Australia, and the United States have begun to present themselves as guests. Accordingly, they now acknowledge the Native people of the land. As I expressed earlier, this sensibility manifests as trans-Indigenous acknowledgment and recognition. This is a crucial move in reckoning with settler colonialism in Oceania and elsewhere, and it is a major component of critical youth studies. Trans-Indigenous acknowledgment allows Pacific Islander youth, as *Kuuyam* or guests, to challenge the whiteness of urbanization and the violence of settler colonialism in Los Angeles.[96]

CONCLUSION

In April 2015, the Tongva scholar Cindi Alvitre first introduced me to the phrase the "East Coast of Oceania." Along with Maylei Blackwell, Mishuana Goeman, and Wendy Teeter, I had co-organized a symposium on the navigation cultures of American Indians and Pacific Islanders at UCLA. The event was one of several activities we had planned as part of our digital humanities project, Indigenous Los Angeles.[97] Alvitre represented one of many speakers from the Chamorro, Chumash, Native Hawaiian, and Tongva societies of California. During the program, she casually mentioned that her community views Los Angeles as the eastern coastline of Oceania. Having worked closely with Palauan artists and other Pacific Islanders, Alvitre already knew much about Pacific Islanders from Micronesia and elsewhere. More importantly, she reminded us that the Gabrieliño-Tongva people are a seafaring society and that their community shares much in common with Pacific Islanders. As the moderator of this program, I then vividly recalled the audience quietly responding, "oh," "yeah," and "wow." Chris Vaimili, a Sāmoan organizer for Empowering Pacific Islander

Communities, was one such person. In response to Alvitre's remarks, he said, "It is amazing that we can look at something that was essential to our existence in the islands, like the canoe, and draw similarities with the indigenous people of California. It makes you think about how connected our people were with one another before Western contact."[98]

These and other connections—however explicit or implied—also inform this anthology's juxtaposition of Native youth and Native cities in Oceania and the diaspora. Once again, they urge us to foster cross-regional, interdisciplinary, and trans-Indigenous conversations about youth identities and their ever-changing agencies, contributions, and performances. As the following chapters illustrate, Pacific Islander youth address climate change, advocate for culturally relevant curricula, communicate across borders, create policies for safer streets, develop multimedia, endure traumatic experiences, entertain the global elite, foster cultural solidarity, resist mass incarceration, and more. And that is how they rep, island style.

NOTES

1 Gilbert Herdt and Stephen C. Leavitt, eds., *Adolescence in Pacific Island Societies* (Pittsburgh, PA: University of Pittsburgh Press, 1998).

2 Helen Lee and Aidan Craney, "Pacific Youth, Local and Global," in *Pacific Youth: Local and Global Futures*, ed. Helen Lee (Acton, ACT: Australian National University Press, 2019), 1.

3 Most research projects about Pacific Islander youth represent them as devoid of agency and prone to crime, illness, violence, and death. Even memoirs written by Indigenous persons, as with Tuhoe "Bruno" Isaac's *True Red: The Life of an Ex-Mongrel Mob Gang Leader* (Pukekohe, New Zealand: True Red, 2007), adhere to fatalistic narrative structures that obscure complex circumstances and conditions. While this is not the venue to assess the pathological contours of this body of work, their parochialism partly stems from their relative exclusion of youth as co-principal investigators and from their disavowal of colonialism, militarism, and racism.

4 The main temporal exception concerns the gross offenses committed by youth, particularly murder, at which time many countries would accordingly treat them as "adults" in courts.

5 Lee and Craney, "Pacific Youth," 6.

6 Liza Keānuenueokalani Williams, "Currencies of U.S. Empire in Hawai'i's Tourism and Prison Industries," in *Gendering the Trans-Pacific World*, ed. Catherine Ceniza Choy and Judy Tzu-Chun Wu (Leiden: Brill, 2017), 155.

7 Awad Ibrahim, "Critical Youth Studies: An Introduction," in *Critical Youth Studies Reader*, ed. Awad Ibrahim and Shirley R. Steinberg (New York: Peter Lang, 2014), xvi.

8   Angela Y. Davis, *The Meaning of Freedom: And Other Difficult Dialogues* (San Francisco: City Lights Books, 2012), 18–19.

9   Eve Tuck and K. Wayne Yang, "Introduction to Youth Resistance Research and Theories of Change," in *Youth Resistance Research and Theories of Change*, ed. Eve Tuck and K. Wayne Yang (New York: Routledge, 2014), 17.

10 Stuart Hall, "The Work of Representation," in *Representation: Cultural Representations and Signifying Practices*, ed. Stuart Hall (London: Sage Publications, 2009), 19.

11 Halifu Osumare, *The Africanist Aesthetic in Global Hip-Hop: Power Moves* (New York: Palgrave Macmillan, 2007), 27.

12 Osumare, *Africanist Aesthetic*, 22.

13 Vicente M. Diaz, *Repositioning the Missionary: Rewriting the Histories of Colonialism, Native Catholicism, and Indigeneity in Guam* (Honolulu: University of Hawaiʻi Press, 2010), 163.

14 Caroline Ralston, "Changes in the Lives of Ordinary Women in Early Post-Contact Hawaii," in *Family and Gender in the Pacific: Domestic Contradictions and the Colonial Impact*, ed. Margaret Jolly and Martha Macintyre (Cambridge: Cambridge University Press, 1989), 54.

15 Margaret Jolly and Martha Macintyre, introduction to *Family and Gender in the Pacific: Domestic Contradictions and the Colonial Impact*, ed. Margaret Jolly and Martha Macintyre (Cambridge: Cambridge University Press, 1989), 10.

16 Latu Latai, "From Open *Fale* to Mission Houses: Negotiating the Boundaries of 'Domesticity' in Samoa," in *Divine Domesticities: Christian Paradoxes in Asia and the Pacific*, ed. Hyaeweol Choi and Margaret Jolly (Acton, ACT: Australian National University Press, 2014), 309.

17 Chris Brickell, *Teenagers: The Rise of Youth Culture in New Zealand* (Auckland: Auckland University Press, 2017), 19.

18 Brickell, *Teenagers*, 19.

19 Ibrahim, "Critical Youth Studies," xvi.

20 Ibrahim, "Critical Youth Studies," xvi.

21 Ibrahim, "Critical Youth Studies," xvi.

22 Sunaina Marr Maira, *The 9/11 Generation: Youth, Rights, and Solidarity in the War on Terror* (New York: New York University Press, 2016), 17.

23 Carol M. Worthman, "Adolescence in the Pacific: A Biosocial View," in Herdt and Leavitt, *Adolescence in Pacific Island Societies*, 29.

24 Gilbert Herdt and Stephen C. Leavitt, "Introduction: Studying Adolescence in Contemporary Pacific Island Communities," in Herdt and Leavitt, *Adolescence in Pacific Island Societies*, 5.

25 Margaret Mead, *Coming of Age in Samoa: A Psychological Study of Primitive Youth for Western Civilization* (1928; New York: Harper, 2001), 137.

26 Mead, *Coming of Age in Samoa*, 139.

27 Herdt and Leavitt, "Introduction," 4.

28 Herdt and Leavitt, "Introduction," 4.

29 Herdt and Leavitt, "Introduction," 7.

30 Lee and Craney, "Pacific Youth," 10.

31 Tuck and Yang, "Introduction," 17.

32 Kalissa Alexeyeff and Niko Besnier, "Gender on the Edge: Identities, Politics, Transformations," in *Gender on the Edge: Transgender, Gay, and Other Pacific Islanders*, ed. Niko Besnier and Kalissa Alexeyeff (Honolulu: University of Hawai'i Press, 2014), 2.

33 Fa'anofo Lisaclaire (Lisa) Uperesa, "Fabled Futures: Migration and Mobility for Samoans in American Football," *The Contemporary Pacific* 26, no. 2 (2014): 283.

34 Cameron Noble, Natalia Pereira, and Nanise Saune, *Urban Youth in the Pacific: Increasing Resilience and Reducing Risk for Involvement in Crime and Violence* (Suva, Fiji: AusAID, 2011), 4.

35 Richard Curtain and Patrick Vakaoti, *The State of Pacific Youth 2011: Opportunities and Obstacles* (Suva, Fiji: UNICEF and Secretariat of the Pacific Community, 2011), 8.

36 Noble, Pereira, and Saune, *Urban Youth in the Pacific*, 4.

37 Frances King Espiritu, "From Childhood to Chief," in *Pacific Voices Talk Story: Conversations of American Experience*, 4 vols., ed. Margo King Lenson (Vacaville, CA: Tui Communications, 2007), 4:57.

38 Cluny Macpherson and La'avasa Macpherson, "Towards an Explanation of Recent Trends in Suicide in Western Samoa," *Man* 22, no. 2 (June 1987): 324.

39 Rachana Agarwal, "Adoptive Transfers and Affective Experiences of Palauan Youth," *The Asia Pacific Journal of Anthropology* 18, no. 4 (2017): 340.

40 Agarwal, "Adoptive Transfers," 340.

41 Alison Cleland and Khylee Quince, *Youth Justice in Aotearoa New Zealand: Law, Policy and Critique* (Wellington: LexisNexis NZ Limited, 2014), 32.

42 Cleland and Quince, *Youth Justice in Aotearoa*, 32.

43 Cleland and Quince, *Youth Justice in Aotearoa*, 32.

44 Agarwal, "Adoptive Transfers," 340.

45 Curtain and Vakaoti, *State of Pacific Youth*, 12.

46 Noble, Pereira, and Saune, *Urban Youth in the Pacific*, 18.

47 Refer, for instance, to Subini Ancy Annamma, *The Pedagogy of Pathologization: Dis/abled Girls of Color in the School-Prison Nexus* (New York: Routledge, 2017); Elizabeth Comack, Lawrence Deane, Larry Morrissette, and Jim Silver, *"Indians Wear Red": Colonialism, Resistance, and Aboriginal Street Gangs* (Halifax and Winnipeg, Canada: Fernwood Publishing, 2013); and Miroslava Chávez-García, *States of Delinquency: Race and Science in the Making of California's Juvenile Justice System* (Berkeley: University of California Press, 2012).

48 Karen Umemoto and Paul Ong, "Asian American and Pacific Islander Youth: Risks, Challenges and Opportunities," *aapi nexus* 4, no. 2 (Summer/Fall 2006): vi.

49 Meda Chesney-Lind, Lisa Pasko, Nancy Marker, Pavela Fiaui, and Steven Connery, *Understanding Gangs and Delinquency on Oahu*, vol. 1, *A Report to the Twenty-Second Hawai'i State Legislature* (Honolulu: Center for Youth Research, 2003), 44.

50 Christine J. Yeh, Noah E. Borrero, Patsy Tito, and Lealaisalanoa Setu Petaia, "Intergenerational Stories and the 'Othering' of Samoan Youth in Schools," *Urban Review* 46 (2014): 149.

51 Katherine Irwin and Karen Umemoto, *Jacked Up and Unjust: Pacific Islander Teens Confront Violent Legacies* (Oakland: University of California Press, 2016), 164.

52 Rick Bonus, *The Ocean in the School: Pacific Islander Students Transforming Their University* (Durham, NC: Duke University Press, 2020), 2.

53 Laura M. Furlan, *Indigenous Cities: Urban Indian Fiction and the Histories of Relocation* (Lincoln: University of Nebraska Press, 2017), 23.

54 Refer to Patrick Wolfe, "Settler Colonialism and the Elimination of the Native," *Journal of Genocide Research* 8, no. 4 (2006): 387–409.

55 Kelly Lytle Hernández, *City of Inmates: Conquest, Rebellion, and the Rise of Human Caging in Los Angeles, 1771–1965* (Chapel Hill: University of North Carolina Press, 2017), 7.

56 Hernández, *City of Inmates*, 7.

57 Vicente M. Diaz, "Oceania in the Plains: The Politics and Analytics of Transindigenous Resurgence in Chuukese Voyaging of Dakota Lands, Waters, and Skies in Miní sóta Makhóčhe," *Pacific Studies* 42, nos. 1/2 (April/August 2019): 3. For a fuller discussion of trans-indigeneity, refer to Chadwick Allen, *Trans-Indigenous: Methodologies for Global Native Literary Studies* (Minneapolis: University of Minnesota Press, 2012).

58 Diaz, "Oceania in the Plains," 37.

59 Paul Jones, *The Emergence of Pacific Urban Villages: Urbanization Trends in the Pacific Islands* (Manila, Philippines: Asian Development Bank, 2016), 10.

60 Jones, *Pacific Urban Villages*, 10.

61 Jones, *Pacific Urban Villages*, 15.

62 Frantz Fanon, *Black Skin, White Masks*, trans. Richard Philcox (New York: Grove Press, 2008), 90.

63 Fanon, *Black Skin, White Masks*, 91.

64 Miriam Kahn, *Tahiti beyond the Postcard: Power, Place, and Everyday Life* (Seattle: University of Washington Press, 2011), 44–45.

65 Aleardo Zanghellini, "Sodomy Laws and Gender Variance in Tahiti and Hawai'i," *Laws* 2, no. 2 (2013): 51–68.

66 Makiko Kuwahara, "Living as and Living with *Māhū* and *Raerae*: Geopolitics, Sex, and Gender in the Society Islands," in Besnier and Alexeyoff, *Gender on the Edge*, 94.

67 Curtain and Vakaoti, *State of Pacific Youth*, 27.

68 Patrick Vakaoti, "Young People's Participation in Fiji: Understanding Conceptualizations and Experiences," *Journal of Youth Studies* 20, no. 6 (2017): 700.

69 Kuwahara, "Māhū and Raerae," 108; and Fiona Beals and Bronwyn Wood, "Negotiating Agency: Local Youth Activism in Aotearoa-New Zealand," in *Super Girls, Gangstas, Freeters, and Xenomaniacs: Gender and Modernity in*

Global Youth Culture, ed. Susan Dewey and Karen J. Brison (Syracuse, NY: Syracuse University Press, 2012), 199.

70 Noble, Pereira, and Saune, *Urban Youth in the Pacific*, 28.

71 Jones, *Pacific Urban Villages*, 12.

72 Christine Jourdan and Johanne Angeli, "Pijin and Shifting Language Ideologies in Urban Solomon Islands," *Language in Society* 43, no. 3 (2014): 268.

73 James Rimumutu George and Lena Rodriguez, "Hybrid Youth Identity in the Maori/Pacific Island Diaspora in Australia: A Study of Young Urban Polynesian Men in Sydney," *New Zealand Sociology* 24, no. 1 (2009): 10.

74 Damon Salesa, *Island Time: New Zealand's Pacific Futures* (Wellington: Bridget Williams Books, 2017), 7.

75 On the professionalization of young Tongan rugby players in Japan, for instance, refer to Niko Besnier, "The Athlete's Body and the Global Condition: Tongan Rugby Players in Japan," *American Ethnologist* 39, no. 3 (2012): 491–510.

76 Melissa Matutina Williams, *Panguru and the City / Kāinga Tahi, Kāinga Rua: An Urban Migration History* (Wellington: Bridget Williams Books, 2015), 17.

77 Williams, *Panguru and the City*, 16.

78 Brickell, *Teenagers*, 190.

79 Brickell, *Teenagers*, 190.

80 Jarrod Gilbert, *Patched: The History of Gangs in New Zealand* (Auckland: Auckland University Press, 2013), 292.

81 Belinda Borell, "Living in the City Ain't So Bad: Cultural Identity for Young Maori in South Auckland," in *New Zealand Identities: Departures and Destinations*, ed. James H. Liu, Tim McCreanor, Tracey McIntosh, and Teresia Teaiwa (Wellington: Victoria University Press, 2005), 192.

82 Nicole Poppenhagen and Jens Temmen, "Introduction—Across Currents: Connections between Atlantic and (Trans)Pacific Studies," in *Across Currents: Connections between Atlantic and (Trans)Pacific Studies*, ed. Nicole Poppenhagen and Jens Temmen (Abingdon, UK: Routledge, 2019), 6.

83 Nitasha Tamar Sharma, "The Racial Imperative: Rereading Hawai'i's History and Black-Hawaiian Relations through the Perspective of Black Residents," in *Beyond Ethnicity: New Politics of Race in Hawai'i*, ed. Camilla Fojas, Rudy P. Gueverra Jr., and Nitasha Tamar Sharma (Honolulu: University of Hawai'i Press, 2018), 123–24.

84 Gabriel Solis, "The Black Pacific: Music and Racialization in Papua New Guinea and Australia," *Critical Sociology* 41, no. 2 (2015): 303.

85 April K. Henderson, "Gifted Flows: Making Space for a Brand New Beat," *Contemporary Pacific* 22, no. 2 (Fall 2010): 297.

86 Henderson, "Gifted Flows," 297.

87 Kyle T. Mays, *Hip Hop Beats, Indigenous Rhymes: Modernity and Hip Hop in Indigenous North America* (Albany: State University of New York Press, 2018), 28.

88 Mays, *Hip Hop Beats*, 89.

89 On blackness and Indigenous social movements in Oceania, refer to Robbie
    Shilliam, *The Black Pacific: Anti-colonial Struggles and Oceanic Connections*
    (London: Bloomsbury, 2015); and Melani Anae, Lautofa (Ta) Iuli, Leilani
    Burgoyne, eds., *Polynesian Panthers: The Crucible Years, 1971–74* (Auckland:
    Reed Publishing, 2006).

90 Darnell Hunt, "Introduction: Dreaming of Black Los Angeles," in *Black Los
    Angeles: American Dreams and Racial Realities*, ed. Darnell Hunt and
    Ana-Christina Ramón (New York: New York University Press, 2010), 4.

91 Margo King Lenson, ed., *Pacific Voices Talk Story: Conversations of an
    American Experience*, 4 vols. (Vacaville, CA: Tui Communications, 2001),
    1:171.

92 Ilana Gershon, "Compelling Culture: The Rhetoric of Assimilation among
    Samoan Migrants in the United States," *Ethnic and Racial Studies* 30, no. 5
    (September 2007): 790.

93 Edward W. Soja, *My Los Angeles: From Urban Restructuring to Regional
    Urbanization* (Berkeley: University of California Press, 2014), 215.

94 Claudia Jurmain and William McCawley, *O, My Ancestor: Recognition and
    Renewal for the Gabrielino-Tongva People of the Los Angeles Area* (Berkeley,
    CA: Heyday Books, 2009), 238–39.

95 Jurmain and McCawley, *O, My Ancestor*, 191.

96 Charles Sepulveda, "Our Sacred Waters: Theorizing Kuuyam as a Decolonial
    Possibility," *Decolonization: Indigeneity, Education and Society* 7, no. 1 (2018):
    40–58.

97 For more information, refer to "Mapping Indigenous LA," UCLA American
    Indian Studies Center, https://mila.ss.ucla.edu/.

98 Quoted in 'Alisi Tulua, "Ancestors in Training," *Marianas Variety*, Septem-
    ber 24, 2015, www.saipantribune.com/index.php/ancestors-in-training/.

PART I

GOVERNANCE, LAW, AND EDUCATION

CHAPTER 1

KŌTI RANGATAHI

Whanaungatanga Justice and the
"Magnificence of the Connectedness"

STELLA BLACK, JACQUIE KIDD, AND KATEY THOM

IT WAS A BRISK BUT SUNNY MAY MORNING IN 2015 WHEN WE WERE invited to attend Kōti Rangatahi, a marae-based youth court held at Hoani Waititi marae. Marae are culturally significant meeting places for Māori, the Indigenous population of Aotearoa New Zealand. This marae opened in 1980 in the western urban area of Tāmaki Makaurau (Auckland), the largest city of Aotearoa, in response to the many dispossessed and landless Māori who found themselves away from their whenua (land) bases. We also came to learn that Hoani Waititi marae was named after a prominent rangatira (leader) from Te Whānau-a-Apanui. This rangatira viewed education and the maintenance of Māori identity as essential to Māori success. Drawn together by our passions in health, social justice, and inequality research, we now gathered at the waharoa (gateway) of the marae. We were particularly interested in what was taking place on this marae and how its community uplifted Māori youth who had found themselves before the court. This experience would become our first of many observations of ngā Kōti Rangatahi of Aotearoa.

As people arrived and waited with us to be welcomed onto the marae through the formal process of a pōwhiri (welcome ceremony), the air was thick with nervous energy. Men in suits appeared, and made-up women chatted among themselves, projecting an air of self-confidence. Others seemed disinterested in Māori cultural protocols given their busy preoccupations with their electronic devices. We recognized, as well, lawyers and youth advocates in the crowd. Others evoked friendlier dispositions, as with the rangatahi (Māori youth) and their whānau (family). Later, we learned that government social workers had accompanied the young people and their relatives. Staff from nongovernmental organizations also helped rangatahi to complete their family group conference plans.[1] One lady we spoke with was advising a teenager on how to get his driver's license. Another man was a youth mentor who had been working closely with a male rangatahi over several months. They told us how they hoped that the young people would each receive a 282 sentence of discharge without conviction that day.[2]

As the minutes counted down to the start of the pōwhiri, we introduced ourselves to a Pākehā (non-Māori) mother and her son. She gushed about how positive Kōti Rangatahi had been for them. They initially hesitated to come to the marae because they were not Māori, but she was grateful that the marae tangata whenua (local people) had embraced them.[3] We also watched Whaea Ada,[4] a female elder, move deliberately and swiftly among those waiting, as if she was gathering pipi (clams) by the handful and placing them in her basket. Though small in stature, Whaea Ada instructed everyone to gather closer to ensure we could all hear the judge, who was about to join us. Such was her mana, or authority, that adults and youths alike knew she meant business. The judge was well known for tirelessly advocating for the inclusion and normalization of Māori beliefs and practices in an otherwise Pākehā-dominated legal system.

We share our impressions of Kōti Rangatahi at Hoani Waititi marae to invite further exploration and understanding of marae-based youth justice in Aotearoa. To do so, our chapter is structured into four sections, all of which include passages taken from notes and reflections. In the first section, we contextualize Māori and Pākehā justice, address the co-option of Indigenous concepts by white settler states, and explore the development of Kōti Rangatahi as a judicial initiative. In the second section, we foreground our interviews and observations in a kaupapa Māori (Māori practices, values, and worldviews of being Māori) methodology and demonstrate how the concept of whanaungatanga (relationships) underpins the interactions between Māori youth, their elders, and the wider community, thus showing how ngā Kōti Rangatahi promote the development and maintenance of relationships. In the Māori language, whanaungatanga best encapsulates this process, one that has been theorized as a "dynamic and innovative" system of relationships.[5] Whanaungatanga also includes connections to one another, our ancestors, whānau (family, both deceased and living), and the environment. Historically, Māori have primarily formed whanaungatanga connections by way of their genealogies, but for many contemporary Māori, colonization has fractured these vital relationships and identities. Therefore, we recognize whanaungatanga as a foundation from which to restore and strengthen a sense of belonging for Māori youth who may otherwise feel excluded and disconnected.

In the third, findings section, we draw on the expertise of the kaumātua (elders) and youth justice stakeholders to explicate whanaungatanga justice as an Indigenous justice model. Elders represent numerous marae connections across Aotearoa, and the youth justice stakeholders often assume the roles of coordinators, judges, lawyers, lay advocates, police officers, and social workers. We then show how three Māori principles have informed this collaborative effort to understand and practice whanaungatanga justice in the Kōti Rangatahi. We do this by focusing on the following three themes that came out of our research: (1) marae setting and pōwhiri (welcome ceremony) as an engagement process; (2) the whakawhanaungatanga (whaka means to cause; in this case, to cause a relationship to happen) circle as a way of sharing pepeha (the detailing of a genealogy); and (3) Kōti Rangatahi as a whānau-for-whānau (family-for-family) approach. In the fourth and final section, we explore some of the challenges related to valuing whanaungatanga justice. As with Jessica A. Schwartz's ethnography of Marshallese youth hip hop in chapter 6 and Demiliza Saramosing's analysis of Chuukese and Filipino youth bicycling in chapter 10 in this volume, we, too, seek to expand the ways by which Indigenous youth and their families engage the cities of Oceania. The chapter thus intentionally and frequently employs te reo Māori (language) and te Ao Māori (worldview) and concludes by envisioning how whanaungatanga justice can shape criminal justice procedures.

MĀORI JUSTICE AND PĀKEHĀ JUSTICE

Prior to colonization, Māori had their own customs, laws, and traditions that worked to reconcile and restore the relationships between the wronged and the wrongdoer. In Aotearoa, the first law is tikanga, which guides collective social expectations and responsibilities among Māori.[6] Tikanga Māori is a complex system of relational values and laws that interact with one another. Although we mainly focus on whanaungatanga in this chapter, other interconnecting tikanga principles include mana (authority), manaakitanga (generosity and care), noa (ordinary), tapu (restrictions), utu (reciprocity and restoration), wairuatanga (spirituality), and whakapapa (genealogy). As with whanaungatanga justice, tikanga differs significantly from the white settler system of Aotearoa that is rooted in both the Westminster model and the Tiriti o Waitangi, or the Treaty of Waitangi.[7]

The lesser-known Tiriti o Waitangi was signed by representatives of the British Crown and some Māori chiefs in 1840 to assert Māori authority and to enable the monitoring of each political entity. But history indicates this did not happen. The Tiriti had little positive effect for the Māori until breaches were lodged against the Crown in the very judicial system that had stripped away Māori land and fractured social structures and language bases.[8] Such protest crystallized in the Māori social movements of the late twentieth century with some Māori leaders striving to assert Māori authority and to reset the terms of engagement between Māori and the Crown. The words of Sir Apirana Turupa Ngata of Ngāti Porou, commissioned as the first Māori lawyer in 1897, are instructive in this regard. A politician and scholar, he fashioned the now popular whakataukī, or proverb, "E tipu e rea, ko tō ringa ki nga rākau a te Pākehā, hei ora mō te tinana, ko tō ngākau ki ngā tāonga a ō tīpuna Māori, hei tikitiki mō tō māhuna." The proverb encourages Māori to "use the tools (modern technology and knowledge) of the Pākehā" and to "hold fast and retain the treasures handed down by your ancestors and display them with pride." In essence, Tā Apirana urged Māori to embrace Western philosophies in order to advance, while also ensuring to retain, their cultural identity.

However, critics have argued against embracing a Pākehā justice system that has provided little "justice" for Māori. Many also oppose the integration of Māori traditional customs and laws by the Pākehā structures that retain power. The use of Māori concepts and practices by state agencies has even been described as artificial, lacking the requisite Māori knowledge and underlying cultural meanings.[9] A criticism of ngā Kōti Rangatahi concerns the question of who is perceived to wield power, Māori or the state. One study found that the Pākehā justice system, which dogmatically focuses on impersonal administrative tasks, resulted in a detached form of interaction that often overshadowed the Māori spiritual aspects central to maintaining connections with one another and the world.[10] Māori scholars asserted that only a separate Māori justice system that understands the realities of Māori offending and the impacts of colonization can achieve justice.[11] Other colonial governments similarly indigenized their criminal justice systems, leading to the oppression of Indigenous communities.[12]

Presently, Māori make up roughly 12.5 percent of the national population over fifteen years of age. But Māori tāne (men) have made up half of the adult prison population in New Zealand for the last thirty years, whereas Māori wāhine (women) have accounted for 62 percent.[13] The patterns of Māori overrepresentation in apprehensions, arrests, prosecutions, and imprisonment often begin in childhood.[14] In fact, Māori youth are three times more likely to be known to the police before they turn fourteen and six times more likely to be apprehended than non-Māori children.[15] Although the latest data indicates that most children and young people are dealt with outside the court system, this trend does not hold true for Māori youth.[16] Research shows that many youth who progress to court appearances will be Māori with complex problems.[17] Some of the issues that influence Māori youth offending include state care trauma, abuse, victimization, and disadvantage related to income, housing, employment, and education.[18]

A systemic bias about and a targeted approach to Māori therefore exists at all levels of the Pākehā criminal justice system. This carceral frame mirrors the colonial discourse experienced by other Indigenous peoples.[19] Colonialism has left an indelible scar on the minds and bodies of Indigenous people around the world. Aboriginal and Torres Strait people, for example, account for just over a quarter of the total Australian prison population despite being only 2 percent of the nation's makeup. In Canada, the First Nations community makes up just over 4 percent of the national population but represents 28 percent of the prison population.[20] American Indians are also more likely to be incarcerated after appearing in federal or state court in the United States.[21] As Eileen Baldry and Chris Cunneen argue, racism, victimization, and disempowerment constitute the strategies and techniques of colonial patriarchy in white settler states, particularly for Indigenous women.[22] If "justice" is to be realized for Indigenous peoples, then transformation must come by way of their laws, remedies, and languages.

Regardless of the criticisms, intergenerational patterns of Indigenous incarceration exist and continue to cause intergenerational harm to Māori familial networks. To pit proponents of Indigenous sovereignty against advocates using the Indigenous tools within this Pākehā system does not help the very rangatahi (youth) and whānau (families) who need support most. In Aotearoa, much debate took place among rangatira; only when one kuia insisted that the focus should be on rangatahi who were constantly getting into trouble was the use of marae and tikanga supported as an alternative legal process.[23] For example, Indigenous problem-solving, peace building, and restorative practices based on customary law are used globally. The Afghani observe jirga as a process of consensus building[24]; the Kānaka Maoli of Hawai'i practice ho'oponopono, an 'ōiwi (native) form of reconciliation[25]; the Haundenosaunee (Iroquois) honor the Deganawida or Tekanawita the Peacemaker[26]; the Navajo or Dine apply Hozhooji Naat'aani as peace planners to achieve harmony[27]; and the ubuntu or botho (deep respect for humanity) operate as a parallel legal system in Africa.[28] The degree to which common law and Indigenous law are applied in each jurisdiction and locale differs. They all offer contrasting models, whether an integrated or separate legal system of justice, for the inclusion of Indigenous elders, customs, and languages.

NGĀ KŌTI RANGATAHI

Although legislation has long existed to enable judges to hear criminal cases on marae in Aotearoa, this discretion has rarely been taken up.[29] During the 1950s, for instance, tribal and Māori committees operated on marae as quasi-judicial bodies. Although they aimed to resolve local offending and improve Māori welfare, they were largely ineffective because they had little authority in the Pākehā justice system.[30] Along with the authorization and support of rangatira (leaders) and kaumātua (elders), Māori judge Heemi Taumaunu in 2008 made a concerted move to utilize marae as a youth court setting. Although Māori communities debated the intrusion of Pākehā law on marae, they ultimately could not ignore Taumaunu's judicial initiative to increase marae-based care for disconnected Māori youth and their families.[31]

The first Kōti Rangatahi was held at Te-Poho-o-Rawiri marae, Gisborne. Fifteen Kōti Rangatahi now operate throughout the country, with fourteen in the North Island and one in the South Island. In 2010, two Pasifika youth courts were also set up in South and Central Auckland to offer Pacific youth an environment in which the processes of "law, culture and faith" are brought together.[32] As in the Pasifika court that has a Pasifika judge, Māori judges often preside in Kōti Rangatahi, although non-Māori judges are called upon to provide cover when required. Māori judges are pooled from the more than forty youth court judges who primarily work out of twenty-two main centers in Aotearoa.[33] The emphasis on Māori judges sitting in Kōti Rangatahi allows the rangatahi (youth) and the whānau (families) to observe and practice Māori notions of connectedness and justice on the marae.

Youth justice professionals also play a critical role in promoting Kōti Rangatahi. Some of them are employed by the Ministry for Children, formerly known as the Department of Child, Youth and Family. This government agency is charged with caring for our most vulnerable children. Each rangatahi is first appointed a youth advocate; for continuity, the advocate represents the same young person if subsequent offending occurs. A social worker assesses the needs of the rangatahi while the youth justice coordinator works with other youth justice stakeholders, the youth, and families to facilitate the family group conference.[34] A rangatahi is also entitled to help from a court-appointed lay advocate; this may take place after a charge has been laid before the youth court. The lay advocate provides support for the young person and their whānau and ensures the court is aware of any relevant cultural matters. A police prosecutor presents the case against a rangatahi in the youth court.

During the proceedings, the judge is guided by the kaumātua (male and female elders) on marae kawa (protocols). In this setting, kaumātua are valued for their expertise in te reo Māori (Māori language) and mātauranga (Māori knowledge). As Hoani Waititi is a pan-tribal urban-based marae, its kaumātua panel includes a diverse range of elders who represent different iwi (tribal community groups) and hapū (subtribal group made up of extended families) throughout the country. In this manner, as a prominent kaumātua based in the Kōti Rangatahi of the Bay of Plenty stated, "[It's about] promoting with these young people a magnificence of the connectedness of their whakapapa. You might have heard me say, 'he toto rangatira e rere ana kei a koe.' [You are the descendant of chiefs.] You know you have to take them out of that desolate world they're in. They are much more." As this elder illustrates through his use of the noun "magnificence," te Ao Māori philosophies of whanaungatanga (relationship) and whakapapa (genealogy connection) practices underpin the Kōti Rangatahi initiative. These philosophies also expose rangatahi to the "magnificence of the connectedness" in learning who they are and where they come from.

A recent report by a chief science advisor attributed the creation of a direct prison pipeline for young Māori to their cultural disconnections, marginalization in society, ongoing experiences of trauma, and state care.[35] In 2017 alone, Māori made up 64 percent ($n = 1,197$) of all youth charged for property- and robbery-related offenses. Overall, 600 youth received sentences; of this number, 36 acquired an adult conviction for the serious offenses like murder and manslaughter.[36] In the same year, 349 rangatahi opted to attend Kōti Rangatahi, meaning that 40 percent of Māori youth in the Pākehā criminal justice system preferred the genealogy, reconciliation, and justice of Kōti Rangatahi.[37] The numbers were low because Maori youth have been limited to only fifteen Kōti Rangatahi marae locales. In fact, a press release from the former minister of justice and minister for social development indicated that rangatahi who attended Kōti Rangatahi committed 14 percent fewer offenses and were 11 percent less likely to reoffend.[38] In light of these small but positive results, more Māori communities have been calling for their own marae youth courts.

A KAUPAPA MĀORI METHODOLOGY

As mentioned earlier, a kaupapa Māori methodology informs our exploration of the underpinning Māori customs, laws, and traditions in ngā Kōti Rangatahi. This approach affirms Māori voices, philosophies, and practices.[39] This process also involves the consultation of communities prior to the formalizing of the research and seeks their feedback during the data analysis to ensure that their voices are accurately represented.[40] Ultimately, a kaupapa Māori approach strives to honor the voices of those living their contemporary realities over and beyond Western scientific theories that do not value community-based knowledge in Aotearoa.[41] As a kaupapa Māori study, our research depends on kaumātua support for success. For instance, the elders of Stella Black, the principal author, provided valuable research assistance for our team. Their guidance helped us to navigate tikanga customs, particularly during the marae engagement processes.

By following a kaupapa Māori methodology, we observed Māori elders, youth, and families and youth justice professionals. Although we did not speak directly with the rangatahi and whānau, the ethnographic nature of our research allowed us to interact with court participants. Our research also took place in three other marae locales, but for the purpose of this chapter, we focus on Hoani Waititi marae, a sacred and urban meeting place in West Auckland. Early consultation occurred at each of the four marae sites. With our elders' direction, we followed the kawa (protocols) of each marae. Generally, this involved a mihi whakatau (informal welcome) that began with a karakia (blessing), mihi (greeting/introductions), and kaupapa (a presentation about our purpose) and ended with a karakia (blessing). Our gatherings also included the sharing of kai (food). In every site, the elders of the marae asked, "Whose research is this and who are you?" In the end, we received unanimous support to proceed with our research project.[42] The close connection we forged with the tangata whenua at Hoani Waititi marae has especially enabled our ongoing research.

At Hoani Waititi marae, we collected observation data over eight months, enabling us to become familiar with the setting, learn the protocols for each marae, build rapport with the communities, and solidify emerging ideas. Overall, we interviewed a total of nine individuals, with Stella Black conducting most of the interviews. Two group interviews and one individual interview were conducted with elders; one comprised six kuia (female elders), and another concerned two male kaumātua who were crucial to the running of the marae. Other participants included an education officer, marae managers, and youth workers. We also wrote field notes during and soon after our observations.

Afterward, we adapted a basic coding framework that was also used in a wider study comparing two specialist criminal courts in Aotearoa.[43] These codes included a description of participant roles and practices, the cultural and legal models that influenced them, and the challenges that they faced. We then read a selection of the transcripts and compared their emerging ideas and analyzed these points before we merged them into the different NVivo "trees." Stella Black, in particular, completed the same exercise across the merged NVivo database as a secondary check of analysis, and codes were brought together into categories. We then identified themes across the data as well as discussed, tested, and in some cases redefined the data.[44] Jacquie Kidd, our secondary author, and Stella Black then ensured the accurate coding and analysis of cultural interpretations.[45]

In presenting our research findings to Hoani Waititi kaumātua, we drew extensively on the direct quotes of the participants and analyzed their words within the context of ngā Kōti Rangatahi. By doing so, we highlighted the distinct perspectives among the different professional groups. In order to illustrate our three themes, we included our field notes and personal reflections. As per our kaupapa Māori methodology, we also invited the elders at Hoani Waititi to provide feedback about our findings.[46] Seven kaumātua attended. We discussed the long and reflexive process of developing whanaungatanga justice, a Māori concept grounded in the data and expressed in the philosophy of ngā Kōti Rangatahi. We also delivered several presentations at national and international meetings. In our ongoing engagement with the marae kaumātua, we confirmed the magnificent connectedness of whanaungatanga. As we demonstrate, we found that whanaungatanga flourished on the marae, thereby deeply connecting the tikanga relations between rangatahi and kaumātua alike and supporting the healing process for their whānau.

RESEARCH FINDINGS

Three themes surfaced that provide a glimpse into the whanaungatanga justice practiced by the youth justice stakeholders. The first theme focuses on the marae setting and the pōwhiri process. The second theme, the whakawhanaungatanga circle, or establishing connections, refers to Māori cultural values that the marae implemented in Kōti Rangatahi, creating a sense of connection and equality among all parties. The third theme, a whānau-for-whānau approach through whakapapa, describes how the whānau established a sense of belonging for rangatahi and their whānau. Two of the themes begin with our personal accounts, and the last one ends with a vignette drawn from our observation and interview data. We then conclude our chapter by considering several challenges faced in implementing whanaungatanga justice in ngā Kōti Rangatahi.

THEME 1: MARAE SETTING AND PŌWHIRI

Waiting at the gateway of Hoani Waititi marae, we huddled around to listen to the judge explain for those unfamiliar with the pōwhiri process what would happen. He outlined the marae kawa (protocols) that would be observed at this marae. This was helpful as each marae has its own kawa. The judge then pointed out that it is customary for the pōwhiri to take place entirely in te reo Māori (the Māori language). He explained, as well, that the pōwhiri would begin with the kuia (female elders) performing the karanga (call) and inviting us onto the marae atea (courtyard) before entering into the whare tīpuna (ancestral meetinghouse). Speeches would then ensue, concluding with the joining of both the manuhiri (guests) and the tangata whenua (marae hosts).

As we stood ready to enter, the high-pitched lament of the first karanga (call) pierced the air and reverberated across the marae atea (courtyard). We saw the kuia standing at a distance in front of the wharenui (meetinghouse). Her call welcomed us into the heart of the ancestral meetinghouse, aptly named Ngā Tūmanako, or The Dreams. As part of the visiting party, the wāhine (women) followed closely behind Whaea Ada as she replied with an equally powerful call. The interchange made our hair stand on end, and we were again reminded that the pōwhiri was a tapu (sacred) process. As such, the aural vibrations of the energy that surrounded us actively operated at a wairua (spiritual) level. Over the following months, we came to realize that these formal exchanges in te reo (Māori language) became the first set of dialogue to transform rangatahi from "offender to rangatira." Rangatahi then effectively began to view and reshape themselves into rangatira or leaders.

As we removed our shoes and entered Ngā Tūmanako, we were struck by the majesty of this beautifully sculptured wharenui. Intricately carved poupou (wall pillars) and patterned tukutuku (lattice work) panels lined the walls, symbolically representing the multitude of links via waka (canoe), iwi (tribal), and spiritual connections. A karakia (blessing) then signaled the beginning of the speeches as the kaumātua (male elders) on each side delivered their whaikōrero (speeches), paying due respect to, among other things, the land, the wharenui, the dead, and the living. Herein came the second set of counternarratives that changed the labels of the rangatahi (youth) from haututū (troublesome) or hīanga (mischievous) to that of taonga (precious beings). After the speeches, the hosts and guests then came together to share hā (breath of life) through hongi (the pressing of noses). In this manner, the reciprocating of the breath of life between everybody represented a change in their relationships with one another. As one elder of Hoani Waititi marae stated, "Welcome, you are now whānau, which means you are now free to go help clean up in the kitchen." In essence, he indicated that a deeper relationship now existed between manuhiri (guests) and tangata whenua (hosts). Unlike the impersonal and detached forms of Pākehā justice, the pōwhiri unites strangers as a family. But this invitation comes with kin obligations and responsibilities.

In the Kōti Rangatahi setting, many rangatahi did not know which marae they came from, did not understand their whakapapa (genealogy), and did not comprehend the pōwhiri ceremony. This is not surprising given their colonial history and carceral environment. And unlike the youth courts of the Pākehā criminal justice system, Kōti Rangatahi is not a quick process. Much time is set aside for the purpose of fostering whakawhanaungatanga or becoming connected with one another. Beginning with the pōwhiri, the participants in this study acknowledged that marae-based justice, over time, sought to create a respectful and welcoming space within the community. As one elder explained, this "isn't a Pākehā court. You meet at nine o'clock . . . and then work out what we're going to do when we get there. This takes them [the youth justice professionals] out of their comfort zone." In fact, the participants suggested that the youth were respectful on the marae and that they overcame any anxieties after being embraced with aroha (love) during the pōwhiri. Participants commented, as well, that the youth quickly adapted to the marae environment and, in some cases, formed an affinity with the kaumātua.

Participants also described the marae as an equalizing environment in that the same Māori customs applied to everybody, including Pākehā and other non-Māori. This was particularly noted during the pōwhiri when the community gathered. As a child youth and family manager noted, the "young people, their whānau, the professionals, the judge . . . there's no separation so you're all sitting in the same level." The way interactions with the youth are carried out can readily foster an inclusive environment. As one elder stated, "The way that we deal with the kids is like we're talking now. It's not a stand over, I'm a rangatira, I'm this and I'm that, it's 'bro,' that's how we talk to them. To me it's that interactive way that the marae communicates with people that puts people at ease."

Several interviewees noted that the marae became a place where the rangatahi could just be themselves. For example, a police youth aid officer explained that they were not labeled as "offenders" through their time in the Kōti Rangatahi. This distinction was acknowledged in the karanga (the call at the pōwhiri) and the whaikōrero (the speeches held at the pōwhiri), as noted by the police youth aid officer: "When they come on to the marae . . . we don't call them offenders . . . they're called ngā rangatira, 'haere mai ngā rangatira' when we refer to them in our whaikōrero, we don't call them offenders. I call them like our tauira, our students o ngā mātāwaka, actually, you're not offenders, you're ngā uri a ngā tīpuna, you're the descendants of our ancestors."[47] One kuia commented that having Kōti Rangatahi on the "marae is the best thing." By bringing the youth into the wharenui (meetinghouse), rangatahi were able to establish connections to their tīpuna or ancestors embodied in the carved posts on Hoani Waititi marae. The marae thus became a place without prejudice, therefore enabling Kōti Rangatahi stakeholders, elders, and the wider community to restore the respect and status of rangatahi.

THEME 2: WHAKAWHANAUNGATANGA CIRCLE

At Hoani Waititi marae, the kawa (protocols) utilized on Kōti Rangatahi days differ from its usual kawa in that everyone is invited to form a circle for the purpose of introducing themselves, usually in te reo Māori. The time this takes varies depending on the number of people in attendance, but the process can be anywhere from twenty to forty-five minutes. Each person introduces themselves with a mihi (greeting) and pepeha (the detailing of a genealogy), sharing their genealogical links to waka (canoes), maunga (mountains), awa (rivers), moana (oceans), iwi (tribe), hapū (subtribe), marae (meeting place), tīpuna (ancestors), and whānau (family). Each person then recites their pepeha in an individualized and unique way that honors their lineages. Demonstrating the diverse protocols of the marae, one kuia fluent in te reo also admitted at a marae we attended that she was not used to sharing pepeha, as this was not a tikanga practice on her marae, but because she was a guest like us, she followed the protocols of Hoani Waititi marae. Another kuia sang a waiata (song) that traced her lineage connections. As each person took turns and shared their genealogies in te reo, some struggled to recall or pronounce their pepeha. However, nearly all conveyed "ko wai au, nō hea au," or "who I am, where I come from," as a way to identify the genealogies that bind one person to another.

In our observations, the participants powerfully expressed whakawhanaungatanga (to cause a relationship to happen) during the whakawhanaungatanga circle. During these exchanges, their offering of aroha (love) became most evident in the sharing of their personal stories. The following observations from our field notes exemplify their whanaungatanga justice and connectedness:

> A visiting international Professor made a connection with a youth advocate, after realizing they grew up around the corner from each other in a large city of America. (Field notes, September 2015)

> A vivacious kuia [female elder] who was passionate about rugby league encouraged a rangatahi [youth] to join the local club. What ensued was a lot of jokes, laughter and cheerfulness among the kaumātua, judge, and the police. Humor came naturally and was often utilized to balance the seriousness of a court proceeding. (Field notes, October 2015)

> A lay advocate spoke about the impact of suicide in his whānau, it brought home the very real impacts rangatahi face and the role everyone has in providing support. (Field notes, May 2016)

As these exchanges reveal, it was not uncommon for people to trade stories about how they were drawn and connected to one another. Their personal insights about suicide left those gathered in somber silence. On other occasions, humor, as noted above, was utilized to balance the serious nature of a situation or, as demonstrated in the previous example, to ease nerves. As one experienced social worker disclosed, "I've seen them [the youth] engage a lot more in the marae setting, whether it's communicating by talking. There's humor, I think that helps a lot to engage somebody, for them to engage and feel like they're part of it."

Speaking in front of a large group of people also proved to be a daunting task for many attendees at Kōti Rangatahi. As the participants realized, not only the rangatahi became nervous when they shared their pepeha. Adults, too, appeared anxious during this protocol session. A social worker noted, "It's cool for our young people to know that as their social workers or as their mentor or their lawyer or whatever, that we're trying to speak te reo too. And sometimes we sound real fresh and that's okay, and if we're not embarrassed it's even better because then we're reaching them not to be embarrassed." For the rangatahi who had never before appeared on a marae, neither the judge nor our hosts at Hoani Waititi required them to share their pepeha during the whakawhanaungatanga circle. Yet the rangatahi often did because they tended to follow the lead of the preceding speakers. As we learned, this tactic and other strategies that involved assistance of a key worker were often observed in the rangatahi court at Hoani Waititi marae to help rangatahi recall their pepeha.

Indeed, the whakawhanaungatanga circle connected each person in attendance to their ancestors and other people and places. Establishing linkages was often a profound experience for Māori and non-Māori alike because it meant relating to someone who knew more about their lineage or finding common ground. Their personal stories reminded us about the purpose of Kōti Rangatahi, namely, to help rangatahi in their struggle with their everyday lives by connecting them to their own sacred identities.

THEME 3: WHĀNAU-FOR-WHĀNAU APPROACH

After the completion of the pōwhiri at Hoani Waititi marae, Rewi and his whānau patiently waited outside for his case to be called. He and his family were then invited into the wharenui (meetinghouse). Rewi, a young Māori and the subject of our closing vignette, then delivered his pepeha before introducing his whānau and other supporters. He also acknowledged his koro (grandfather) and relatives for traveling three hours to assist him at this marae in West Auckland. The judge asked if he "deserves that kind of care, that his aging koro would travel that far just to support him in Kōti Rangatahi." Rewi did not answer; he just shuffled from foot to foot as he looked down at his feet. His lay advocate and lawyer then provided their updates. Afterward, the kaumātua spoke to Rewi. As the kuia (female elder) began to talk, Rewi leaned in to hear her: "Rewi your koro and whānau are here to support you, and everyone is helping you to learn your pepeha, so that you know 'ko wai koe, nō hea koe' [who you are and where you come from]." Another kaumātua then turned to Rewi and said, "When I saw you during the break, you appeared lost, and you asked for an orange juice, and we didn't have that in our wharekai [eating house] to give you. I believe you are in the right place here in te Kōti Rangatahi, but I challenge you to look around you and take in what the marae has to offer you here and now because it can fill you up and sustain you for life."

Before closing, the judge queried if anyone had anything more to add. Rewi's grandfather then stood and was brought to tears. He declared, "He's a tutu (rebellious) boy, easily distracted, but we all really love him," then grabbed Rewi, and as they embraced, Rewi snuggled into his koro's chest. There was joy in the meetinghouse. And as Rewi completed his very last appearance in the Kōti Rangatahi, he received a 282 or discharge without conviction. The community then invited Rewi to hongi (sharing of breath) and kihi (kiss) all the members of the Kōti Rangatahi panel. The police prosecutor shook Rewi's hand and wished him well, as did the court supervisor, the court registrar, the judge, and, finally, the kaumātua (elders) and kuia (female elders).

In the second theme, we focused on the power of the whaka-whanaungatanga circle to establish connections between oneself and others. In the vignette about Rewi, observational data further demonstrates how relationship building and holistic well-being underscore marae-based justice. The vignette also describes how ngā Kōti Rangatahi is a whānau-for-whānau approach led by kaumātua. In this respect, Kōti Rangatahi did not duplicate the impersonal features of the Pākehā justice system. Rather, kaumātua are viewed as the cultural experts who model cultural values and practices. The kaumātua who took part in this research ranged in age from their fifties to eighties and represented many tribal affiliations. In addition, the kaumātua had diverse backgrounds and a wealth of experiences as academics, factory workers, managers, and teachers. Some worked closely with whānau in a range of social services and programs.

Regardless of how culturally disconnected rangatahi might be, one Ngāpuhi (Northland tribe) kaumātua stated he could always establish whaka-papa (genealogical links) for the rangatahi by relating their connections to their ubiquitous tīpuna, Chief Kupe.[48] As this elder explained, chief Kupe traveled from Hawaiki to the land we now call Aotearoa. He further clarified, "A lot of people say pepeha is the identity, tikanga, when you learn tikanga, pepeha is the first thing you learn; yes, and that's the identity. Identity, it comes from whakapapa, tātai whakaheke go right back, and that's where I take our young people, back to Kupe." As a participating youth justice coordinator reported, the genealogical links of the youth became enhanced by way of their whakapapa knowledge: "Through whakapapa, that's how we operate. We practice by whakapapa first and foremost." Another participant added that their practice was based on whakapapa, which is key to whanaungatanga and making connections: "I think it's all about connection. I think that's the one word that encompasses everything of what this [Kōti Rangatahi] is all about. Connection and all its forms, connection to whakapapa, to your lineage, connection to your urban marae, and connection to your community through community work and different things."

Within the Kōti Rangatahi setting, the kaumātua thus established numerous whakapapa connections with the rangatahi. By addressing questions of "Who am I?" and "Where do I come from?" rangatahi expressed emotional reactions, created new friendships, and renewed their ties with the kaumātua, meaning that they felt comfortable among the elders. Over several months, we even witnessed transformations in the demeanor of some young people, from being shy and withdrawn to being more confident about their journey of self-discovery and cultural identity. Such interactions embody what we mean by whanaungatanga justice, that is, as a kaumātua said, "whānau being used to help whānau." As one social worker put it, "I think it's really a family atmosphere, and I can say that the kai [food] the marae is providing is really . . . you know, it breaks the ice of the family to share everything . . . release your ideas and feelings and be really connected to the others."

As we have shown, these three main themes demonstrated whanaungatanga justice in action within the Kōti Rangatahi setting. The marae space both enabled and represented many layers of connectedness across temporal and spatial planes. In the pōwhiri process, we heard the narratives that upheld the power of the youth as future leaders. We also saw how the marae required the youth justice professionals to "walk their tikanga," meaning that they had to put aside their superiority and engage at a relational level with rangatahi and their whānau. The whakawhanaungatanga circle also rightly proved to be a challenging arena for adults, let alone for rangatahi. Yet this forum powerfully motivated the youth to learn and practice their genealogies. Traditionally, Māori are an aural and oral society, where ancestors repetitively recited whakapapa history and ancient karakia (incantations). It makes sense that a similar process could be used in this pan-tribal marae setting. Knowing that we can connect to one another, the last vignette offers a model by which we can operationalize whanaungatanga justice as a whānau-for-whānau approach led by kaumātua.

RESOURCING AND VALUING WHANAUNGATANGA JUSTICE

Despite the clear value of ngā Kōti Rangatahi, participants raised concerns about the limitations in resources to support tikanga values within this court setting and the marae more generally. For instance, the marae hosts spoke about the difficulty in ensuring enough people were available to welcome, engage, and feed their guests. Quite often, marae-based health and social services called on their staff to fulfill many of the roles for Kōti Rangatahi. As a result, some staff lost time and productivity with their core businesses. And whenever the marae lacked additional services, the hosts heavily relied on the tangata whenua (locals) and their resources to ensure optimum manaakitanga (hospitality). In some situations, Kōti Rangatahi even struggled to have basic support whenever several of the marae kaumātua were unavailable because they needed to attend tangihanga (funeral).

Another issue raised during the interviews relates to the financial shortfall in meeting the cost of manaakitanga or the generosity for Kōti Rangatahi. The Ministry of Justice would pay a set amount to each Kōti Rangatahi marae, and each marae would determine how to best use these funds, such as with the preparation of food. As one participating elder noted, "we always make sure there is reasonable kai because we know our kids are always hungry" while also noting that funding does not fully cover the cost of hiring the marae and catering. This meant that the marae usually "ran at a loss." Another participant added that catering for the rangatahi court differed from catering for other marae purposes. For example, a marae may collect koha (e.g., gifts like food or money) during a funeral or hui (gathering) from attendees as a form of reciprocity. Only one marae in this research collected koha before the Kōti Rangatahi pōwhiri; this kawa (protocol) was not followed in the other marae sites. Thus, the marae that participated in this research faced challenges in balancing their financial shortfalls despite receiving nominal financial assistance from the Ministry of Justice. A kaumātua had the following to say about the lack of adequate investment in Kōti Rangatahi:

> If it fails, a kid fails, and then they'll say, "We sent them down to the marae, they went through the Kōti Rangatahi, and they still failed." They don't look at what were the lack of resourcing that were here, what was the lack of support. . . . It's a real unbalanced way of thinking the system's got. They want to use the things that work, but they don't want to invest in it because it's going to show that they're inadequate to actually deal with it. Like we can, we can do a better job than the system can.

As these sentiments illustrate, some marae participants felt that the government disregarded the mana (authority) of the marae and its people. Over the span of this kaupapa Māori study, the kaumātua panel went through some changes in membership, but there was a core group of four kaumātua who provided consistency in Kōti Rangatahi. Many elders agreed with the sentiments expressed by a kaumātua who noted, "i tāku wairua, he konei," meaning "my spirit is within this work." However, one kuia (female elder) said she felt her contribution within Kōti Rangatahi was "not valued" and left in order to use her skills elsewhere. Across the entire research project, this sentiment was echoed by other elders who agreed it was difficult to balance the needs of the rangatahi with the financial difficulties. The kaumātua suggested that the government could strengthen the kaumātua panels as well as offer stipends to acknowledge their leadership roles on the marae.

CONCLUSION

Kōti Rangatahi is an Indigenous innovation spearheaded by Māori judges, rangatira (Māori leaders), and kaumātua (elders) as a culturally appropriate approach to meet the needs of rangatahi and their whānau. In our study, we found that whanaungatanga served as a foundational tikanga value and justice principle that can be applied by the elders and youth alike. Within the context of ngā Kōti Rangatahi, we conceptualize these acts of "whanaungatanga justice" as a culturally appropriate way to welcome rangatahi and their whānau and to support their dialogue and healing. Whanaungatanga justice occurred between the rangatahi through core relational skills that took place on the marae, within the pōwhiri, and in the whakawhanaungatanga circle. Participants especially indicated that the marae setting provided an "ahua," or atmosphere, that was safe, respectful, and comfortable. In contrast to the hierarchical and detached forms of Pākehā justice, participants suggested that the marae represented a neutral setting that encompassed a spiritual space of equal participation and infinite potential.

The whānau-for-whānau approach that characterizes whanaungatanga justice places the elders as part of the collective and enables them to draw on their mātauranga (knowledge) to help the youth connect or in some cases reconnect as Māori, even when their genealogical links to the marae were not evident.[49] In our study, we found that the kaumātua or elders were very skilled in establishing the whakapapa connections of the rangatahi regardless of where they came from. This was done by referring to far-reaching traditional accounts, including oral stories and the visual records within the wharenui (meetinghouse) and whakairo (carvings). We also observed that the participants accepted Māori justice as a way to care for the future generations of rangatahi.

If we are to engage disconnected rangatahi and their whānau, then we must advance a collaborative mindset and approach from the outset.[50] By doing so, we can uphold the kōrero (voice) and mātauranga (knowledge) of the kaumātua, the rangatahi, and tangata whenua (local people) across the different marae. Whanaungatanga justice should also keep all Māori out of the Pākehā criminal justice system and connect them to te Ao Māori (Māori world) where their tikanga or culture prevails. This can happen if whanaungatanga justice occurs through the pōwhiri engagement process and related Māori protocols of connecting the genealogies of the old and young. Like the conciliatory processes of other Indigenous youth examined in this anthology, whanaungatanga justice represents a magnificent tikanga value that can and should be used in every legal process in Aotearoa.

NOTES

1   This research did not include youth service perspectives from nongovernmental organizations.
2   Section 282 of Oranga Tamariki Act 1989 gives the court the power to discharge a charge in the youth court.
3   As the study progressed, we did not meet another non-Māori rangatahi participating in Kōti Rangatahi.
4   Pseudonyms have been used in this chapter to protect the anonymity of the research participants.

5   Leonie Pihama, Kuni Elaine Hineatauira Jenkins, and Alamein Middleton, *"Te Rito" Action Area 13 Literature Review: Family Violence Prevention for Māori Research Report* (Auckland: Auckland UniServices, 2003).

6   Ani Mikaere, "Tikanga as the First Law of Aotearoa," *Yearbook of New Zealand Jurisprudence* 10 (2007): 24–31.

7   Stella Aroha Black, Jacquie Kidd, Katey Thom, Alice Mills, Tracey McIntosh, and Khylee Quince, "Researching Ngā Kōti Rangatahi–Youth Courts on Marae," *Ethnographic Edge* 1, no. 1 (2017): 33–45.

8   See New Zealand Māori Council v. Attorney General 1 NZLR 64 (1987), known as the Lands case.

9   Juan Marcellus Tauri and Robb Webb, "A Critical Appraisal of Responses to Māori Offending," *International Indigenous Policy Journal* 3, no. 4 (2012): 1–16.

10 Haimona Hone-Hiki-Tia-Te-Rangi Waititi, "Toitū Te Mana Rangatahi: Marae-Based Youth Courts—Negotiating Pathways for Rangatahi Offending" (master's thesis, psychology, Victoria University, 2012).

11 Moana Jackson, *The Māori and the Criminal Justice System: He Whaipaanga Hou; A New Perspective* (Wellington: Department of Justice, 1987–1988).

12 Wanda D. McCaslin and Denise C. Breton, "Justice as Healing: Going Outside the Colonizers' Cage," in *Handbook of Critical and Indigenous Methodologies*, ed. Norman K. Denzin, Yvonna S. Lincoln, and Linda Tuhiwai Smith (Thousand Oaks, CA: Sage Publishing, 2008), 518.

13 Ministry of Corrections, 2019, *Prison Facts and Statistics: March 2019*, www.corrections.govt.nz/resources/research_and_statistics/quarterly_prison_statistics/prison_stats_march_2019.

14 Alison Cleland and Khylee Quince, *Youth Justice in Aotearoa New Zealand: Law, Policy and Critique* (Wellington: LexisNexis, 2014).

15 Philip Spier, *Offending by Children in New Zealand* (Wellington: Ministry of Social Development, 2016), 1.

16 Ministry of Justice, *Children and Young People in Court: Data Highlights for 2018*, December 2018, www.justice.govt.nz/assets/Documents/Publications/children-and-young-people-in-court-data-highlights-dec2018-v1.0.pdf.

17 Ministry of Justice, *Youth Justice Inidcators Summary Report*, April 2018, www.youthcourt.govt.nz/assets/Documents/Publications/Youth-Justice-Indicators-Summary-Report-201804.pdf.

18 Peter Gluckman, *It's Never Too Early, Never Too Late: A Discussion Paper on Preventing Youth Offending in New Zealand* (Auckland: Office of the Prime Minister's Chief Science Advisor, 2018), www.pmcsa.org.nz/wp-content/uploads/Discussion-paper-on-preventing-youth-offending-in-NZ.pdf.

19 Chris Cunneen, "Racism, Discrimination and the Over-Representation of Indigenous People in the Criminal Justice System: Some Conceptual and Explanatory Issues," *Current Issues in Criminal Justice* 17, no. 3 (2006): 329–46.

20 Ivan Zinger, *Office of the Corrrectional Investigator Annual Report 2017–2018* (Ottawa, Canada: Correctional Investigator, 2018), www.oci-bec.gc.ca/cnt/rpt/annrpt/annrpt20172018-eng.aspx.

21 Addie C. Rolnick, "Untangling the Web: Juvenile Justice in Indian Country,"
    N.Y.U. Journal of Legislation and Public Policy 19 (2016): 49–140.

22 Eileen Baldry and Chris Cunneen, "Imprisoned Indigenous Women and the
    Shadow of Colonial Patriarchy," *Australian and New Zealand Journal of
    Criminology* 47, no. 2 (2014): 285–89.

23 Katey Thom, "New Zealand's Solution-Focused Movement: Development,
    Current Practices and Future Possibilities," in *Therapeutic Jurisprudence: New
    Zealand Perspectives*, ed. Warren Brookbanks (Wellington: Thomson Reuters,
    2015), 335.

24 Ali Wardak, *"Jirga*: A Traditional Mechanism of Conflict Resolution in
    Afghanistan," Centre for Criminology, University of Glamorgan, 2003.

25 K. Kaʻanoʻi Walk, *He Waʻa Hou: An Alter-Native Court for Hawaiʻi* (Honolulu:
    Ka Huli Ao Center for Excellence in Native Hawaiian Law, 2012).

26 Christopher Buck, "Deganawida, the Peacemaker," in *American Writers:
    A Collection of Literary Biographies*, ed. Jay Parini (Farmington Hills, MI:
    Charles Scribner's Sons, 2016), 81–100.

27 Philmer Bluehouse and James W. Zion, "Hozhooji Naatʼaanii: The Navajo
    Justice and Harmony Ceremony," *Conflict Resolution Quarterly* 10, no. 4
    (1993): 327–37.

28 Christa Rautenbach, "Legal Reform of Traditional Courts in South Africa:
    Exploring the Links between *Ubuntu*, Restorative Justice and Therapeutic
    Jurisprudence," *Journal of International and Comparative Law* 2, no. 2 (2015):
    279.

29 Colin Keating, *Judicial Functions on Marae, Address by the Secretary for
    Justice to the Conference on Indigenous Peoples and Justice* (Wellington:
    Ministry of Justice, 1999), www.firstfound.org/vol.%201/keatring.htm. There
    are few recorded examples, as with meetings at the Putiki marae in Whan-
    ganui and the Te Haroto marae on the Napier-Taupo Road.

30 Richard S. Hill, *Maori and the State: Crown-Maori Relations in New Zealand/
    Aotearoa, 1950–2000* (Wellington: Victoria University Press, 2009), 4.

31 Heemi Taumaunu, *Rangatahi Courts of Aotearoa/New Zealand: An Update,
    21st Pacific Judges Forum* (Auckland: Ngā Kōti o Aotearoa/Courts of New
    Zealand, 2014).

32 For the Kōti Rangatahi and Pacifika youth court judges, elders, and youth
    speaking about these court processes, see "Rangatahi Court," YouTube video,
    posted by "Ministry of Justice," June 23, 2016, www.youtube.com/watch?v
    =oRWe2dY8Cgw&feature=youtu.be.

33 The District Court of New Zealand, "The Judges," www.districtcourts.govt.nz
    /about-the-courts/the-district-court-judiciary/the-judges.

34 Cleland and Quince, *Youth Justice*, 114.

35 Gluckman, *It's Never Too Early*, 7.

36 Ministry of Justice, *Youth Prosecutions Statistics: Data Highlights for 2017*
    (Wellington: Ministry of Justice, 2018), www.justice.govt.nz/assets
    /Documents/Publications/youth-prosecution-statistics-data-highlights
    -2017.pdf.

37 Ministry of Justice, email message to Stella Black, June 22, 2018.

38 Te Ururoa Flavell and Amy Adams, "Ka Whakanuia Ngā Kooti Rangatahi: Celebrating What's Happening in Rangatahi Courts," Beehive.govt.nz: The Official Website of the New Zealand Government, July 8, 2016, www.beehive.govt.nz/release/ka-whakanuia-ng%C4%81-kooti-rangatahi-%E2%80%93-celebrating-whats-happening-rangatahi-courts.

39 Maui Hudson, Moe Milne, Paul Reynolds, Khyla Russell, and Barry Smith, *Te Ara Tika: Guidelines for Māori Research Ethics: A Framework for Researchers and Ethics Committee Members* (Auckland: Health Research Council of New Zealand, 2010).

40 Hudson et al., *Te Ara Tika*, 14.

41 Anaru Eketone, "Theoretical Underpinnings of Kaupapa Māori Directed Practice," *MAI Review* 1, no. 1 (2008): 336.

42 Black et al., "Researching Ngā Kōti Rangatahi," 41.

43 Katey Thom, Alice Mills, Michele Yeoman, and Stella Black, *Te Kōti O Timatanga Hou/The Court of New Beginnings Process Evaluation: Qualitative Findings* (Auckland: University of Auckland, 2018).

44 Virginia Braun and Victoria Clarke, "Using Thematic Analysis in Psychology," *Qualitative Research in Psychology* 3, no. 2 (2006): 77–101.

45 We are aware that post-analysis feedback from marae kaumātua would be essential to add another layer of collective analysis to the data.

46 Hudson et al., *Te Ara Tika*, 14.

47 Our translations include rangatira (leader), whaikōrero (speech), tauira (student), ngā (plural), ngā mātāwaka (descendants of many waka or tribal affiliations), ngā uri (smaller tribal grouping), and ngā tīpuna (ancestors).

48 Māori oral history records that Kupe was a great explorer who traveled to Aotearoa from his homeland in Hawaiki. See Ranginui Walker, *Ka Whawhai Tonu Matou: Struggle without End* (Auckland: Penguin Books, 2004), 34–37.

49 Matiu Dickson, "The Rangatahi Court," *Waikato Law Review: Taumauri* 19, no. 2 (2011): 86–87, https://researchcommons.waikato.ac.nz/handle/10289/7464.

50 Andrew Becroft and Sacha Norrie, "The Youth Courts of New Zealand in Ten Years Time: Crystal Ball Gazing or Some Realistic Goals for the Future?," paper delivered at the National Youth Advocates/Lay Advocates Conference, Auckland, Aotearoa New Zealand, July 13–14, 2015.

CHAPTER 2

"RAISE YOUR PEN"

A Critical Race Essay on Truth and Justice

KEPA ʻŌKUSITINO MAUMAU, MOANA ʻULUʻAVE-
HAFOKA, AND LEA LANI KINIKINI

> For we know that the law is spiritual.
>
> —ROMANS 7:14

INTRODUCTION

LEA LANI KINIKINI

Diasporic Pacific Islanders and Native Hawaiians are a severely under-studied population in the mass incarceration crisis of the settler United States. One study, itself a rare occurrence, even showed a 250 percent increase in the incarceration of Asian Americans and Pacific Islanders, thereby demonstrating how the United States has targeted these communities as deviant.[1] At the same time, the US federal classification of "Asian Americans," under which Pacific Islanders are grouped, lacks disaggregated data. Given that the Asian American category generally represents East Asian Americans, as with its equally problematic "model minority" stereotype, the tracking of specific Pacific Islander incarceration rates have been underreported. In fact, academics and public policy officials have only begun to confront the incarceration and deportation of Southeast Asians and Pacific Islanders before and since 9/11. Additionally, Asian Americans constitute 1.5 percent of the population in federal prisons, yet, at the time of this writing, no significant effort at the national level has been made to disaggregate data about Pacific Islanders.[2]

The stark facts of mass incarceration in the settler United States are just as disturbing: the lifetime likelihood of incarceration for Black men is 1 in 3, for Latino men it is 1 in 6, and for white men it is 1 in 17, with all men being 1 in 9. In settler Canada, an Indigenous person is ten times more likely to be incarcerated in a federal penitentiary than a non-Indigenous person.[3] And American Indians constitute 2.9 percent of the total population in US federal prisons but only account for 1.6 percent of the country's demography. As these statistics reveal, we must interrogate how race-based incarceration affects Indigenous communities, as with Tongans, the subjects of our chapter and the community with which we identify as artists and writers.[4]

According to the critical race theorist Randall Kennedy, race-based incarceration adheres to an anti-Black racism and the "unequal enforcement of the law" as the principal means by which the courts, the government, and the police classify "nonwhite races." From this vantage point, the settler United States practices an unequal enforcement of the law wherein African Americans and other nonwhites receive "arbitrary, capricious, and openly discriminatory treatment" as criminal suspects.[5] Critical race theory (CRT), one of our methodologies, holds that an analysis of US settler law and justice requires an intensive counternarration to reveal the concealed class, gender, and race oppressions behind mass incarceration. Derrick Bell, another critical race theorist, similarly writes that in order to combat legal and political injustices, we should revolutionize society by way of "illustration, anecdote, allegory, and imagination."[6] As with Stella Black, Jacquie Kidd, and Katey Thom's vital usage of the Māori language in chapter 1 and as with Moses Ma'alo Faleolo's selfless support of grief-stricken young Sāmoan men in chapter 8, we also propose a radical counternarration of how Salt Lake City has represented Tongan boys and young men.

Given the high rates of Tongan incarceration in the United States, a colonial and racial process that renders Tongans as necropolitical subjects, we offer Tongan forms of storytelling that compassionately foreground their lives within and beyond the law. Indeed, every story has a soul. But many souls are required to give life to their stories. In our chapter, we represent three racial justice writers of Raise Your Pen (RYP), a grassroots coalition based in Salt Lake County. RYP is a response to the judicial murder of Siale Maveni Angilau, a young indigenous Tongan man who was gunned down by a federal marshal during the final trial that targeted a legal fiction called the "Tongan Crip Gang." With our focus on the federal grand jury indictment and racketeering and conspiracy prosecution of sixteen Tongan and Native Hawaiian young men in Salt Lake County, we therefore give life to the story of Siale Maveni Angilau and his extended family. We then identify and analyze the concealed dimensions of inequity, racism, and injustice in these trials and show how the court, housed in the land of the indigenous Ute, charged these youth as "members" and "associates" of what the law describes as a "gang" or a "continuing criminal enterprise."[7]

In these ways, we critically align CRT approaches with an ancient Oceanic belief that regards the artist as the "vehicle through whom the gods create."[8] Tongan poetics refer to this artistry as *faiva*, literally meaning one's ability to create spatial dimensions. Tongan poetics also use *heliaki* or an Indigenous kind of concealed discourse in which one says one thing but means another. This Tongan cultural practice parallels the Native Hawaiian poetics of *kaona*, wherein a deep understanding of the Native Hawaiian language can help one unpack its implied meanings in the genealogies and metaphors of chiefly and everyday speech. But unlike the law's concealed discourse that seeks to incarcerate Tongans and other nonwhite communities, *heliaki* and *kaona* reveal the hidden art, love, poetry, spirits, and even intentions of the speakers and the listeners. As master storyteller Emil Wolfgramm writes, Tongan storytelling achieves "an emotional climax in which the spirit of the presentation permits the audience *to experience the unseen world*. This is called *'asi* ('to behold the presence of the unseen')." At its highest level, continues Wolfgramm, Tongan art reflects "the spiritual angst of the composition, an ideal acknowledged by such responses from the audience as *Malie faiva. Ko e langi kuo tau!* ('Bravo, well done. The heavens are being attained!')."[9]

Throughout this chapter, we utilize literary, visual, and life writing forms of Tongan storytelling in our efforts to bring life to the incarcerated young Tongan men of Salt Lake City and the settler United States. For these reasons, we follow Wolfgramm's depiction of Tongan storytelling dynamics wherein "audiences readily *fu* (clap with cupped hands) in beat to the meter of the story poem and in reply to the traditional signal of *Tupa!*"[10] We do so not only to memorialize our loved ones with poetry and protest. Moreover, we also demonstrate the wider agentic powers of things unseen in the Tongan world, as illustrated in the saying, *kelekele 'oku u'u*, literally, "the land bites." In our conclusion, we reflect on how the land, as reflected in this proverb, metes out justice for the Tongan youth who are subjected to police surveillance, racist trials, and mass incarceration. We ruminate, as well, on the concealed discourses of the snake in US law enforcement and sovereign jurisdiction more generally, demonstrating how they become intertwined with the power of the land.

Tupa! (Clap quickly!) Let the story be told.

PART I: UNSETTLING JURISDICTIONS

LEA LANI KINIKINI

> To understand the story, the place must be understood; the
> jurisdiction, or the extent of the power to make legal decisions
> and judgments, must be displayed.
>
> —LEA LANI KINIKINI

Salt Lake County spreads out like an immaculately planned grid emanating from ground zero: the Salt Lake Temple. To the east of the Salt Lake Temple lie "the haves" on what is called the eastern "bench," a reference to authority, money, power, and reverence. To the west lie the "have nots" and the racial minorities. For all its manicured piety, an intangible dust penetrated the orderly grid. The lake for which Salt Lake City derives its name is a remnant of an ancient sea, filled with an evaporating brine leveled from a desiccated underworld named by the Ute as Pi'a-pa, or "Great Water." They also called it Ti'tsa-pa, or "Bad Water." The settler territorialization of Utah is equally great and bad. While the first Mormons were organized, they were also squatters until the Organic Act of the Territory of Utah of 1850 legitimated their presence under previous claims of allodial title over Native land. The Utah Organic Act was the most extensive land grab since the Louisiana Purchase of 1803. Today, the federal District of Utah encompasses the State of Utah and consists of twenty-nine counties covering over 82,000 square miles. By 2011, a population of 2.8 million resided in the district. Salt Lake City and its suburbs also make up Salt Lake County, the district's largest urban center. More than 70 percent of its public land is situated within the boundaries of "Indian reservations."

Like other settler jurisdictions blighting Turtle Island, the train tracks of commerce and industry in Salt Lake County separate housing for the working poor and the middle and upper classes. The federally instituted "Zone Improvement Plan codes" or ZIP codes formalized such class divisions in the 1960s by way of district markers based on income. Private and public entities likewise assigned social value and economic investments through the census, credit card campaigns, education, law enforcement programs, voter registration, and other urban policies. Although narrativized as a more efficient way to sort mail by the postmaster general, ZIP codes actually reflect how settler "planners and public officials persisted in their efforts to find a legally defensible way to regulate residences by race."[11] The first three digits delineate about 900 geographic areas, and the last two target specific areas, often colloquially known as "neighborhoods" but not always identified as distinct charters, municipal codes, and "covenants." The gridded streets locked in not only federal postal codes but also represented sites owned by the Church of Jesus Christ of Latter-Day Saints. As the dominant religion of Tongans in the county, Mormonism spatially maintained its division of religious "wards," which further segregated Tongan migrants.

In particular, Glendale, an industrial neighborhood of Salt Lake County, was the starting point for gang task force surveillance in the late 1980s, which then spread to West Valley City. Glendale falls in the Zone Improvement Plan Code of 84104 and has 7.5 percent of its area designated for residential homes.[12] This sparse residential pattern made finding Tongan children as targets shockingly simple. By the early 1990s, legal precedents from California and other state and federal lawmaking bodies flowed into Glendale. They "cracked down" on "gang-related" crime, issued mandatory life sentences for some persons, and lowered the age threshold for incarceration by "certifying" children as adults who could receive adult penalties and prison sentences. By 1991, the "ethnic enclaves" in Salt Lake City like Glendale, Poplar Grove, Rose Park, Granger, Kearns, and West Valley became "target areas" for federally funded "initiatives" like the Weed and Seed program under the US Department of Justice. Salt Lake City was chosen as a case study in the Weed and Seed program. Weed and Seed's target area was 6.4 square miles heavily populated by Tongan and Latin American migrants. Analysts had determined that this target area had seen "an influx of criminal groups from California and illegal immigrants from Mexico . . . [who were] reportedly responsible for an increase in drug trafficking within the city."[13] The reference to criminal groups from California is a thinly veiled reference to the interstate migration of Mexicans and Pacific Islanders. Initiatives like these, along with the increasingly militarized Utah state police and its adherence to California's paramilitary style of law enforcement, meant that Tongan families, and particularly children and especially boys, faced considerable, nay excessive, hyper amounts of surveillance. Police subsequently racially profiled families, including our own, to create registers of names, document traffic arrests, photograph marks on the body, and collate a technical pool of data for "gang databases."

Comparably, European American settler "Mormons" (Church of Jesus Christ of Latter-Day Saints) had also violently displaced Utes, Paiutes, Goshutes, Shoshone, and Diné/Navajo peoples in the mid-nineteenth century.[14] Their missionaries documented, as well, the migration of Tongans and other Pacific Islanders. A few decades after the 1849 takeover, for instance, the first Native Hawaiian Mormons settled a town called Iosepa, quite a ways westward of Salt Lake City. Iosepa was the first Pacific settlement in the lands of Utah. Tongans associated with the Mormon faith later settled in Salt Lake City after World War II, yet they mainly transited through the gateway cities of Los Angeles and San Francisco. Many Tongans also worked at the Los Angeles International Airport and eventually resided in nearby Inglewood. By the late 1990s, they had developed circular, kinship, and interstate networks between California and Utah as well as cultivated all sorts of social and political formations germane to capitalism's ebbs and flows. One counterculture included the Tongan youth gangs, as with the territorialized set called Raymond Avenue.

In the United States, Tongan gangs descended from the genealogy of Black American gangs in urban Chicago, Los Angeles, and San Francisco. They also forged reversals of the elite and powerful secret societies. Likening themelves to the Freemasons and other political parties, Tongan youth appropriated and created secret names and handshakes, hyperviolent altering rituals, color-coded ritual dresses, dances, and oral traditions. The police often surveilled and brutalized Black and Tongan youth, especially boys and young men, as poor, working-class communities. With their shared history of police violence, coupled with the heroin rush of the late 1970s and the crack epidemic of the 1980s, some Tongans and Black Americans found class unity in their struggle as youth gangs. As a response to these youth formations, Tongan parents usually sent their troubled children from Los Angeles to safer places like Glendale, Utah. By 1988, the "Tongan Crip Gang" had emerged as an enemy of the state of Utah after an arson and graffiti incident near East High School on 1300 East.[15]

Tupaheo! (Clap again.)

PART II: LEGAL FICTIONS

LEA LANI KINIKINI

> Salt Lake County, Utah jurisdiction in the land of the Utes,
> Paiutes, Goshutes, Shoshone, and Diné/Navajo

In 2010, a grand jury charged seventeen individuals, purported "members" and "associates" of a "Tongan Crip Gang," with a twenty-nine-count indictment under the Racketeer Influenced and Corrupt Organizations Act (RICO Act 18 USC 1961–68).[16] In the trials, the media and many people, including Tongans, referred to the act as RICO. The charges alleged that these individuals robbed convenience stores from 2002 to 2009 at which firearms were brandished and discharged. Under the State of Utah's jurisdiction, most of the defendents were already serving lengthy sentences when they were wrangled again under RICO. As per the federal mandatory minimums, they faced decades-long sentences on top of state sentences wherein they could spend up to or in excess of fifty years in prison.

During the press conference for the grand jury indictment, federal prosecutors "contend[ed] that TCG [Tongan Crip Gang] [was] a criminal enterprise that ha[d] built itself into a gang that has terrorized Utah for the past 20 years."[17] According to the officers of the court, the indictments symbolized the occult emblem of reptilian decapitation, marking the eradication of Tongan criminality. As District Attorney Lohra Miller boasted, "We have cut off the head of the snake."[18] Miller's chilling metaphor discounted the expectation that the trials would be a space to stand the tests of truth and justice.

Journals and newspapers chronicled the event and labeled the young men as "gang members," focusing on their non-European origins and playing on the stereotype of the "Polynesian giant." Newspaper writers reported daily from the trials, penning scripts driven by their classed and racist views of Tongan youth. At the same time, some attorneys labored to defend individuals subsumed by the legal title of "gang member." As the *Salt Lake Tribune* noted on September 7, 2011, Defense Attorney Fred Metos "asked jurors to try to look at each defendant separately instead of lumping all into the same category. He said prosecutors will create an atmosphere of 'fear and foreboding' that will play on jurors' emotions and implored them not to judge the defendants on their appearances—calling the group 'physically large people with long hair and foreign names.'"[19] However, the prosecutors categorized the defendants as criminals marked by vague racial body decorations and comportment.

The alleged "TCG" case also included the federal "gang expert" witness Officer Break Merino, whose testimonies raised contentious issues about his credibility. Officer Merino rose to his position in a career that included coaching little league football teams in Glendale, a neighborhood heavily populated by Tongan immigrants. In this manner, he surveilled and gained police intelligence of Tongan parents and children, particularly boys. His "expert" opinions thus helped federal prosecutors in a case that "made his career."[20] Yet Officer Merino's expert testimony rested solely on inadmissible hearsay and research gathered through undocumented conversations. Hearsay is an important legal doctrine. One legal scholar calls such undisclosed hearsay "stealth hearsay." When applied to race-based incarceration of youth gangs, stealth hearsay interlocks the oppressions built into the legal realm, strips rights and forecloses possibilities for justice through a deft slippage between constitutional and evidentiary law, and creates serious legal inequities in the allowance of unreliable evidence—"junk science"—that leads to incorrect or unfair outcomes.[21]

The above examples illustrate a few of the manifold issues in the RICO trials, all of which reveal the race-based incarceration of Tongan youth in Salt Lake City. For the remainder of our chapter, we continue to share a narrative based on CRT and Tongan forms of storytelling. But, first, it is important to memorialize our youth:

> This work is in memory of two young indigenous Tongan men
> made part of the RICO trials on Ute Lands:
> Siale Maveni Angilau
> and
> Filikisi Paea Hafoka Jr.

Filikisi Hafoka Jr. and Siale Maveni Angilau tragically lost their lives as a result of the federal prosecutions. Already serving a sentence for robbery at the Utah State Prison, Filikisi was re-tried and, after a trial, re-sentenced to an additional ten years under RICO, and this time remanded to a federal penitentiary in Virginia. On one of his first days at the penitentiary, a mob stabbed Filikisi during a prison riot. He was taken to a Tennessee hospital after the attack and passed away two weeks later, surrounded by his family.[22]

Siale Maveni Angilau was the last to stand trial under RICO. On the first day of trial, federal prosecutors called a witness to testify about "gang rituals and initiations." Siale, who was not shackled because the new courthouse defense tables had not yet been furnished with "modesty drapes," stood up and acquired a pen, a pencil, and highlighter from his attorney's tabletop. Fleet of foot, Siale "flew" into the witness box, crossing space and time. The shackled witness skittered sideways. Four shots resounded.[23] A federal marshal yelled, *"Drop the pen! Drop the fucking pen!"* Siale collapsed, "bleeding profusely" and being "unable to drop the pen." A deputy tried to handcuff him, but Siale was covered in blood, the FBI report stated.[24] Siale reportedly died later that day at a local hospital.

The judicial murder of Siale Maveni Angilau made national and international headlines. News reports emphasized that he was "armed with a pen" and characterized him as a "gang member." In August 2019, the *Salt*

Lake Tribune published another article calling the judicial murder a "christening" of the new courthouse, reiterating that its ten-story facility served "as a symbol of federal justice in Utah."[25]

According to the investigative report, it also remains unclear as to why the federal officers held Siale Angilau at the Weber County Jail during the trial. Given that the federal witness also awaited the case in this jail, Judge Tena Campbell described this move as irregular if not uncustomary. On the morning of the trial, the court records then showed that Siale's lawyer complained that Siale did not have access to his legal material and that he was refused a shower. Said Judge Tena Campbell, Siale was "in a pissy mood."

As members of the Raise Your Pen coalition and the Tongan community, we believe that this transfer to the Weber County Jail intentionally put Siale in direct physical proximity to the federal witness, Vaiola Tenifa. As the person selected to testify about "gang initiation rituals," Tenifa assisted the court's attempts to build a legal fiction called the Tongan Crip Gang.

PART III: "LETTER TO SIALE"

MOANA 'ULU'AVE-HAFOKA

> A US marshal shot and killed a Pacific Islander gang member
> Monday when the defendant tried to attack a witness with a pen
> inside the new federal courthouse in Salt Lake City. Siale Angilau,
> 25, a member of the Tongan Crip Gang, was shot several times in
> the chest about 9:25 a.m. MT [Mountain Time] after charging the
> witness [a fellow TCG member] in an "aggressive, threatening
> manner," the FBI said. He died several hours later at a hospital.
>
> —*USA TODAY*, APRIL 21, 2014

Dear Siale,

It's been ten years since we attended high school together—the high school we were bused to on the east side of Salt Lake City. We hardly knew each other. I was always tucked away in a corner writing in my black and white speckled notebook. You were surrounded by boys who respected and girls who crushed.[26]

You died last week. Shot eight times by a courtroom marshal when you reached for a pen at the defense table. And you weren't even supposed to be there. Your guilty plea had already been heard at the state level, but the federal courts wanted you, too. Wanted you and the whole Tongan Crip

Gang. So they used as a witness, a brother turned foe, and riled you up, then took you down.

While you lay heaving on a gurney, I sat in a lightly air-conditioned classroom at Harvard University where I was learning how to save black and brown poor kids from their own selves. "Give them a pen," I say, "it's the only way to save them." I dreamt of coming to Harvard ever since I was a kid and my mother gave me a pen and paper and said, "*Go and write the world*." I thought if I can just get *there*, just get *here*, it would mean something—*I* would mean something. I could re-write the narrative of the working-class brown kids from the Westside of Salt Lake City who were all bad and no good.

But it's the pen that killed you. The media took your image, plastered it across the country, called you a "known danger," made you a footnote to the story everyone already knows, evidence of the pathology of brown bodies.

They say you were the problem. They say now that you're gone our Salt Lake City community is safe from the savage gangsters, safe from hate, safe from violence. But what about the ones who shot you? We Westsiders hide from their bullets guided by the narrative that brought you down. We hide our boys that look like you deep in our hearts so they won't get them, too.

Most accept the narrative that tells us that killing brown-skinned men like you will save the family, the community. But few seem to notice the dismantling of our family—the Tongan family. It has been unraveling since we came to this country. When our mothers became maids and our fathers became landscapers, they built other people's homes and other people's dreams. We had to be grateful because we believed it was just a matter of time when it'd be our homes and our dreams.

Years later, when our parents, sick and tired, repaired their own disintegrating homes, we were gone. We already found out those dreams were never going to be ours. So we took to the streets.

Siale, is that why you reached for the pen?

We underestimated the story behind the bullets. You knew you did some bad things and you weren't trying to excuse yourself. You lunged forward knowing the punishment was never going to match the crime. Was it worth the risk? I wish I could've written you into a more submissive part in the story. Head down, your *please* and *thank yous* in place. Be friendly, but not too friendly—lest they misread your kindness for trickery. Cover your tattoos with white collared shirts. Behave for the teacher, then the police officer, and finally the judge.

But your spirit was too big, too strong, too knowing of injustice. You had to do things your own way.

I followed the narrative, stayed in my corner, in my books. Started on my way to suburbia—separate, token, gritty, lucky, and afraid. Afraid that you might be right, that three letters behind my name wouldn't change the fact that I was a working-class kid from the Westside of Salt Lake City and will always be. And I needed to own it, not re-write it.

My Facebook feed is filled with your image. I'm reconnecting with our old high school friends. Sharing story and struggle, the beautiful and the difficult. The Tongan family is mourning together; we're seeing each other, again. No news coverage here. We want to write the wrongs on our timeline.

Funny thing, though, as skewed as the news is, they got one thing right about you, the judge, the marshal, the jury, too. The most dangerous person in the United States of America is a brown body armed with a pen.

Your Glendale sister,

Moana

Tupaheo! (Clap again.)

PART IV: DISAPPEAR

LEA LANI KINIKINI

No sooner had we dug our heels into the American Dream, they began to disappear. I began using fingers to count the number of brothers, sons, cousins, and fathers who disappeared. I ran out of fingers. I began counting on my toes. I ran out of toes. Children as young as thirteen began disappearing into a life "behind the fence."

But their specters haunted me in newspapers, on television, in tiny bites wrapped up on both sides with officials making "statements." First they went into alternative high schools, then youth corrections and state and federal penitentiaries. The machinery was automated, with bureaucratic chutes and black holes, and sometimes we never saw them again.

A good deal were from prison put on US Immigration and Customs Enforcement (ICE) holds, shackled and flown to homes they hadn't seen since they were infants.

Growing up in the 1990s was like one long episode of *The Twilight Zone*, only more Orwellian.

Seeing our stories gilded on the evening news, the familiar voices of the disappeared were rarely, if ever, heard. I dreaded the thought of mind control, of the Orwellian future as technology grew into tiny bytes of sound and image. What I knew was the whole story was not being told. I distanced myself from the news reports, full of rubbish, I thought.

Then came the years of visits, behind strong panes of plexiglass, weeks marked by collect calls, the reams of handwritten letters. Then came the quiet rage. A blue rage. A rage against American capital, Walmarts, schools, the news apparatus, the legal vices, prisons, and the racial and class segmentation.

The millennium came and went. A quiet dis-ease followed as computers that were meant to melt down never did.

And then 9/11.

After 9/11, I realized that the pat downs, the search and seizures, the data surveillance, and the invasions of privacy that affected poor communities of color during the mass incarceration buildup and the domestic "war on drugs" were increasingly applied to larger swathes of the population in the "war on terror."

The "new" millennium's settler security state had turned on itself, a frenzied cannibal eating its own.

As the late Lakota political activist and leader Russell Means said, "Welcome to the American Reservation."

With the disappearance of our brothers, our freedoms disappeared too.

Tupaheo! (Clap and let the time renew.)

PART V: FIXSTACK MERCY ME 924(C), HR 4261 SAFE JUSTICE ACT

KEPA ʻŌKUSITINO MAUMAU

> In our constitutional order, a vague law is no law at all.
>
> —ASSOCIATE JUSTICE GORSUCH,
> United States v. Davis et al. decision (June 24, 2019)

Preface: After standing trial, Kepa ʻŌkusitino Maumau, one of the seventeen individuals named on the federal indictments in 2010, was imposed by far the longest bondage term of fifty-seven years due to heightened mandatory minimum penalties for possessing a firearm in connection with a "crime of violence" under the Hobbs Act robbery 18 USC 924(c)(3)(B). Disregarding factual events, this statute defines "crime of violence" as that which "by its nature, involves a substantial risk that physical force against the person or

property of another may be used in the course of committing the
offense." From a federal prison in Louisiana, the state with the
second highest incarceration rate (also the site of the largest slave
revolts in the early nineteenth century), Kepa pursues justice
through the power of the written word and activates his sovereign
mana or power in countering the unconstitutionality of the legal
deficiencies in his case. In these ways, Kepa actively engages with
racial justice despite the severe restrictions about writing inside a
federal prison. In 2018, he then published articles for community
newspapers on education. Kepa wrote the following resistance piece
for the 924(c) Mercy Me campaigns and the Safe, Accountable, Fair,
Effective Justice Act (SAFE Justice Act HR 4261). Each advocates for
sentencing reform, with the latter awaiting action in Congress.[27]

I had requested letters of support from willing family members and friends
to be sent to my judge Tena Campbell as I awaited her ruling on my
motion.[28] The letters were intended to demonstrate the strong support system I was to return to if granted the opportunity. 'Inoke Hafoka, along
with members of the Glendale Turkey Bowl Committee (GTBC), Glendale
Youth Football (GYF), and Raise Your Pen (RYP), organized a write night
at the Glendale Library to facilitate this demonstration. These amazing
organizers provided paper, writing utensils, computers to print, envelopes
and postage stamps to send everyone's letters. It was a magical night; the
coming together of our community and good cheer, spirits, love and support; they sparked positive action and created a home where no child in
our family gets left behind. This hope gave life to believe that one letter will
make a difference. And it did. You were just made to believe otherwise.

Can you imagine how my judge must have felt after receiving your letters?
You have a value and force as a united people! I don't think she has experienced
this much love and support for a defendant in the history of her career! You
made a positive impact that changed the landscape of how our love is perceived.
This love is not influenced by the negative views of outsiders. This is rooted in
truth. You all deserve to know what happened with my motion. And you
might wonder what happened with the letters Tena Campbell received. I
imagine she was caught by surprise before she became overwhelmed.

The illustration that follows conveys a message with deep meaning.
There is a mind out there that will connect and decipher it.

I couldn't believe it either. I knew we did not qualify for RICO but it
required a reasoning I could not articulate. It is like one of those movies

where a patient who is mistakenly placed in a mental asylum tries to convince doctors that he is not crazy. Only the audience knows. I am not RICO material. It has been misapplied. I had to ask myself, "How many have been caught up in its illusory webs? And how many will there be after me?" "Was I supposed to be fearful enough not to question its use?" Someone had to stand up to the bully's abuse. So I stood. It's not easy on my family and friends but it was necessary to bring the injustice to light. Along the way, invaluable lessons have been learned. Our justice system works for or against us depending on the individuals wielding its power. In

FIGURE 2.1. (*opposite, top*) Judge Tena Campbell receives letters. The illustration begins with my judge reflecting on all of your letters . . . (Image credit: Kepa Maumau, *Mercy Me: An Illustrated Story*)

FIGURE 2.2. (*opposite, bottom*) Lawyer Benji petitions. My lawyer contacted me one day, asking permission to make additional arguments in my motion. Of course, I agreed! It was like an angel from heaven was sent to assist me out of a bottomless pit. My lawyer came running in because he had . . . (Image credit: Kepa Maumau, *Mercy Me: An Illustrated Story*)

FIGURE 2.3. (*above*) Sentencing flashbacks. (Image credit: Kepa Maumau, *Mercy Me: An Illustrated Story*)

retrospect, my judge had to make sense of everything that took place up to this point. It may be noteworthy to consider that it is not easy for the governing authority to acknowledge that a flaw exists within its body.

What if RICO was misapplied? Siale Angilau was killed in court at his RICO trial. That might've meant that Vaiola Tenifa would have no need at that trial for Siale to lunge at. And if that's true, Siale would've never been killed that day. What about the lawsuit that was pending against the government? You have excessive force but now you have misapplied law that leads to excessive force. It is not a pretty picture. There are many things to consider in addition to your letters.

FIGURE 2.4. (*above*) Judge Campbell denies motion. (Image credit: Kepa Maumau, *Mercy Me: An Illustrated Story*)

FIGURE 2.5. (*opposite, top*) Lawyer Benji responds. (Image credit: Kepa Maumau, *Mercy Me: An Illustrated Story*)

FIGURE 2.6. (*opposite, bottom*) Judge Campbell rule bound. Does it really matter that there has been a misapplication of law? Yes, of course, it does because individuals learned in law are purported to know what they are doing. (Image credit: Kepa Maumau, *Mercy Me: An Illustrated Story*)

Well, you see, that's the thing. It's not new evidence. It's Been right before your eyes this whole time. And the eyes of the Plaintiff executing this case, the one responsible for upholding the law.

I've taken existing facts from the record and applied the law to it.

And it clearly outlines that these guys did not qualify for the R.I.C.O. to begin with...

My client also pointed out that the process for qualifying the detective as an expert was flawed.

You make a valid point and you might be right but let me explain how this works.
The rules say that if you come under actual innocence, you have to meet a few requirements.

One of those requirements is it has to be new evidence. So although you might be right, you've taken facts that were available from the beginning. Why it was not brought up from the beginning, I cannot Say. But at this stage in the proceedings, it is old evidence.

Therefore, you cannot use Actual innocence. It now becomes mere legal insufficiency.

FIGURE 2.7. (*top*) Benji questions: Hmm . . . this is interesting. You may want to take some time to reason through this one. (Image credit: Kepa Maumau, *Mercy Me: An Illustrated Story*)

FIGURE 2.8. (*bottom*) Benji paces point by point. (Image credit: Kepa Maumau, *Mercy Me: An Illustrated Story*)

FIGURE 2.9. (*top*) Technical bars: Piercing the veil of justice. (Image credit: Kepa Maumau, *Mercy Me: An Illustrated Story*)

FIGURE 2.10. (*bottom*) On two hands: Siale and Kepa. (Image credit: Kepa Maumau, *Mercy Me: An Illustrated Story*)

FIGURE 2.11. (*top*) How do you sleep at night? (Image credit: Kepa Maumau, *Mercy Me: An Illustrated Story*)

FIGURE 2.12. (*bottom*) Karl Malone delivers. Guess who delivered all of your letters to Tena Campbell? (Image credit: Kepa Maumau, *Mercy Me: An Illustrated Story*)

IN REM JURISDICTION: REVERSAL OF SOVEREIGNS

LEA LANI KINIKINI

> For the priesthood being changed, there is made of necessity, a
> change also of the law.
>
> —HEBREWS 7:12

> You will tread on the lion and the adder; the young lion and the
> serpent you will trample underfoot.
>
> —PSALM 90

As we end this chapter, we return to District Attorney Lohra Miller's invocation of the potent emblem of a decapitated snake. Interestingly, a snake
continues to maintain an ability to bite after death. Certain reptiles refuse
to die after decapitation and still remain animate, able to effect action.
Some even regrow their bodies. It's perhaps possible that Miller did not
realize they were, in fact, invoking an occult symbol representative of life
not merely after death but in defiance of death. The metaphor of reptilian
decapitation in the occult is not a symbol of death; rather, especially in the
context of the federal government, the decapitated snake has been used as
a symbol of political dismemberment or the jurisdictional redrawing of
sovereign territories since the eighteenth century.

During the early English colonization of non-Christian worlds, the
papal authority of the doctrine of discovery and *inter caetera* informed
English possessions of land and property. Thereafter, colonies that removed
themselves from the jurisdiction of the Crown came to be known as decapitated snakes. In this regard, the snake became a cartographic emblem that
conveyed allodial title from the realms and subdivisions claimed under
the English Crown. As a symbol of independence and even continued colonization, the snake struck down the Kingship of the British Crown and
marked the emergence of what would become a new order under US settler
jurisdiction. The decapitated snake not only reflected a break from a dis-
embodied sovereign; more tellingly, the snake represented another sovereign. In the settler United States, these sovereigns manifest as reservations,
overseas territories, and even gangs.

Then and now, snakes, as emblems of power, liberate and re-unify
political will and reverse established jurisdictions. For example, on May 9,
1754, a drawing of a segmented and decapitated snake with the caption
"JOIN, or DIE" was published in the *Pennsylvania Gazette*. Oft cited as the

first political cartoon published in American newspapers, it was accompanied by an exchange of rivaled verse between Great Britain and British America. Derided as the "Head of the Serpent we know *should* be bruised," the British colonies in North America accompanied a rejoinder:

> Tho' the prudent catch snakes by the back or the tail—
> To direct to the head!—our GOOD KING *must* indite 'em—
> They forgot that the *head* would most certainly bite 'em.[29]

As the federal prosecutor's invocation of reptilian decapitation reveals, the RICO trials led to the judicial murder of Siale Angilau. Yet, as our analysis of decapitated snakes illustrates, a reversal of sovereignty is at stake. In other words, despite the necropolitical attack direct to the head, *the head still bites.* Nevertheless, we find it difficult to convey the effects and subtleties of Siale Maveni Angilau's death to his relatives. In March 2018, a summary judgment even dismissed the Angilau's family's wrongful death lawsuit against the federal marshal who killed Siale and concluded that the marshal's actions were "not unreasonable."[30] In response to requests by the media and Angilau's family, the federal government then released the court video footage of Siale scaling the witness stand. The video stream, now public, appears on multiple news outlets, websites, and YouTube, with more than three million views to date. It spells a haunting story. Oddly, all of the video footage contains a strange audible warp that sounds like it's saying "wall," which is "law" backwards.

For many Tongans, a general feeling exists about the land, namely, that the "world of things" is animated with agentic powers. Such mana adheres in the saying *kelekele ʻoku uʻu*, literally, "the land bites." In this sense, the "world of things"—what Anglo-Saxon law calls *in rem* jurisdiction—indicates that a rule "of things" was laid long ago in contrast to a rule "of persons," or *in personam* jurisdiction:

> This seems to indicate the existence of a time in Anglo-Saxon law when
> inanimate objects (and animals, too) were tried in lawsuits *as defendants.*
> There is little doubt but that all primitive thought regarded the immediate
> cause of an injury as capable of being tried in a lawsuit. To this thought
> there came the idea that there must have been some kind of motion,
> perhaps to enable the mind to read animation into the thing . . . if one
> assumes that the ship is endowed with life and personality the law at
> once becomes intelligible.[31]

An action *in rem* is a proceeding that takes no notice of the owner of the property but determines rights *in* the property that are "conclusive against all the world." As Tongans often say, *kelekele 'oku u'u*. Remember, jurisdiction "is the power and legal authority to declare what is law in a given situation. It has been declared that the ultimate basis of jurisdiction is the physical power to enforce."[32] The legal authority, in a given situation, rests on the *physical* power to enforce. But what about the powers that stand *behind* the world of things, *behind* the world of people, *behind* the world of state governments, principalities, municipalities, corporate entities, armies, navies, warmongers, and Gang Task Forces?

And what of Native land? Does land have agentic powers to effect enforcement? Does the unjust titling of land provide a counternarration, if not life story, for resisting the legal claims of the settler state? Maybe, just maybe, there is a spiritual world that controls *things* and has power to effect action upon persons, such as illness or death. Tongans know this world as *faikehe*, or "the other side" that encompasses all supernatural entities. In this world, that which is not seen retains the mana and power to determine the truth and enforce justice.[33] As we say, "things have a way of working themselves out." *Kelekele 'oku u'u*: the land bites.

CODA: THE LAND BITES (*IN REM* JURISDICTION)

LEA LANI KINIKINI

What happened to Mr. Break Merino, the Salt Lake City police officer and "gang expert" who helped federal prosecutors in the RICO trials examined in this chapter?[34] In the years following his testimony, the Salt Lake City Police Department fired Merino after he succumbed to post-traumatic stress disorder and caused a cortisol buildup to blind his left eye. Perhaps the "mote" that Mr. Merino found in his brother's eye became a beam in his own?[35] Whether his blinding is poetic justice for the prosecution of Tongan youth or mere coincidence remains a matter of interest. It is perhaps one of the many invisible "strands of human lives" that can connect or disconnect justice in the world behind "things." Mr. Merino was not the only individual whose career was in some ways enhanced by the press and prosecutions.

What can we say, as well, about Lohra Miller, the popularly elected and police-endorsed federal district prosecutor? At the same time she prosecuted the legal fiction called the Tongan Crip Gang, she was simultaneously surrounded by a number of "controversies . . . and allegations of behind-the-scenes shenanigans," as one liberal news publication phrased it.[36] As early as 2005, Miller was subjected to numerous police investigations. Specifically, the police allleged that she held alcohol parties for children, ran an illegal and unlicensed day care and law office out of her home, and accepted unethical campaign donations. Salt Lake County councilmen alleged that Miller even "invented an imaginary crime wave to justify increasing her office budget. An anonymous citizen hired a private investigator to look into her 'shenanigans' motivated by 'a sincere desire for truth and public accounting of public officials.'"[37] Eventually, Miller was officially cleared of criminal charges. Her neighbors also maintained her innocence in their gated community.

Nevertheless, the former district attorney of Salt Lake County remains a contested figure, as reflected in the American Civil Liberties Union's lawsuit about her illegal charging of unlimited fees to indigent defendants.[38] As of 2019, Miller lives in Boca Raton, Florida, and works as the chief executive officer of a cloud-based crime prevention (pre-crime) computer program. The company works with retail companies that partner with jurisdictions to curtail crime by using cloud-based technology, databases, and facial recognition software.[39] Lohra Miller's replacement, District Attorney Sim Gill, then instituted a Conviction Integrity Unit (CIU) to allow those who have been wrongfully accused of crimes the opportunity to review their convictions. The CIU also encourages a culture of transparency, citing that the "diverse backgrounds" and legal expertise of panel members would ensure impartiality. As Gill explained, "We have an affirmative ongoing obligation, as ministers of justice, not only to the community but to the process itself."[40]

After Siale's passing, many brothers, sisters, and loved ones in Salt Lake City rallied around 'ofa (love) to counteract the moral panic around Tongan children and young people. In an attempt to counter such hate and fear, the community chose the high school graduation photo of Siale. The image showed him wreathed from the heart to the crown with kahoa and lei, traditional emblems of love and respect in Tonga and Hawai'i, respectively.[41] The Raise Your Pen Coalition, established by Siale Maveni Angilau's family, now works with Tongan and other Pacific Islander children to ensure their safety and protection from all forms of violence, seen and unseen, written and spoken. As we have demonstrated, every soul deserves a story in the mass incarceration crisis of the settler United States. In this regard, Filikisi Hafoka Jr., who lost his life in a prison riot in Virgina, will never be forgotten. His brother, 'Inoke, is a doctoral candidate at the University of California, Los Angeles, and is an author in this volume (see chapter 9). 'Inoke also works with the Tongan community to use education to heal the collective trauma experienced by the past three decades of police surveillance, racist trials, and mass incarceration in Salt Lake County.

In June 2019, the United States Supreme Court stated that 924(c) firearms enhancement clauses are "unconstitutionally vague." This decision opens a pathway of relief for Kepa 'Ōkusitino Maumau, whose case similarily reflects the fate of several thousand incarcerated men and women whose lives have been hampered by unconstitutional sentencing.[42] These are just a few of the positive outcomes that highlight the agency and redemptive power of Tongan storytelling and grassroots organizing. In our case, literary, visual, and life writing, coupled with critical race theory methodologies, revealed the concealed discourses of the judicial murder of Siale Maveni Angilau. That is to say, we show how the mass incarceration crisis informed the policing of immigrant communities in Glendale, the fictionalizing of the Tongan Crip Gang, and the killing of Tongan boys and young men. But given our emphasis on bringing life to the stories of Siale and others, we creatively offered the art, criticism, and poetry of Raise Your Pen; revealed the alternative sovereigns that are reborn after the death of a snake; and flagged the power of land in the unseen world of Tongans.

Taken together, we have sought to change the will of the heart (*loto*) and the will of the crown (*'ulu*) in the years following the sixteen indictments, the judicial murder of Siale Angilau, and the inequitable sentences handed down by federal judgments. Given our humility and *'ofa/alofa/aloha/aroha* (compassionate love to the other), our means of resistance lies in equalizing the heart (*loto*) with the crown (*'ulu*) as the base for agentic power. This resistance is wrought not through the angry bite of imposing venomous codes among the Tongan youth. Rather, such resistance comes through the loving allowance of *hā*, or the gift of sharing breath, carrying truth, and delivering justice—what in Tonga is *manavā*. And in love we can find and achieve truth and justice. From this stance, our generation can resist the mass incarceration crisis and preserve our Indigenous genealogies, our true codes.

Malie faiva. Ko e langi kuo tau!

POSTSCRIPT

LEA LANI KINIKINI

> Where there is no law, there is no transgression.
>
> —ROMANS 5:4

On February 18, 2020, Judge Tena Campbell granted Kepa 'Ōkusitino Maumau a re-sentencing hearing based on the extraordinary factors of Kepa's youth at the time of the offense. She then ordered him to be transported from a Louisiana penitentiary to a jail in Utah. On March 13, the day the US settler state declared a national emergency due to the outbreak of the novel coronavirus disease (COVID-19), Kepa arrived in Salt Lake County. John Gleeson, the counsel for Kepa, then participated in a telephonic hearing on May 4. Gleeson, a former federal judge, also prosecuted and convicted John Gotti, the Gambino Mafia boss, in 1992. Now representing Kepa, Gleeson provided a "doorway of justice" for our fellow co-author and illustrator. At the hearing, Judge Campbell then stated that she was legally bound to uphold a fifteen- to twenty-five-year portion of the mandatory minimum in the current fifty-five-year sentence of Kepa. Citing recent case law under the First Step Act of 2018, however, Gleeson argued that Kepa's mandatory minimum sentence must be evaluated as a "choice" and not as a requirement. Judge Campbell then asked both sides to submit briefs, and a second telephonic hearing was scheduled the following week. Three days before this hearing, COVID-19 raged inside Kepa's jail, and he was put into quarantine. On May 11, Judge Campbell allowed oral arguments to proceed without Kepa present. Nevertheless, members of his family and wider community, including a newspaper reporter, called into the telephonic hearing to express their 'ofa (love) for Kepa. Both briefs then concluded that Judge Campbell was not bound by the fifteen-year minimum. After weighing the oral arguments, presentence reports, and supplementary materials, Judge Campbell then granted Kepa a sentence reduction to time served in twelve years of his original fifty-seven-year sentence. Gleeson, Kepa, the Raise Your Pen Coalition, and many other supporters subsequently opened the doors of justice for thousands of Black and Brown people similarly affected by mandatory minimums under 924(c).

On May 22, 2020, Kepa 'Ōkusitino Maumau was delivered from captivity, *crown intact.*

NOTES

1 This statistic excludes Native Hawaiians. Refer to Angela E. Oh and Karen Umemoto, "AAPIs: From Incarceration to Re-entry," *Amerasia Journal* 31, no. 3 (2005): 43–59.

2 Federal Bureau of Prisons, "Inmate Race," accessed June 2, 2019, www.bop.gov /about/statistics/statistics_inmate_race.jsp.

3 Karlie Gurski, "Guilty by Design: A Critical Race Analysis of the Over-Incarceration of Indigenous Peoples in an Era of Reconciliation" (master's thesis, University of Alberta, 2017), 4–5.

4 Thomas P. Bonczar, "Prevalence of Imprisonment in the U.S. Population, 1974–2001," *Bureau of Justice Statistics*, accessed June 2, 2019, www.bjs.gov /content/pub/pdf/piusp01.pdf.

5 Randall Kennedy, *Race, Crime, and the Law* (New York: Vintage Books, 1997), 111–14.

6 Derrick A. Bell, "Who's Afraid of Critical Race Theory?," *University of Illinois Law Review* (1995): 893.

7 Because of space constraints, we do not examine the Native Hawaiian youth in these trials.

8 Erenora Puketapu-Hetet, *Maori Weaving* (Auckland: Pitman Publishing, 1989), 2.

9 Emil Wolfgramm, "Comments on a Traditional Tongan Story Poem," *Mānoa: Writing from the Pacific Islands* 5, no. 1 (Summer 1993): 171 (emphasis added).

10 Wolfgramm, "Comments," 172.

11 Christopher Silver, "The Racial Origins of Zoning: Southern Cities from 1910–40," *Planning Perspectives* 6, no. 2 (1991): 189. Refer, as well, to Ruth Knack, Stuart Meck, and Israel Stollman, "The Real Story behind the Standard Planning and Zoning Acts of the 1920s," *Land Use Law Zoning Digest* 48, no. 2 (1996): 3–9.

12 Salt Lake City Engineering Division, "Community Council Districts," online open data digital GIS file, accessed August 11, 2020, https://gis-slcgov .opendata.arcgis.com/datasets/8a6d4c855ac64dc9a0462b9b1f49bedf_4.

13 US Department of Justice, *National Evaluation of Weed & Seed: Salt Lake City Case Study Research Report* (Washington, DC: National Institute of Justice, 1999), www.ncjrs.gov/pdffiles1/nij/175700.pdf.

14 Hokulani K. Aikau, *A Chosen People, A Promised Land: Mormonism and Race in Hawai'i* (Minneapolis: University of Minnesota Press, 2012).

15 On media coverage of this incident and its link to a "gang element" in 1987, refer to "Tongan Crips Gangster Member Arrested in February Car Arson," *Deseret News*, April 21, 1989, www.deseret.com/1989/4/21/18803868/tongan -crips-gangster-member-arrested-in-february-car-arson; and "Gang Element Downplayed in Vehicle-Burning Incident," *Deseret News*, February 14, 1989, www.deseret.com/1989/2/14/18795256/gang-element-downplayed-in-vehicle -burning-incident.

16   "Grand Jury Returns Indictment Charging Members, Associates of Tongan Crip Gang with RICO, Other Violations," US Attorney's Office District of Utah, May 12, 2010, https://archives.fbi.gov/archives/saltlakecity/press-releases/2010/slc051210.htm.

17   Melinda Rogers, "Jury Convicts Some Gang Members on Racketeering Charges," *Salt Lake Tribune*, October 7, 2011.

18   Stephen Hunt, "'We have cut off the head of the snake' of Tongan Crip Gang," *Salt Lake Tribune*, May 13, 2010. See also Clinton S. Hinote, *Cutting Off the Head of the Snake: Applying and Assessing Leadership Attack in Military Conflict* (Maxwell Air Force Base, AL: School of Advanced Air and Space Studies, 2013).

19   Melinda Rogers, "Is the Tongan Crip Gang a Criminal Enterprise?," *Salt Lake Tribune*, September 7, 2011.

20   Erin Alberty, "Betrayal Comes Full Circle, Says a Salt Lake City Gang Investigator Who Developed PTSD, Then Lost His Job," *Salt Lake Tribune*, July 15, 2018. On the court's decision to admit Officer Break Merino as an expert witness, see Fangupo, "Motion to Exclude as Break Merino as Expert Witness," ECF No. 362 in 2:08-cr-758 (D. Utah, 2011); and Order and Memorandum Decision Case No. 2:08-CR-758-TC (D. Utah, 2011), https://ecf.ksd.uscourts.gov/cgi-bin/show_public_doc?2012cr10089-643-3; both in Kamahele v. United States, Case No. 2:15-cv-00506-TC (D. Utah, August 9, 2017), https://casetext.com/case/kamahele-v-united-states.

21   Julie A. Seaman, "Triangulating Testimonial Hearsay: The Constitutional Boundaries of Expert Opinion Testimony," *Georgetown Law Journal* 96 (2008): 827.

22   'Inoke Hafoka, "Tokoua Brother Testimonial," YouTube video, posted by "I. Hafoka," December 10, 2012, www.youtube.com/watch?v=7adDaQvduAQ&t=1s.

23   Initially, eyewitnesses reported eight shots, which may have been attributed to the echo in the courtroom chambers. After extensive petitions by Angilau's family, the court then publicly released its video footage in March 2018 and confirmed that four shots had occurred.

24   "FBI Angilau Summary," May 23, 2014, www.documentcloud.org/documents/6283520-FBI-Angilau-Summary.html.

25   Nate Carlisle, "Utah's Fatal Courthouse Shooting Might Never Have Happened If the Drapes Had Arrived Earlier," *Salt Lake Tribune*, August 18, 2019.

26   This letter is reprinted from Moana 'Ulu'ave, "Open Letter to Siale," YouTube video, posted by "LELE Pacific," April 30, 2014, www.youtube.com/watch?v=dREpH-OeW2g&t=17s; also published on the blogsite *KiwiMormon*, May 3, 2014, www.patheos.com/blogs/kiwimormon/2014/05/utah-where-being-a-brown-brother-with-a-pen-can-cost-you-your-life.

27   Kepa Maumau, "My Education Continues," *Westview Media News*, February 7, 2018, https://westviewmedia.org/2017/item/236-my-education-continues. See also "Summary: H.R.2944—114th Congress (2015–2016)," accessed

December 17, 2018, www.congress.gov/bill/114th-congress/house-bill/2944?q
={%22search%22%3A[%22safe+justice+act%22.

28 This section is reprinted from Kepa Maumau, "#FIXSTACKING MERCY ME
924(C): HR 4261 S.A.F.E. Justice Act," Spark Adobe, accessed December 15,
2018, https://spark.adobe.com/page/oRv3JKJgoX1xk/?fbclid=IwAR2RPFkWL
CPqwWmN828jRSVUXTOPzVHooQ3FyvADaFwPoWxxMgptgpgxxHc.
See also Maumau, "My Education Continues."

29 Karen Severud Cook, "Benjamin Franklin and the Snake That Would Not
Die," *British Library Journal* 22, no. 1 (1996): 88–111, www.bl.uk/eblj
/1996articles/pdf/article5.pdf.

30 Nate Carlisle, "Video of 2014 Salt Lake City Courthouse Shooting to Be
Released, but Judge Dismisses Lawsuit Brought by Family of Slain Defendant,"
Salt Lake Tribune, March 9, 2018.

31 Morris E. Cohn, "Jurisdiction in Actions *in Rem* and *in Personam*," *St. Louis
Law Review* 14 (1929): 175 (emphasis added), https://openscholarship.wustl
.edu/law_lawreview/vol14/iss2/5.

32 Cohn, "Jurisdiction," 171.

33 Andy Mills, "'Akau tau': Contextualizing Tongan War Clubs," *Journal of the
Polynesian Society* 118 (March 2009): 39–40.

34 See note 20.

35 Matthew 7:3–5.

36 Stephen Dark, "Salt Lake DA Lohra Miller's Bullet-Dodging Faces Test," *Salt
Lake City Weekly*, October 27, 2010, www.cityweekly.net/utah/salt-lake-da
-lohra-millerandrsquos-bullet-dodging-faces-test/Content?oid=2150184.

37 Ted McDonough, "Illegally Blond: The Wild Party at Salt Lake County
Attorney Lohra Miller's House Goes On. And On," *Salt Lake City Weekly*,
March 18, 2008, www.cityweekly.net/utah/feature-illegally-blond-the-wild
-party-at-salt-lake-county-attorney-lohra-millerandrsquos-house-goes-on
-and-on/Content?oid=2134845.

38 Webb v. Lohra Miller, October 12, 2010, www.acluutah.org/images/Webb_v
_Miller_Complaint.pdf. See also the press release announcing the settlement,
"Utah Association of Criminal Defense Lawyers and Salt Lake County Settle
Discovery Fees Lawsuit," February 8, 2011, www.acluutah.org/images
/020911PRDiscoveryfees.pdf; and the ACLU notice of the resolved case, July 1,
2011, www.acluutah.org/legal-work/resolved-cases/item/167-webb-v-lohra
-miller.

39 Lohra Miller website, accessed September 7, 2019, http://lohramiller.com.

40 Jessica Miller, "Salt Lake County Launches a Conviction Integrity Unit to
Review the Cases of People Who Say They Are Innocent," *Salt Lake Tribune*,
October 8, 2018.

41 Eric S. Peterson, "To Write a Wrong: The Raise Your Pen Group Wants to
Rewrite the Tragic Story of Siale Angilau," *Salt Lake City Weekly*, April 29,
2015, www.cityweekly.net/utah/to-write-a-wrong/Content?oid=2790387.

42 United States v. Davis et al. Syllabus, decided June 24, 2019, www
.supremecourt.gov/opinions/18pdf/18-431_7758.pdf.

CHAPTER 3

PASIFIKA LENS

An Analysis of Sāmoan Student Experiences in
Australian High Schools

VAOIVA PONTON

WITH THE GROWING ENROLLMENTS OF MĀORI, PASIFIKA, AND
Sāmoan students in the schools of Melbourne, a coastal city in the state of
Victoria, Australia, educators must consider their cultural and migration
experiences as part of their curriculum and policies. This knowledge can
improve their educational goals and can establish links to communities
that are not well known in Melbourne. Moreover, the "one size fits all"
approach of the Western education system often fails to engage diverse
learners, form effective communication strategies, and establish a sense of
belonging for new immigrants. Having lived as a teenager and having
worked as a high school teacher in Melbourne, I am very familiar with
these educational challenges. In an effort to raise awareness about these
issues in Victoria and abroad, I subsequently pursued a doctor of education at the University of Melbourne. I then examined Sāmoan student
experiences in two homework study groups (HSGs) in Melbourne in 2011.
In my study, I asked, What learning strategies did Australian educators
and Sāmoan youth associate with positive outcomes? What factors and
symbols influenced effective learning for the Sāmoan youth? And how did
the preferred learning methods of the Sāmoan youth generate rapport
with caregivers, educators, and parents?

This chapter is based on my study about the learning experiences and extracurricular activities of the Sāmoan participants in HSGs that I led. With my focus on the northern and western suburbs of Melbourne, I recruited nine teenagers from the Sāmoan churches and youth groups of these areas. They constituted an ideal sample given that they often sought support as well as represented the next generation of leaders in their Sāmoan communities.[1] In this manner, the Sāmoan youth embodied what the Tongan sociologist Karlo Mila-Schaaf calls "polycultural capital," or the ways by which second-generation Pasifika youth use traditional and cross-cultural knowledge to maximize their opportunities. As Mila-Schaaf explains, polycultural capital applies to some second-generation Pasifika youth who "identify and negotiate in ways that serve their interests. Polycultural capital is associated here with cross-cultural resources, knowledge, skills, and agency to potentially realize cumulative advantage."[2] The youth participation therefore reflected their previous history of accepting assistance from educators, if not their willingness to gain additional economic, political, and social capital.

For this study, I solicited the insights of these Sāmoan youth also because they often spent their weekends playing sports or rehearsing for cultural events. Every Sunday, for instance, they attended church services as well as participated in choir practice held on Fridays. In this regard, the youth were expected to follow the norms of *fa'aSāmoa* (Sāmoan customs) every day and especially on the weekends. Given that their community events predominantly occurred during the latter, I envisaged the HSGs as extensions of their Sāmoan cultural practices. I likewise utilized a researcher-practitioner approach wherein I became immersed in their learning experiences as a Sāmoan university researcher, high school teacher, and adult figure.

In this chapter, I show how my program not only supported the academic growth of Sāmoan youth in "college," the US high school equivalent of the Australian school system, but also assisted them in promoting their "cultural and community identification" with educational settings more generally.[3] Furthermore, I selected a library space for the HSGs to allow the participants to engage in meaningful discussions about Sāmoan culture and Australian education.[4] Their discussions highlight how Melbourne's educational systems have negatively affected Sāmoan students. For this reason, I first discuss how Australian schools engage Sāmoan and other Pasifika students before I examine how the youth and some of their parents reflect on *fa'aSāmoa* and education in the HSG sessions. My research thus finds that the existing educational programs do not support Sāmoan students as learners but instead contribute to the high rates of discrimination they experience in Melbourne.

As this volume illustrates, Sāmoans and other Pasifika youth regularly face white racism in the schools of Oceania and the diaspora. In chapter 9, Arcia Tecun, Edmond Fehoko, and 'Inoke Hafoka partly discuss this urgent matter in their examination of *faikava* in Aotearoa New Zealand and the United States. Against this literature that highlights the educational "failings" of Pasifika students, my chapter seeks to better understand the educational experiences of a group of Sāmoan students in Melbourne. I show how a homework study group can keep the students engaged while undertaking academic tasks.[5] More importantly, my reflections and recommendations for effective engagement can be applied to other Pasifika students.

EDUCATION IN AUSTRALIA AND THE VICTORIAN EXPERIENCE

Driven by the desire to improve their educational, employment, and living conditions, Pasifika families often migrate to Australia, New Zealand, and the United States. The adults have also earned some success in these areas, leading other families and friends to join them. For the children, however, they have experienced much adversity, a lack of belonging, and cultural misunderstandings. As studies in Queensland, Australia, reveal, Sāmoan students experience cultural barriers in schools where the populations represent low socioeconomic backgrounds.[6] Because of their struggles in living between Australian and Sāmoan practices, many Sāmoan students achieve low levels of academic success in Australia.[7] One study even noted that a "significant cohort of Samoan students is at risk of not meeting nationally agreed benchmarks for literacy as these students progress through school."[8]

Scholarship on the educational system of Aotearoa New Zealand similarly report on the low academic achievement of Sāmoan youth.[9] In recognition of the learning needs of Pasifika and Sāmoan students, the New Zealand Ministry of Education implemented the Pasifika Education Plan 2013–2017 (PEP). The PEP aimed to "put Pasifika learners, their parents, families and communities at the centre of the education system, where they can demand better outcomes."[10] The New Zealand Ministry of Education thereby recognized Pasifika people as a highly skilled workforce that contributes to the country's economy and society. In Australia, however, no comparable program exists. Educators consequently view the PEP as a starting point for the schools of Victoria. In fact, data on the achievement patterns about and the qualitative responses to learning by Sāmoan youth are missing in the primary, secondary, and tertiary levels of Victorian schools. As for the Aboriginal groups, the government recognizes their specific cultural areas during the opening "Welcome to Country" statements made at events. Protocol demands that we acknowledge the Aboriginal people at community ceremonies, celebrations, and school assemblies in Melbourne and nationally.

Determining the precise number of Pasifika people in Australia is difficult due to the way in which they self-identify on the census database.[11] Unlike New Zealand's efforts to better document Pasifika and Sāmoan people, the broad categorizations of "ethnic" and "other" in Australian census materials obscure data about where they live, what jobs they occupy, and what levels of education they attain.[12] Despite these limitations, the distinguished policy fellow James Batley nevertheless revealed that Sāmoans constituted the largest group of people claiming Pacific Islands heritage in Australia.[13] By comparing data from the 2006, 2011, and 2016 censuses, he found that the number of Sāmoan people had increased from 39,997 in 2006 to 75,753 in 2016. In Victoria alone, the area of this study, the people who identified as Sāmoan grew from 10,730 in 2011 to 17,182 in 2016.[14]

As a result, significant reports have been published about the need to maximize learning for Sāmoan students. Christine Barrett highlights two major reports, *Schools in Australia: Report of the Interim Committee for the Australian Schools Commission* and *Review of Funding for Schooling— Final Report*.[15] They reveal the urgency to remove the obstacles to learning that are "wrought by difference, disability and disadvantage."[16] The question for educators in Victorian schools was, What is being done for Sāmoan students to increase their success in education? In this respect, these reports sought to foster strategies that support Sāmoan and other Pasifika students in Australian schools. Otherwise, all schools in Victoria are guided by the Australian Curriculum. They also incorporate aspects of the Victorian Essential Learning Standards (VELS), which outline what students should learn and what educational development level they should achieve at each year level. Students in Victorian schools can then pursue a high school education through the Victorian Certificate of Education (VCE) pathway, with the option of pursuing university studies once completed. They can also attend high school through the Victorian Certificate of Applied Learning (VCAL) pathway, which enables them to select units in industries or trades. For students to navigate the schools of Victoria and to gain successful educational outcomes, they require the support and patience of educators. With respect to the Sāmoan students in my study, they should have teachers who cater lessons to their preferred learning styles.

In light of these challenges, new educational research seeks to support Sāmoan students with their educational outcomes.[17] This body of work contests earlier curricula and policies that attribute blame to the students for their assumed lack of enthusiasm at school. This scholarship likewise asserts that unless educators in Australia understand the lived experiences and cultural practices of the students, effective learning is unlikely to take place.[18] This is particularly the case with regard to Pasifika, Māori, and Sāmoan students, who appreciate the importance of teachers relating to them and understanding their perspectives and backgrounds.

Interestingly, the Australian Curriculum has a unit of study called "Polynesia" that schools can incorporate in their curriculum as part of Humanities study (year 8). In Victorian schools where the Australian Curriculum and Victorian Essential Learning Standards (AusVels) are followed, teachers abide by the Progression Points and descriptors for units of work. In assessing students for the Polynesia unit, the teachers therefore determine whether students are capable of reaching the required level of achievement for this lesson. Ultimately, then, the teachers decide whether to incorporate the study of Polynesia in their Humanities curriculum. During the fifteen years I have taught in Victorian high schools, very seldom did teachers pursue this opportunity. Whether teachers feel adequately equipped to teach this as a unit to students, as well as how the Pasifika community can work with schools to utilize their expert knowledge about Pasifika languages, customs, and performances, needs to be investigated. Until these matters are addressed, the teachers cannot fully embrace this opportunity to incorporate Pasifika, Māori, and Sāmoan topics in their classrooms.

Effective learning takes place when teaching styles reflect the learning preferences of Sāmoan students, namely, the educational models premised on their home, church, and wider community environments. These factors influenced the approach that I took in designing the HSGs for Sāmoan students in Melbourne. I also followed the work of Mei Kuin Lai, Stuart McMaughton, Meaola Amituanai-Toloa, Rolf Turner, and Selena Hsiao, who argue for the improvement of literacy skills among Indigenous and ethnic minority groups in schools.[19] They likewise recommend that educators evaluate the impact of programs over longer periods of time. In other words, they stressed that teachers must model student expectations and learning styles as a way to prepare the youth to become independent learners. Teachers can thus better incorporate cultural resources and build the students' "sense of self-efficacy and more general engagement and motivation."[20] Their methodology especially applies to students from schools in low socioeconomic areas where teachers tend to lower their academic expectations of the students. Hence, as with my HSGs, I set high expectations for the Sāmoan students.[21]

HOMEWORK STUDY GROUPS IN MELBOURNE

In general, parents rarely question the issuing of homework to students. Instead, they frequently believe that the more homework a child receives, the better off they will be academically. Only "good" teachers, it is assumed, administer a lot of homework, a process reflective of a "quality" education.[22] In the educational literature, however, scholars debate whether students of different educational levels can equally benefit from completing academic tasks outside of school hours.[23] One such study focused on the importance of students being given homework that could be completed with the assistance of their parents.[24] The research revealed that parents often found it difficult to assist their children with the completion of their homework since the parents lacked the educational skills or the time to help. Additionally, many students complained that they were assigned "busy" work.[25] In this manner, teachers need "to be sure that homework assignment [is] made in such a way that parents are not involved in the responsibility of teaching."[26] As a result, this study called for clearly defined homework policies that informed teachers, parents, and students of "the goals, purposes, and procedures to be followed by the faculty in making out-of-school assignments."[27]

However, a range of factors can positively influence the academic outcomes of students who complete their homework. These dynamics include supportive parents who not only supervise homework time but also guide their children whenever they experience difficulties in and beyond the classroom settings.[28] One study analyzed how an after-school program functioned "within the broader context of what children do after school each day."[29] The research revealed noticeable academic improvements in students who attended the after-school homework program on a regular basis. The study also found that the youth improved their social and personal attributes, reiterating the productive elements of homework programs. In this vein, after-school homework programs serve four major functions: (a) increase safety and supervision; (b) enhance cultural and community identification and appreciation; (c) develop social skills and increase competency; and (d) improve academic achievement. Programs typically address one or more of these functions as well as vary by their designs and student needs.[30] Educators in Australia are now beginning to focus on after-school homework as a strategy to better support students.

For my study, I define homework as "any assignment from the regular classroom teacher that is intended to occur outside of regular school hours, regardless of where that assignment is completed."[31] The University of Melbourne Human Research Ethics Committee and the Department of Education and Early Childhood Development also approved the ethics proposal of my study. With my focus on the outer suburbs of Melbourne, I then approached the college director of the then largest college in Melbourne in the western suburbs (Springs College) to seek permission to recruit Sāmoan students for this study. Of the four campuses in the college, fourteen students attended the weekly study sessions at first. This number then declined over the weeks. When recruitment commenced for students in the northern HSG, I approached a religious minister (*faifeau*) at a Sāmoan church. A pilot study also occurred three months prior at the minister's property to gauge youth interest as well as parental support. Whereas one HSG represented a Sāmoan youth group (Camden) in northern Melbourne, the other HSG involved students from colleges in the western suburbs of Melbourne. In each case, they brought their homework or unfinished schoolwork to the group where they worked in a supervised environment. Given my qualifications as a secondary school teacher and academic, I assisted them with their homework. I also addressed their individual student learning needs and, where relevant, recommended a tutor whenever they needed additional help from their teachers.

In total, nine students eventually participated in group discussions and observations.[32] For this chapter, I have replaced participants' names with pseudonyms, a practice that I also applied to the school and church community. We agreed to meet at two public libraries—one in the northern suburbs and one in the western suburbs. I then booked meeting rooms where we could meet each week. The students thus had quiet and private spaces to study. These libraries proved to be ideal meeting places too. As one participant, Letisha, later stated, the library space "forced them to do work." Moreover, the youth readily accessed resources because of the availability of computers, books, or printing facilities. Peta, another participant, confirmed the supportive environment of the library, saying, "I think the location was very helpful. It had everything we needed. Also, I liked that we had our own space to work in."

Initially, nine Sāmoan students expressed an interest in participating in the HSGs; they also signed the appropriate consent forms to do so. But because only five parents signed their related consent forms, I only interviewed five students. Moreover, only one student, Eloise, was eighteen at the time of the study. The participants met every week during the school terms.

PARTICIPANT RESPONSES USING SĀMOAN SYMBOLISM AND MEANING

How might we cultivate the learning styles of Sāmoan youth and support their academic achievements in Melbourne? In the HSGs, I not only helped the students complete their homework assignments but, more vitally, also organized focus groups on Sāmoan youth identity and the symbolism of *fa'aSāmoa* or Sāmoan customs. In my collection of data, I specifically selected a few symbols taken from interpretations of Sāmoan symbolism in studies by the Sāmoan poet and writer Albert Wendt and from information provided by a cultural retailer in Sāmoa.[33] As images can have different meanings depending on the viewer, I used these symbols to metaphorically reflect upon the experiences of the participants during our homework study sessions and focus groups; their responses shed insights on the powerful symbolic meanings of Sāmoan traditional designs in the diaspora. Each symbol, full of meaning, has been used by Sāmoans over time to express chiefly and religious power, decorate fabrics, use in paintings and tattoos, and carve into decorative homeware. Despite the censorship of missionaries and other colonial officials, these symbols persist today. They also stem from the historical reference that is widely known as *tatau*, or tattoo. For my purposes, the circulation of these Sāmoan images not only reaffirmed the youth's sense of belonging but also allowed them to open up about their cultural, educational, and familial challenges and insights.

When selecting the images from artistic drawings by Lisha Sablan on her retail website, I specifically chose the meanings that best related to the participants.[34] That is, I showed a printed copy of the images to the participants, solicited their responses about the images, and asked if they felt happy about including their symbolic interpretations in this study. Therefore, I only highlight images that the students unanimously approved and that described the experiences of their families in Australia. As I will show, traditional *tatau* (tattoo) patterns and decorative motifs also represent the educational journeys of these Sāmoan participants.[35] While my usage of symbols clearly illustrates a unique methodological framework for explaining Sāmoan educational experiences in Australia, the notion of using symbols to represent traditional Sāmoan values and beliefs is not new. By examining Sāmoan youth perceptions of these symbols, we can then better understand their awareness of and appreciation for *fa'aSāmoa*, HSGs, and education in Australia.

IDENTITY

In an attempt to investigate how Sāmoan students self-identify as young people in Melbourne, I arranged a focus group at the northern HSG. Although only four students participated in this session, their discussions highlighted the importance of having a safe space in which to share information and hear honesty in the words spoken. Their views echoed those of other Pasifika young people I have had experiences with and also paralleled my own as a teenager growing up in Melbourne. The students also stated that they identified as Sāmoan even though they were born in Australia or New Zealand. They saw the notion of identity as stemming from the language in which they were addressed at home, since parents spoke to them in the Sāmoan language even though the youth tended to respond in English. Furthermore, they identified as Sāmoan because they often practiced *fa'aSāmoa* by attending church, community, and youth events during the weekends.

The majority of Sāmoans who live overseas belong to a church community. Whether they are Catholic, Methodist, or Mormon, they view churches as the closest approximation of *fa'aSāmoa* and village life. Churches therefore serve as the best source of support for Sāmoans in the diaspora. When Eloise was asked what *fa'aSāmoa* meant to her, for instance, she stated "everything's *fa'aSāmoa*, like everything is in Sāmoan 'cos our parents are Sāmoan and they can't really speak English so . . ." For Eloise, her parents encompassed the values of *fa'aSāmoa* and accordingly raised her in Australia. Reflecting on the role of the church, she observed, "I thought being Sāmoan is like going to church, umm, knowing where you come from, it's all about family, yeah." Hence, she frequently attended family events, such as weddings, funerals, choir practice, and *lotu*, or church services.

In our discussion, some of the participants identified the specific gender roles young people are expected to adopt as *fa'aSāmoa*, regardless of the country in which they're living. The expression of one's identity is seen in one's actions, which include attending church or community events and respecting cultural practices and expectations wherever that person is and wherever such events occur. An example of this is evident in preparing for special occasions, such as a Sāmoan concert, song rehearsals, and dances in the Sāmoan language. When young people attend a rehearsal, for instance, both males and females are expected to wear an *ie lavalava*, or a sarong. They can also cover their pants with an *ie lavalava*. As the youth observed, girls are also expected to be more conservative with their clothing. As per the norms of *fa'aSāmoa*, this practice shows that a person has been raised well and respects themselves and others around them.

Following their attendance at HSG sessions, the participants in the northern HSG then left for weekly concert rehearsals at their minister's house, specifically his garage. For many Sāmoan households, the garage serves as a public space for family events, including rehearsal sessions led by this particular pastor. I also found that they were preparing for a fundraising concert. In this way, the girls were also expected to wear traditional attire. They subsequently dedicated long hours to these rehearsals, practicing usually two to three times per week during the evening. They even ended their church practices at 10:00 p.m. or later, so they had very limited time for their homework. Given the centrality of these cultural practices, it is important that students and teachers alike become aware of *fa'aSāmoa* and its obligations.

In the HSGs, I also found that the youth did not perceive the ability to speak the Sāmoan language as an important prerequisite for being Sāmoan. Rather, they felt comfortable in their identity so long as they could understand what the adults said in Sāmoan. These responses, derived from the focus group interview, demonstrate what the students meant by "Sāmoanness." When I asked how they practiced *fa'aSāmoa*, the participants referred to their ability to speak and understand the Sāmoan language:

ATAMAI: I don't know, basically like go to church, do chores, mainly chores—umm, yeah, that's it. We can speak English to our parents but they like us to speak in Sāmoan.

> PONTON: Do they speak to you in Sāmoan?
> ATAMAI: Yep, but I always reply back in English or half in English, half in Sāmoan.
> PONTON: Is that for all of you?
> SALAMASINA: Nah, I speak in English [responds to mother in English when she speaks in Sāmoan].

At times, however, their parents could not respond to them in English because the parents' English fluency was not as great as for Sāmoans born in Australia, New Zealand, or the United States. Nevertheless, these parents indicated that the youth should know how to speak Sāmoan so they could perform cultural ceremonies without viewing these practices as foreign. Knowledge of their language also allowed the youth to appreciate its nuances. When an interview was conducted in the Sāmoan language with one of the mothers (La'ei), for example, she spoke about her daily discussions with her children in which she advised them to do well in school. She even asked her daughters, who were participants, if they had homework to complete, but the question was not really about homework. In my presence, the mother was really asking her daughters if they were excelling in school, and the young women understood the essence of her query. As reflected in the youth experiences, it was not uncommon for Sāmoans born in Western countries to know and understand the Sāmoan language when spoken to but to respond in English rather than in Sāmoan. Given the centrality of the English language in Australia, the participants felt more confident responding in English to adults who spoke to them in Sāmoan.

The parents of the participants in my Melbourne study also supported the educational aspirations of their children.[36] Their mothers, in particular, regularly engaged with their children's schools by attending parent and teacher meetings and interviews.[37] At the same time, they issued a caveat for me and the HSGs. That is, while they agreed that it was their responsibility to impart *fa'aSāmoa* to their children, they believed that it was the teachers' obligation to provide a good education for the youth. Natia, one of the mothers, even stated that although she respected that she and her family now lived in Australia, it was not necessary, nor did she encourage, the blending of culture and education in the schools. Exemplifying the complex roles of Sāmoan parents in my study and in Australian education, Natia did not seek to interfere with the teachers; nor did she expect them to intervene in her family matters. In the end, I determined that the youth in my study ultimately came from caring environments, allowing them to communicate their opinions and develop their self-confidence. While the values of *fa'aSāmoa* encourage youth development, it remains to be seen as to how teachers and parents alike in Victoria could implement Sāmoan topics in their classrooms and lesson plans when some mothers view *fa'aSāmoa* and education as two separate entities.

BEING EMPOWERED THROUGH EDUCATION

One symbol I shared with the HSGs was the *gogo* (figure 3.1). The *gogo* represents a bird that is free to spread its wings and soar high in the sky. This bird symbolizes freedom and direction, a Sāmoan pattern found in the *tatau* (tattoo) and a metaphor of the participants' ability to express their voices. Furthermore, the *gogo* symbolizes the importance of sharing their hopes, concerns, and fears.

In my group interview with four of the participants from the northern HSG, they discussed what it meant to be raised as a female by their parents who practice *fa'aSāmoa*. Specifically, they mentioned that any discussion about being "weak" would bring shame upon one's family. Moreover, if

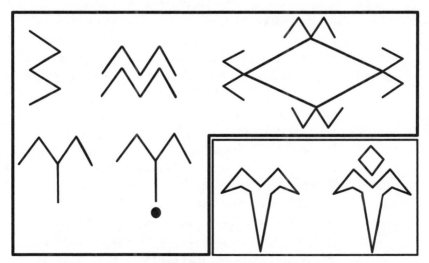

FIGURE 3.1. *Gogo.* According to Lisha Sablan, the "arctic tern," or *gogo*, is a symbol of protection and guidance. The bird was often seen during long ocean voyages, and voyagers would often follow the birds to land. Each symbol shows variants commonly used in the Sāmoan *malu*. The bottom-right symbols are variants commonly seen in male tattoos, textiles, and other surface prints. (Image credit: Lisha Sablan)

one were to bring such shame, this act would be considered worse than death, as illustrated in this exchange:

> ELOISE: I suppose 'cos they're a lot more isolated and just pressure I guess.
>
> PONTON: Are they different from your pressures?
>
> TEUILA: Oh well here we have the support, like we have like heaps of people, it's easy to talk to people like counselors and stuff when you need help. It's like easy to access those kind of people but I think in Sāmoa it's not that easy 'cos like they're fobs ["fresh off the boat"], they aren't very understanding when it comes to like depression and talking about problems. They're very like, keep it underlying, all that stuff.
>
> PONTON: So do you feel comfortable sharing your problems if you had any with your parents or relatives or like adults?
>
> ELOISE: Parents and stuff?
>
> TEUILA: It depends what type of problem . . .
>
> ELOISE: Yeah, it depends.
>
> TEUILA: Because just say you got pregnant, yeah like now, um yeah good luck trying to tell your parents.
>
> ELOISE: But we, I think Sāmoans are like, young Sāmoan girls nowadays, like, that's the category that they fall in a lot is teenage pregnancy.
>
> PONTON: Why do you think? Is it because of that? They're not really educated in that area, it's not really talked about in the home?
>
> TEUILA: Yeah. I know for us, we get a lot of like, everyone talks to us about safe sex and stuff . . . (laughs)—I don't know if they . . .
>
> PONTON: At school?
>
> TEUILA: Yeah . . . and what happens if they get pregnant.
>
> ELOISE: I think in Sāmoa, they're misunderstood a lot as well.
>
> PONTON: In what area, what do you mean by that?
>
> ELOISE: Um, with like, what Teuila was saying about depression and stuff like, parents don't really talk about it and it's like here, we have like psychologists, and stuff like that—we know where to go for help. But in Sāmoa, everyone is Sāmoan so . . .
>
> TEUILA: I think because Sāmoans think they have this image that like, they're these big tough people and just 'cos they're like huge, you know like, they have to be strong. You know like if

they have problems, don't talk about it 'cos you're supposed to be strong, like, it's like that image is so big and important to them, that it's hard for them to actually open up and tell you what's wrong and it's hard for them to talk about what's wrong because they're not used to talking about what's wrong.

ELOISE: They have so much pride.

TEUILA: Yeah, it's so hard for them to let that down and be straight up and open.

PONTON: Are you saying that's for everyone? Males and females or just . . .

TEUILA/ELOISE: Everyone.

TEUILA: Majority of the people.

ELOISE: But that's another thing with Sāmoans, like they have so much pride they're so like, shame is so much worse than death. Like, you know, if you bring shame on your family, it's like, you might as well just die. [The other girls agree in the background.]

TEUILA: I don't think it's just with Sāmoans, I think it's like with a lot of people; gossip is like another big thing, yeah, but I think that's getting off the subject.

In my position as a teacher and researcher, I know that these cultural matters like shame and pride cannot be taken lightly. Above all, the honesty of the youth revealed how the HSG provided them with the freedom to be treated equally and to realize a world in which they can move without restrictions. While the obligations of *fa'aSāmoa* presented the youth with both opportunities and challenges, the fact that the young women opened up to me in an educational setting proved compelling. As I have shown, very seldom do Sāmoan youth view schools, libraries, and other educational facilities in Australia as places that welcome their cultural beliefs.

I also asked the participants what they plan to do after they complete college. Eloise and Atamai, two girls in year 12, or the final year of high school in Melbourne, noted that they would like to learn the prerequisites for achieving university entry. As I outlined in my observation notes, Eloise and Atamai felt enthusiastic about exploring specific courses toward youth work degrees:

22 August 2011: Eloise and Atamai researched university courses and police academy prerequisites.

22 August 2011: I was pleased with the first half of the study session as I had the chance to assist Atamai with her university preferences. We had a look at the VTAC Handbook and discussed the youth work degrees and courses at TAFE she was considering. Atamai is keen to go to university and works hard in all her subjects. She does need assistance with her English language in writing of essays, which I've been helping her with since she started.

It became apparent to me that the HSG sessions guided the participants in making lifelong choices about pursuing higher education to enter careers that would assist others. During my interviews with parents, I even advised them of their daughters' desire to attend universities. Although the mothers were concerned about paying university fees, I mentioned the option of deferring their payments through the Higher Education Loan Program (HELP) or Higher Education Contribution Scheme (HECS). Because the parents were not aware of these options, they did not consider university pathways for their children. Furthermore, the parents thought that university tuition had to be fully paid at the onset. After I spoke with them and after they realized their daughters' aspirations, the parents felt both relief and appreciation. They then encouraged their daughters to apply for university entry as well as granted me their approval to do all that was possible to ensure their daughters' academic success.

Much like the *gogo*, or the bird, the image of *la*, or the sun (figure 3.2), applies to the students. *La* means power or empowerment; *la* also refers to Tagaloalagi, originally known as the creator before American and European missionaries introduced Christianity to Sāmoa in the 1800s. For the youth in my study, they likewise identified *la* as something they value. Having knowledge of their academic and career choices clearly empowered them. In fact, they often stated, "knowledge is power." For example, recognizing how the after-school program supported her, Letisha expressed that it "helped me a lot to complete homework, organize myself, and keep my grades up." In her case, she utilized the HSG to improve her knowledge of advanced English vocabulary, complete her writing tasks, and read her novels, among other tasks.

Finally, the symbol *Fa'a Aveao* means "starfish" (figure 3.3), but it more generally represents protection. As with the other symbols, I asked what *fa'a aveao* meant to the youth. In our conversations, we talked about how protection usually entails one's ability to *fa'alavelave*, or support, the weddings, funerals, church fundraisers, the bestowal of chiefly titles, and other

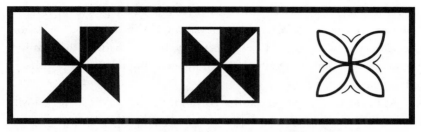

FIGURE 3.2. *La* (the sun). According to Lisha Sablan, ancient Sāmoan mythology tells of Tagaloalagi or Tagaloa, who was the paramount god for the Sāmoans. Tagaloalagi, also known as the Sun God, created Sāmoa as a resting place for his son, Tuli, who took the form of a bird, the Pacific golden plover. In turn, the golden plover became a messenger for Tagaloalagi. The sun, *La*, thus holds a sacred relationship with Tagaloa-lagi and Tuli. Today, the sun offers the most creativity and symbolism in design usage. (Image credit: Lisha Sablan)

FIGURE 3.3. *Fa'a Aveao*. According to Lisha Sablan, the *aveao*, or starfish, is a decorative element and is portrayed as having four or more elaborate legs. The top three symbols are also used in the Sāmoan *malu*, whereas the bottom two are commonly found in textile and *tapa* cloth. (Image credit: Lisha Sablan)

events for extended family members and the wider community. This support occurs through financial means and/or hands-on assistance. For families who believe in supporting those in need, *fa'alavelave* is like an investment. You provide financial, moral, or social help to others, and in the future, when you need assistance, they, too, will give willingly. When it is respectfully used, *fa'alavelave* thus encourages a reciprocal relationship between the giver and receiver whenever tangible or intangible goods and services are exchanged. More importantly, the goodwill of the family is remembered, cementing long-lasting and enduring relationships through such exchanges.

At the same time, however, the girls in this study often struggled with what their mothers perceived as the freedom and protection of *fa'aSāmoa*. During my interviews of two mothers, for instance, they raised concerns about giving their daughters too much freedom to do what their friends were free to do.[38] La'ei stated she did not want her daughters to end up like "girls who have not contributed to supporting their parents financially due to falling pregnant," a remark that reiterated the kind of shame the girls said they would face if they were to get pregnant. The mother had always advised her children to try their best at school because of the many benefits they experienced while living in Australia in comparison with her hard life and that of other parents who had grown up in Sāmoa: "You know, I always think it is such a waste for young girls [not yet twenty-one years old] to fall pregnant before they've matured and understood the responsibilities of parenthood. I feel sorry for their parents who have worked hard all their lives to raise kids in Australia. The least the kids could do is get a job, earn money, and give it back to their parents. The role of the daughter is to look after her parents, make sure they have all they need [financially and physically]."

For these reasons, the parents did not allow their daughters to go out with friends from school or friends they were not familiar with, especially at night. Generally speaking, Sāmoan families seldom give their girls the freedom to "roam" as their brothers and other male relatives do. Eloise, one of the students, underscored this gendered contradiction when she expressed disappointment that her older brother, when he turned eighteen, was allowed to go out with his friends and do anything because he was a male. As did the other girls in this study, Eloise also knew that she would not receive such freedom when she turned eighteen. In the following conversation, the girls highlighted how *fa'aSāmoa* encouraged the parents to overprotect girls and grant more freedom to boys:

PONTON: Do you think girls have the same expectations as boys? Are they treated the same?

ELOISE/SALAMASINA: No! Boys have way more freedom.

PONTON: So what can they do that you can't do?

ELOISE: Boys are able to do a lot more than girls like . . .

SALAMASINA: And they get away with a lot of stuff.

ELOISE: The girls have to . . .

TEUILA: The girls are inside and the boys are like outside . . . I don't know how to explain that in English.

PONTON: Do you want to give an example? Sometimes it's easier to give an example.

ELOISE: Um, [I] just turned eighteen, and it's different from when my brother turned eighteen. When my brother turned eighteen, he was already doing things that he would have started doing when he was eighteen. But for us girls, it's different. I'm eighteen now, but I'm still not allowed to do, like, do certain things, as much as I want to.

PONTON: What sort of things do you want to do?

ELOISE: Like clubbing every weekend [laughter].

PONTON: Anything else you want to do that boys are allowed to do?

ATAMAI: Um, they mainly just get . . .

ELOISE: They just get it easy!

SALAMASINA: They always like, get what they want. They're like mummy's little boy.

TEUILA: The expectations are always higher for the girls from the parents.

As their comments illustrate, the girls found the freedom and protection of *fa'aSāmoa* as clearly favoring the boys and other males. They also flagged the age of eighteen as the beginning of "adulthood," a modern category that stretches back to the missionary period and that now clearly aligns with the metropolitan definitions of responsibility in the Sāmoan diaspora. At the same time, mothers like Sefina, La'ei, and Natia wanted the best for their daughters. Because they saw the benefits of their children receiving educational support in a library, they allowed their children to participate in this study, itself an extension of *fa'aSāmoa* during the weekends. With the support of their Sāmoan *lotu* (church), the parents passed on knowledge about the Sāmoan language, customs, and expectations to their children. The practice of *fa'aSāmoa*, as with the value of *fa'alavelave*, thus represents freedom and protection, albeit in ways that are gendered and uneven.

REFLECTIONS AND RECOMMENDATIONS

Once again, the HSGs benefited the Sāmoan youth and their parents of Melbourne. These library spaces provided opportunities for the youth to develop rapport with one another and to exchange ideas about culture and education. The HSG sessions I led therefore minimized students' confusion associated with their daily learning tasks. As a teacher, I also found that the youth related to me as a Sāmoan educator. Moreover, their learning styles and willingness to talk openly flourished whenever we discussed Sāmoan symbols in the libraries, thereby destabilizing the notion of educational spaces as apathetic or racist venues for learning. Additionally, the libraries provided the youth with resources they did not have at home, such as computers and internet access; in turn, the participants learned how to access information online.

In light of the relative absence of Pasifika and Sāmoan materials in the Australian school system, I implemented teaching strategies from New Zealand and cultural symbols and practices from *fa'aSāmoa* in the HSGs. In this manner, I exposed the students to Sāmoan and Western ideas in ways that furthered their education. They also represented a motivated group of students, all of whom received support from their churches and community groups. For this reason, they completed their "homework" activities, took care of their younger siblings or older relatives, completed household chores, attended church services, and participated in cultural rehearsals.

One tangible educational outcome of the HSG sessions concerned the students' ability to appreciate and practice collective tasks. As they revealed in their interviews, they worked with their families during the weekends. In turn, the parents encouraged them to maintain good attendance in the HSGs, which they did. Schools in Melbourne can learn much about the students they teach when educators move beyond the school gates and welcome wider community engagement. Similarly, the youth have called on their Sāmoan families to create links with their schools.

To be clear, Sāmoan parents have a high regard for the schools in Melbourne even though a few of them view *fa'aSāmoa* as not directly relevant to the education of youth regardless of their socioeconomic backgrounds. On the surface, the latter point can be read as a sign of disinterest. But for many Sāmoan parents, they respect the authority of teachers. Educators in Australia therefore have to account for the language barriers, customs, and time constraints of Sāmoan and other Pasifika parents. Many parents already engage numerous cultural events and often work long shift hours, thereby limiting their involvement in school activities. The onus falls, then, on the teachers of Melbourne. Unless teachers understand the background of their Sāmoan students, the students will continue to struggle in school and be labeled as "at risk" youth.

As studies in Australia, New Zealand, and the United States have long shown, Sāmoan students find difficulty in relating to the curricula of Western schooling because they lack the necessary cultural capital and knowledge to engage non-Sāmoan topics. While they may follow *fa'aSāmoa* and be open to learning other issues, their schools in Melbourne have not reciprocated in kind. Instead, the schools have not taken advantage of the "Polynesia unit"; nor have they foregrounded the polycultural capital of their Sāmoan students or sought the expertise of Pasifika educators. Therefore, I recommend that teachers follow the expectations of the Australian Professional Standards for Teachers and incorporate student prior knowledge into lesson planning so that student engagement is maintained. That is, teachers can ask students to compare texts they read in class to the books, songs, or images of their cultural and home environments. Having utilized this pedagogy as a high school teacher, I know that such cross-cultural comparisons can and do successfully increase student confidence, knowledge, and participation.

Indeed, most schools in Melbourne offer homework study sessions at least one day a week, all of which are supervised by teachers. However, the teachers need to have the empathy and skills necessary to make Sāmoan students feel comfortable in these settings. They likewise need to be more patient in their teaching of writing and reading so the youth can better follow their lesson plans. Furthermore, teachers may have to repeat demonstrations of such tasks until students feel confident to complete them more independently. Laptops, unlimited Wi-Fi, calculators, novels, and other learning tools should also be readily available to the Sāmoan students and other youth who may not have such items in their homes. Above all, the teachers need to learn more about *fa'aSāmoa*.

At a wider policy level, the educational system in Melbourne can implement and revise the applicable parts of New Zealand's Pasifika Education Plan and PowerUP Plus program. These programs take seriously Pasifika and Sāmoan students and are potential starting points for schools in Australia. Teachers and administrators alike can also track the educational enablers and barriers of Sāmoan students in Australia by way of longitudinal studies. While my HSG sessions only offer a microcosm of the ways in which Sāmoan youth view and practice education, much more needs to be done to bridge the gaps between educators and community groups. At the moment, no policy or program exists in Australia that would foster meaningful exchanges between Sāmoan families and educators.

NOTES

1 Cluny Macpherson and La'avasa Macpherson, "Churches and the Economy of Sāmoa," *Contemporary Pacific* 23, no. 2 (2011): 303–38.

2 Karlo Mila-Schaaf and Elizabeth Robinson, "'Polycultural' Capital and Educational Achievement among NZ-Born Pacific Peoples," *MAI Review* 1 (2010): 1–18.

3 Merith Cosden, Gale Morrison, Ann Leslie Albanese, and Sandra Macias, "When Homework Is Not Home Work: After-School Programs for Homework Assistance," *Educational Psychologist* 36, no. 3 (2001): 211–21.

4 Peggy Fairbairn-Dunlop, "The Interface of Pacific and Other Knowledges in a Supplementary Education Site," *Compare: A Journal of Comparative and International Education* 44, no. 6 (2014): 874–94.

5 Fairbairn-Dunlop, "Interface," 875.

6 Karen Dooley, Beryl Exley, and Parlo Singh, "Social Justice and Curriculum Renewal for Samoan Students: An Australian Case Study," *International Journal of Inclusive Education* 4, no. 1 (2001): 23–41.

7 Parlo Singh and Mark Sinclair, "Diversity, Disadvantage and Differential Outcomes: An Analysis of Samoan Students' Narratives of Schooling," *Asia-Pacific Journal of Teacher Education* 29, no. 1 (2001): 73–92.

8 Judith Kearney, Margaret A. Fletcher, and Maya Dobrenov-Major, *Improving Literacy Outcomes for Samoan-Australian Students in Logan City* (Griffith, South East Queensland: Griffith Institute of Educational Research, 2008).

9 Tanya Wendt-Samu, "The 'Pasifika Umbrella' and Quality Teaching: Understanding and Responding to the Diverse Realities Within," *Waikato Journal of Education* (2015): 129–40, https://wje.org.nz/index.php/WJE/article/view/229/220.

10 Ministry of Education New Zealand, *Pasifika Education Plan, 2013–2017* (Wellington: Ministry of Education, 2012).

11 Michael Cuthill and Sue Scull, "Going to University: Pacific Island Migrant Perspectives," *Australian Universities' Review* 53, no. 1 (2011): 5–13.

12 David Takeuchi and Shirley Hune, *Growing Presence, Emerging Voices: Pacific Islanders and Academic Achievement in Washington*, report submitted to the Washington State Commission on Asian Pacific American Affairs (Seattle: University of Washington, 2008).

13 James Batley, "What Does the 2016 Census Reveal about Pacific Islands Communities in Australia?," *DevPolicyBlog*, September 28, 2017, https://devpolicy.org/2016-census-reveal-about-pacific-islands-communities-in-australia-20170928/.

14 "Victoria Ancestry," accessed April 15, 2020, https://profile.id.com.au
    /australia/ancestry?WebID=110.

15 Christine Barrett, "School Social Work in the State of Victoria, Australia:
    65 Years of Student Wellbeing and Learning Support" (PhD diss., University
    of Melbourne, 2014). Refer, as well, to *Schools in Australia: Report of the
    Interim Committee for the Australian Schools Commission* (Canberra:
    Australian Government Publishing Service, 1973); and David Gonski, Ken
    Boston, Kathryn Greiner, Carmen Lawrence, Bill Scales, and Peter Tannock,
    Review of Funding for Schooling—Final Report (Canberra: Department of
    Education, Employment and Workplace Relations, 2011).

16 Barrett, "School Social Work," 28.

17 Wendt-Samu, "'Pasifika Umbrella,'" 40.

18 Peter Allen, Leali'ie'e Tufulasi Taleni, and Jane Robertson, "'In Order to Teach
    You, I Must Know You.' The Pasifika Initiative: A Professional Development
    Project for Teachers," *New Zealand Journal of Educational Studies* 44, no. 2
    (2009): 47–62.

19 Mei Kuin Lai, Stuart McNaughton, Meaola Amituanai-Toloa, Rolf Turner, and
    Selena Hsiao, "Sustained Acceleration of Achievement in Reading Compre-
    hension: The New Zealand Experience," *Reading Research Quarterly* 44, no. 1
    (2009): 30–56.

20 Lai et al., "Sustained Acceleration," 33.

21 Lai et al., "Sustained Acceleration," 44.

22 George W. Bond and George J. Smith, "Establishing a Homework Program,"
    Elementary School Journal 66, no. 3 (1965): 139.

23 Frances L. Van Voorhis, "Interactive Homework in Middle School: Effects on
    Family Involvement and Science Achievement," *Journal of Educational
    Research* 96, no. 6 (July/August 2003): 323–38.

24 Bond and Smith, "Establishing a Homework Program," 142.

25 Van Voorhis, "Interactive Homework," 323.

26 Bond and Smith, "Establishing a Homework Program," 141.

27 Bond and Smith, "Establishing a Homework Program," 140.

28 Van Voorhis, "Interactive Homework," 325.

29 Cosden et al., "When Homework Is Not Home Work."

30 Cosden et al., "When Homework Is Not Homework," 212.

31 Cosden et al., "When Homework Is Not Homework," 211.

32 Student participants were as follows for the two study groups (sex and gender
    in parentheses). Northern HSG: Atamai (female, 17 years), Eloise (female,
    18 years), Peta (female, 16 years), Letisha (female, 14 years), Salamasina
    (female, 14 years), Teuila (female, 14 years). Western HSG: Chris (male,
    17 years), Lagi (female, 16 years), and Mika (male, 16 years). Six were born in
    Australia and three in New Zealand.

33 Albert Wendt, "Afterword: Tatauing the Post-colonial Body," in *Inside Out:
    Literature, Cultural Politics, and Identity in the New Pacific*, ed. Vilsoni
    Hereniko and Rob Wilson (Lantham, MD: Rowman and Littlefield, 1999),
    399–412; and Lisha Sablan and Christopher Sablan, "The Importance of

Samoan and Pacific Symbols—The Legacy of the Lapita People—Samoan
Tattoo, Carvings and Artwork," *Janet's Samoa* (blog), April 21, 2014, http://
blog.janetssamoa.com/samoan-and-pacific-symbols-samoan-tattoo-carvings
-and-artwork/#comment-39.

34 Sablan and Sablan, "Samoan and Pacific Symbols."

35 Mark Adams, Sean Mallon, Peter William Brunt, and Nicholas Thomas,
Tatau: Samoan Tattoo, New Zealand Art, Global Culture (Wellington: Te Papa
Press, 2010).

36 Cluny Macpherson, "From Moral Community to Moral Communities: The
Foundations of Migrant Social Solidarity among Samoans in Urban Aotearoa/
New Zealand," *Pacific Studies* 25, nos. 1–2 (2002): 71–93.

37 The three mothers who consistently drove students to the weekly HSGs
(northern) usually did so after work or they changed their shifts in order to
bring students to the public library where the HSGs took place (two of the
mothers were single parents). When required, the mothers often took turns
driving the students each week.

38 Each mother had two daughters in the homework study group.

PART II

POPULAR CULTURE, SOCIAL MEDIA, AND HIP HOP

CHAPTER 4

SCREEN SOVEREIGNTY

Urban Youth and Community Media in Vanuatu

THOMAS DICK AND SARAH DOYLE

THE URBAN YOUNG PEOPLE OF VANUATU USE OPPORTUNITIES
for media production in ways that resonate with the experiences of Pacific
Islander youth in colonial and settler settings, such as Auckland, Hawai'i,
and Los Angeles, and are distinctly different. For this chapter, the authors
draw on their long-term engagement with artists and producers from Vanuatu. We have lived and worked in Vanuatu for over seven years, and we
have forged relations with the young producers of Further Arts, a nongovernmental organization (NGO) based in Port Vila that endorses ni-
Vanuatu cultural and creative projects.

Linking the academy and the community, we nurture a point of productive tension, which can be challenging but is also liberating. As
unwaged researchers and volunteers at Further Arts, we investigate youth
phenomena in ways that resonate with the ni-Vanuatu youth and work
toward social transformation and decolonization.[1] As with Demiliza Saramosing's analysis of youth solidarity in Kalihi, O'ahu, in chapter 10, we
similarly examine how ni-Vanuatu youth created a sense of belonging by
way of their digital media. But the lives of young people in Hawai'i
described so richly by Saramosing are shaped by different inflections of US
colonialism than those in the sovereign nation of Vanuatu. At the same
time, we recognize that decolonization would entail self-determination for
all Indigenous peoples, including the Kānaka Maoli of Hawai'i.[2] We also

share with other theorists of critical youth studies a strengths-based approach that avoids the pathologizing of youth.[3]

Thomas (Tom) Dick is an Australian producer and founder of Further Arts. He served as chairperson of the board for seventeen years and continues to provide pro bono input for fundraising and development initiatives. For almost a decade, Tom lived in Vanuatu, where he produced several films with local communities. Although he now resides in Australia, Tom regularly travels to Vanuatu to visit family, conduct research, and support the work of the communities with which he is associated, mainly in the north of Vanuatu. Sarah Doyle began volunteering in 2012 with Further Arts as it re-established its physical office space with major project funding. In 2013, as momentum grew with the recruitment of staff and young people in Port Vila, Sarah co-developed a community multimedia facility that fostered youth engagement in the civic space. She has since supported the management of the facility and organization and is currently a Further Arts board member. Together, we have collaborated on projects at Nesar Studio, a community access media production facility located at Further Arts.

In this chapter, we feature some of the key ni-Vanuatu founders in Nesar Studio. They include Marcel Meltherorong, a well-known ni-Vanuatu artist who was a production facilitator, later becoming Further Arts' artistic director and then a board member, and Roselyn Tari, a local media producer who started her career as an intern at Further Arts. We also engage Dely Roy Nalo, who, based in Luganville, the second largest town located in northern Vanuatu, established another independent unit that was administered by Further Arts. We draw, as well, on interviews with Andrew, Gina, Niki, and Onis—all Port Vila youth interested in multimedia who have since become core crew members and/or Nesar Studio production staff. Consistent with daily interactions at Further Arts, we use first names to refer to the young people.

First, we briefly describe the making of Port Vila as a postcolonial and urban city in Melanesia and discuss the public perceptions of youth and flag the relevance of *kastom*. We then offer further details about the establishment of Nesar Studio in September 2013 and show how this studio facilitates and was facilitated by the emergence of young producers. We then explore the contexts and practices of youth multimedia production, demonstrating their importance in Port Vila. We also use the emergent idea of *rimix* (in Bislama, the lingua franca of Vanuatu), a localized rendering of "Indigenous Remix."[4] This framework allows us to understand how young urban ni-Vanuatu negotiated community, institutional, and professional obligations and leveraged opportunities for producing media that asserted their sense of belonging and engagement in civic life.

We argue that ni-Vanuatu *rimix* constitutes an element of "screen sovereignty" wherein Indigenous youth produce and disseminate digital media in new ways that reflect their own desires, identities, and languages. The idea of screen sovereignty draws on the work of Jolene Rickard, who pioneered the idea of visual sovereignty, later advanced by Michelle Raheja.[5] Kristin Dowell also shows that screen sovereignty has proven to be a salient framework for scholars of Indigenous media, and Ginsburg has applied the term *media sovereignty* to the Indigenous media sector in Australia, asserting that Indigenous media sovereignty contends with legal questions of rights, control, possession, and authority, albeit with respect to the making of media.[6] Our contribution to this literature on popular culture and to the study of Native youth in cities in Oceania more generally concerns the ways in which the young media producers of Nesar Studio practice a spatially anchored form of screen sovereignty in urban Vanuatu. In this manner, the ni-Vanuatu youth have begun to co-opt resources to produce media and stories about their lives and the lives of people that matter to them. More vitally, as we intend to show, their access to, appreciation for, and partial ownership of media has helped them to navigate the creative, spatial, and virtual worlds of Port Vila, Vanuatu, and beyond.

PORT VILA: THE NATIVE CITY

Port Vila, commonly known as Vila, Vila Taon, or Taon (town), is splashed upon an isthmus on the southwestern side of the island of Efate in the Shefa province. The city rests on the ancestral lands of Ifira (the northern side of the city) and Pango (the southern side of the city). On the western side of the isthmus are the concentric bays of Fatumaru, Vila, and Mele. On the eastern side a lagoon extends north before dog-legging east. The southern end of the isthmus opens onto a peninsula on which is located Pango, one of the five peri-urban villages that border Port Vila. The others are Ifira, on an island to the immediate north of Pango, Erakor on the eastern side of the lagoon, Mele to the northwest, and Mele-Maat to the immediate north of Mele. Port Vila occupies the majority of the land between these villages. The proximity of Indigenous communities to the city shapes a sense of belonging and exclusion that variously inform young people's expressions of screen sovereignty. In this manner, Port Vila's settler cityscape partly resonates with the British and French colonial era, when their "policies attempted to regulate or exclude [the ni-Vanuatu] presence in town through ordinances controlling movement, residence and dress."[7] Today, Port Vila is bounded by these peri-urban villages. A central business district situated on the picturesque Seafront is now surrounded by residential areas. The literature refers to these residential areas as "settlements"; however, we choose to call them "communities," as this is the term most residents use.[8]

Over the last three decades, Port Vila has developed into a bustling, cosmopolitan capital city and is somewhat anomalous in Vanuatu where over 70 percent of the population lives in rural villages. With its population of around 50,000 people and its patisseries, duty-free shopping, bars, and nightclubs, Port Vila is more comparable to a small city in Aotearoa New Zealand and Australia than it is to a Melanesian village. However, this view of a cosmopolitan world city can be contrasted with the communities within Port Vila and Luganville (Vanuatu's second largest urban area), some of which are structured on a "Melanesian village model" that coalesces around shared languages and common connections to home islands.[9]

With regard to young people in urban areas, they have engaged media at younger ages through their usage of mobile phones and access to youth centers.[10] Yet a few of them successfully participate in the formal media sector. Nevertheless, young people have been forming their own associations. But just as youth in Port Vila organize and enact change, community leaders, the police, and government officials have frequently questioned their legitimacy and have criticized their lack of professionalism. For example, in 2006, a group of young people created a political association called Vanuatu Roots with the intent to show the government the kinds of violence that young people faced in Port Vila's communities. One of the members of Vanuatu Roots, Owen, explained, "The government always talks about the future, but it is their future not our future. They say that us youth today are the future of the nation, but when you throw out the future of the nation in class-six then what do you expect? So we formed Vanuatu Roots because we know that we must move to do something. We must bring forth our ideas, bring out our life, find an alternative way of living and work it."[11] The Vanuatu government shut down the association after only a few months, citing that they were a group advocating the smoking of marijuana. This example demonstrates how ni-Vanuatu youth have often been perceived as an internal threat to authority and order, as though they are not a constitutive part of Port Vila society. In another instance of governmental censorship in 2017, the then minister of internal affairs attributed many social problems to "organized youth gangs who may or may not have better things to do, but instead formed organized groups, then take alcohol or drugs that leads to unwanted social problems and crimes."[12] The article quoted the minister declaring, "We want to crackdown on all these organized or loose youth gang activities and disband them, put full stop to such behaviours and return total peace and harmony at community levels throughout Port Vila."[13]

Compounding the challenges of the government, some youth have also struggled to assert their voices and agency in the city. Onis recognized that young people have talents but highlighted their lack of opportunities to develop those talents. As Onis stated, "Young people have skills but there is just nowhere for them to go for guidance and support. When you feel like there is nowhere to go, that's when the passion we have just gets burned into nothing, and that's really hard." Indeed, there are few opportunities for young people in urban Vanuatu, the minimum wage is very low, and the cost of living is high. In these ways, young people embodied the colonial impact and the tensions of decolonization.[14] Many youth became disillusioned and disempowered through the rapid modernization of urban life, if not felt excluded from decision-making processes and the production of media.

Because of the misrepresentations of urban youth degenerating into violence and anti-social behavior and the relative lack of educational resources, young people increasingly developed strategies of resistance. One strategy was "co-opting." Some youth, for instance, co-opted the Voices for Change program and established a permanent space for media training and production. In the residential communities, including Anabrou Sesivi, the community where the Further Arts office is located, the young people co-opted language and repurposed it for their use. As we observed, they also referenced the conditions of Black youth in the Caribbean and North America, appropriated the Black English of street music such as reggae and hip hop, and called their smaller neighborhood groups *skwad* (squad) or *geto* (ghetto). In contrast to the governmental misconceptions of gangs, the ni-Vanuatu youth perceived *geto* as sites of creativity, community engagement, youth agency, and profound social growth.[15] As we intend to show, the youth have been actively creating their own sense of belonging by co-opting the language and resources of the city. In the next sections, we turn to a particular dynamic in this process of co-opting power, itself a manifestation of screen sovereignty. Specifically, we ground these ideas in *kastom*, explore *rimix* as a performative expression of co-optation, discuss the emergence of Further Arts and Nesar Studio, and analyze youth video productions in Vanuatu.

KASTOM, RIMIX, AND NESAR STUDIO

The somewhat ambiguous term *kastom* encapsulates the multiplicity of cultural practices in the diverse linguistic and cultural milieu. It is used by ni-Vanuatu to "characterize their own knowledge and practice in distinction to everything they identify as having come from outside their place."[16] In reality, there are as many *kastom* systems as there are languages, as each of the 113 language groups currently found in Vanuatu represents a people with different oral histories, cosmologies, and traditions. The national government and the modern cash economy have been overlaid onto these complex traditional systems. Many urban youth wish to know their *kastom* but do not have the opportunity to learn it, as *kastom* is perceived as a system spatially anchored to a rural location. Knowing the language of one's "home island" or place of origin is linked to learning about one's *kastom*. However, the use and understanding of vernacular languages among urban youth is increasingly diminishing. Currently, Bislama, English, and French are more widely spoken, leading the youth to commonly say, "*paspot i lus*," meaning "I have lost my passport." This phrase implies that a person does not have permission or a "visa" to visit her or his home island. But for the youth who have come from their islands to Port Vila, they seem to retain a greater sense of *kastom* than their counterparts born in the city.

Despite the perception of a widening gap between urban and rural life, artists in Oceania increasingly use new technologies that draw from their contemporary creative practices and "traditional" knowledges. In Vanuatu, these conceptual innovations, many of which originate from outside sources, come together in the emergent idea of *rimix* (remix). We first noticed its use around a decade ago in the backstreets, *nakamals* (kava bars), and the *geto*. In a conversation with Marcel, he explained, "The way [foreign researchers] talk about bringing '*kastom*' into contemporary practice does not make sense to me. It is not about the past and the present. I am living now. I am creating *kastom* art now. *Rimix* is about me being able to bring innovations from outside my culture, from outside Vanuatu."[17] As

Marcel suggested, the performative use of the creolized *rimix* of Bislama can thereby disorient the accreted tensions and misunderstandings of terms like *kopiraet* (referring to customary protocols restricting knowledge and property transfer), *copyright*, and *kastom*.[18] As anthropologists have argued, these terms refer to different orientations of power and regulation, and they are not direct translations. With *rimix*, we found that people used the term performatively to reframe the tensions between the worn binaries of tradition (*kastom*) and modernity in Vanuatu. *Rimix* is now a term that both young and old ni-Vanuatu people use to refer to the creative reuse of Indigenous and foreign knowledge in contemporary creative arts in Vanuatu. Ni-Vanuatu people working in cultural organizations like Further Arts and the Vanuatu Cultural Centre facilitate multiple forms through which Indigenous peoples can express screen sovereignty.

As we plan to demonstrate, *rimix* soon found a home in Further Arts and its many projects. Founded in December 2000, Further Arts is a local NGO that supports the creative activities of ni-Vanuatu and Melanesian producers, artists, and musicians and seeks to develop sustainable livelihoods. Initially, Further Arts focused its programming on urban, young musicians—a category that was almost exclusively male at that time. From 2010, responding to growing interest in photography, Further Arts began engaging urban youth in media and multimedia production activities in parallel with major music festivals, cultural events, and social movements. In 2012, Further Arts was awarded a grant through the European Union (EU) for approximately VUV 12 million (about US$100,000) (for the "Voices for Change" program) and received further funding from a range of donors through the Dynamics of Civic Engagement program (approximately VUV 6 million, or roughly US$50,000). The staff and board members of Further Arts, including both authors, intentionally designed these programs to amplify the voices of the youth through skills building in leadership, governance, citizen journalism, and activism. Through the Voices for Change program, Further Arts thus provided the resources, the impetus, and, perhaps most importantly, a physical space for young people and community activists to pursue their goals.

However, the senior leadership, who were focused on the functional obligations of managing projects with multiple donors and stakeholders, were surprised when a new group, which came to be known as Nesar Studio, formed. This group grew out of production activities written into the Voices for Change project with the aim of increasing technical and production skills of young people. Around this time, Libby Gott, an Australian volunteer, joined Further Arts as the creative communications development officer, working closely with Marcel. By April 2013, Libby had negotiated for two interns to join Further Arts from Youth Challenge Vanuatu's Ready for Work youth employment program: Christelle, an administrative assistant, and Roselyn, a production assistant. Over the ensuing months, the predominantly male-oriented Further Arts facility then shifted to accommodate young urban women as well.

The core Nesar Studio team initially included creative and administrative staff, and a number of youth formed the core production crew (figure 4.1). Since the setup of Nesar Studio, Libby and Roselyn have moved on to other positions in the media industry, and a steady stream of young people has come through the organization. All of the young producers in Further Arts and Nesar Studio were born in the two decades after Independence in 1980, have lived in one of the peri-urban villages or residential communities, and have achieved a basic level of education. When asked how she came to be a part of Nesar Studio, Gina explained, "Back in 2016, I followed Further Arts on Facebook and saw how they helped young

FIGURE 4.1. Founder of Nesar Studio, Marcel Meltherorong (left), with crew member, Andrew Tamata (right), in the studio. (Photo credit: Further Arts 2014)

people who are interested in media. So I messaged them asking if I could participate in any training, and in June last year I got an invitation to join a Women in Media course. After that, I became a regular part of Further Arts crew. And very recently, I got a job with Further Arts Nesar Studio as production coordinator." Niki had this to say about Nesar: "For skills on media and filming, there was nowhere for youth to make their own videos. Nesar—it's the only place we can come and learn by actually creating our own media." Contrary to the authorities' negative views of the youth, they actually aligned with existing institutions that provided them with legitimacy. The members of the Youth Against Corruption Vanuatu organization, a group that shares many members with Nesar Studio, created opportunities for their members to participate in each other's activities. These partnerships allowed the youth to work interdependently and to produce media.

Young media producers also accessed Nesar Studio, used a range of digital tools, and developed livelihood opportunities in the creative industries. In Marcel's words, "That's what I wanted this studio to be: A space to speak, to tell our stories . . . through video, studio recording, music . . . everything. It's all story. Vanuatu people have an oral culture, we are storytelling people. So it's a space for this. And it's not only for promoting and distributing stories; it also has an archival function. Maybe people want to record stories so they can show them to their children in 10 years' time." The media environment in Vanuatu is difficult for the youth to penetrate. As Onis said, "I couldn't find anywhere." This is partly due to technical barriers, such as the media's focus on either the French or English language as well as a lack of education. Gina summed up the situation: "It was really hard. I went to the technical college but they only offered a (print) journalism course, without film or photography elements. The University of the South Pacific didn't have anything. I tried all the different institutions in Vanuatu, but I couldn't find any media courses." These quotes show how the establishment of Nesar Studio signaled a significant disjuncture for youth- and community-driven media in Port Vila and Vanuatu. What is perhaps less clear is the central role that the youth themselves played in the emergence of Nesar Studio. It was largely in response to the interest expressed by a core group of young people who participated in the initial media training, namely, Marcel, Sarah, and Libby, who recognized that multimedia was an appropriate and accessible medium for the youth. At this time, Australia's High Commission in Vanuatu supplied five laptops to the studio in-kind, and other basic equipment was procured through EU funding.

In September 2013, for instance, Marcel named and launched Nesar Studio as a community access multimedia facility so that young people in Port Vila could access media and multimedia tools, resources, and education. Marcel explained, "'Nesar' means 'nasara' in the language of Vao. 'Nesar' and 'nasara'—the words mean a place where people come together . . . to celebrate, to perform dances and songs, and to witness ceremonies or rituals and other things like that. It's a public space—open to everyone, there are no restrictions." As these words reveal, Nesar Studio became an urban *rimix* of the village *nasara*, evoking other Indigenous interrogations of media and sovereignty, as with Raheja's "virtual reservations."[19] In an age of increased telecommunications and media platforms, Nesar emerged to transmit youth knowledge. Marcel again stated,

> But the other reason that I gave the studio this name is that during the masterclass that I did at FIFO in Tahiti [in 2013], the first thing they told us was that in Oceania, there are so many stories and films, most are being told by non-Indigenous researchers and outsiders. There are very few producers, writers, and creatives from Oceania who are telling their histories and documenting stories because they are busy doing other things. Maybe working in national broadcasters, news reading, or journalism, or whatever, but they are not making documentary films and telling the stories and histories of Oceania, in the words of Oceanian people, from the perspectives of Oceanian people.

Marcel also clarified that Nesar Studio was not about the authority vested by the government or the church. By invoking the significance of the village *nasara*, he demonstrated that other young people held the power and creativity to make their stories. Nesar Studio was and is fundamentally about "theoretical notions of sovereignty that are also rooted in the arts."[20] Nesar Studio thus embodies an ontological disjuncture and technological liberation for the youth across the rural and urban spaces and the customary and popular practices of Vanuatu. As Homi Bhabha writes, the spaces in between "provide the terrain for elaborating strategies of selfhood—singular or communal—that initiate new signs of identity, and innovative sites of collaboration, and contestation, in the act of defining the idea of society itself."[21] In the following section, we explore how

Nesar Studio generated creative ways to express a screen sovereignty spatially anchored to an urban location.

EMERGING YOUNG MEDIA PRODUCERS

Developing the capacity of young media professionals in Vanuatu is not a simple process. Stakeholders must navigate divergent interests and compete for resources within an environment in which the digital media and creative industries are poorly understood by state actors and supported in an ad hoc fashion by development partners at both national and regional levels. The bodies that do advocate for this sector, including the Vanuatu Cultural Centre, Secretariat of the Pacific Community, and the Pacific Arts Association, have not been consistently effective. This means that the role of nurturing young media professionals is in the hands of civil society actors, either in cooperation with, or struggling alongside, the dominant media companies.

Young Nesar Studio producers participated in the studio to learn new skills and develop opportunities for personal and professional development. Niki said that Nesar Studio "gives young people a chance to express ourselves." Many members noted that they do not have any other prospects for employment or education so the studio became a base for them to access opportunities for learning or paid work. Since opening, the studio has created three full- and part-time staff roles to coordinate production activities and several interns in various administration and production roles. The core media crew continues to change as members come and go as they please, contingent upon available training programs or project work offered by the studio.

Whether or not structured activities and programs are offered, the studio space is a platform for members to explore media, work on personal projects, or collaborate with others. When asked how she came to be involved in media work, Gina talked about how excited she was to find a local institution that engaged the visual aspects of media: "To be honest, I was really happy when I found Further Arts because I am personally more interested in the visual than the verbal. I like seeing short video clips, photos, memes more than reading and writing. I like seeing the ways that different people express their different perspectives through photography." Media professionals, photographers, and filmmakers from Australia, Canada, Fiji, Italy, France, New Zealand, the United States, and West Papua have introduced new and alternative techniques. They have worked with the crew on projects and provided technical training. These experiences enriched studio members' understanding of media as a global phenomenon and enabled them to *rimix* foreign approaches with their Indigenous worldviews to create unique media. Going beyond a traditional documentary format whereby the person holding the camera generally retains storytelling power, the youth by default utilized the camera as a device for attenuating local stories. Although they understood broadcast, dissemination, and distribution as abstract possibilities with limited impact, the youth appreciated how the camera enabled them to tell their own stories and create new subjects and knowledge. For instance, the ni-Vanuatu youth interviewed the lived realities of the community, including musicians shot in their community homes instead of performing on the stage and women at the market shot behind their counters instead of standing in front of the brightly colored produce. These mid-range shots also evidenced the preferred localities of their subjects (figure 4.2).

Footage captured and then edited by the youth almost always portrayed the rawness of daily life in Vanuatu. By entering the Port Vila market

FIGURE 4.2. Photograph titled *Grandma*, first-prize winner in the category of photography at the National Portrait Exhibition. (Photo credit: Gina Kaitiplel / Further Arts 2017)

house with a video camera, for example, the young producers sought out the real stories of the women who spent their entire week living and sleeping there, some selling fresh produce and others cooking throughout the day. They intended to create content that was accessible primarily for the ni-Vanuatu audience, avoiding the need to address language and literacy barriers. This content can then be *rimix*ed for wider use, such as the Traditional Entertainment and Kastom Support (TEKS) Unit photographic essay and text co-developed for the international *Langscape* magazine, demonstrating a powerful bridge between local forms of knowledge and the global systems of academia, media, and publishing.[22]

CREATIVE STORYTELLING AND THE NAMATAN SHORT FILM FESTIVAL

Some of the most interesting creative productions have been short films produced for submission to the annual Namatan Short Film Festival and Competition (known locally and henceforth as Namatan), run by the Vanuatu Broadcasting Television Corporation and the Australian High Commission in Port Vila. Since Namatan's inception in 2012, Further Arts facilitated and gave resources to competition filmmakers and Namatan's annual training workshop. Nesar Studio members have submitted fictional narrative films across genres, including comedy, romance, drama, horror, and adventure. These films drew on local culture, life, and stories while others *rimix*ed foreign ideas in the pursuit of entertainment. Such films included *Bush Party* (2013), a piece about a girl's birthday party that was overrun by zombie-like characters, and *The Kiaman* (2013), a film about a couple witnessing con artists trick a man and steal his computer from a public place. The music and action sequences also reflected the influence of popular culture and mainstream aesthetics. As Andrew explained, "I watch many foreign films and take ideas from them to come up with my own filmmaking ideas."

Fiction and documentary films also communicated local voices and stories. *True Colors*, which won first place in the 2014 competition, depicted a broken family in Vanuatu confronting domestic violence and separation. The director, Roselyn, said that she based the film on the reality for many young Port Vila families. Through her filmmaking, she showed people that "this way of living is not right." When the film was publicly screened and she won, she felt proud and really happy about it. Film became the medium for Roselyn to express her voice.

With respect to Namatan, it is unique in Vanuatu. The festival also provides the missing platform for ni-Vanuatu filmmakers to broadcast their films. It has galvanized young people to share ideas and stories through film. For the training workshop that has preceded the competition, Nesar Studio has hosted interested individuals with little prior knowledge of film production and given them the skills for script development. The competition has further incentivized participation through prize giving. Without this platform, there would not be a growing number of people interested in filmmaking and other visual media. The festival is central to the expansion of the emerging Vanuatu film industry, motivating young film producers working with Nesar Studio who are otherwise too busy working on media projects commissioned by Nesar Studio, Further Arts, and other organizations.

DOCUMENTARY PRODUCTIONS FOR THE NGO SECTOR

Most of the Further Arts' projects are documentary videos, radio programs, and photographic works on Vanuatu culture, society, and events. Occasionally, members are required to develop written reflections and blog pieces on their process and content. However, the current members of Nesar Studio are more interested in the audio-visual application of media. Given that Vanuatu is an oral culture, these kinds of media disseminate information more widely than written literacy-based media. Videos in particular amplify the unheard stories of the community, such as the slave trade in the Pacific, the struggles for freedom in West Papua, and everyday expressions of Melanesian identity. Take, for example, the youth participation in the TEKS Unit.

In collaboration with communities from northern Vanuatu, Nesar youth recorded traditional knowledge practices via rural mini arts festivals and urban *kastom* performances. Footage, photos, and interviews depicted and explained *kastom* ceremonies, songs, dances, and art to create appealing and informative media in collaboration with the communities. TEKS Unit leaders, all consisting of indigenous ni-Vanuatu, established respectful relationships with community members and stressed the importance of the multimedia productions to sustain and promote traditional knowledge, particularly for young people and future generations. In effect, this practice maintained power in the hands of the communities and allowed them to control how their traditions were transmitted to produce new meaning.[23] Dely, the founder of the TEKS Unit, said that "my identity has always been a drive. I love my culture, I am proud of who I am. And that motivates me to make other people be proud of themselves."

Dely's intentionality resonated with the Nesar Studio members. For example, Gina talked about what this partnership was like for her, explaining that "it has been an exciting journey for me as a young woman who has never been to other islands except for my home island. One of the highlights from my time here is doing projects in seven different islands from north to south of Vanuatu documenting *kastom* knowledge—music, food, and dance—through video, CD productions, and books." Furthermore, Roselyn expressed that through the TEKS program, she attained a greater understanding of *kastom* on different islands of Vanuatu. TEKS also inspired her to learn more about her own cultural identity and family's *kastom* of which she has little knowledge. Reflecting on this matter, Dely said that "many young people never thought about *being* somebody today. But now they are, thanks to all the training and the positive influence it had on them; it makes them who they are now."

The TEKS media productions did not intend to replace the practice of young people going through traditional ceremonies to obtain cultural knowledge. Rather, the collective showed the ni-Vanuatu youth of Port Vila that they never lost their passports, could access the *kastom* of their home islands, and should continue to value and make use of their cultural heritage. In this way, cultural multimedia compelled the young people to consider their own modes of cultural knowledge, interdependency, and political agency. While the youth themselves did not use this language, we have found that the youth-oriented media exemplified screen sovereignty insofar as they produced and disseminated digital media that mainly reflected their own desires, identities, and languages over the perspectives of outsiders. As Gina expressed, she tries "to apply the skills [gained through the Nesar training] to achieve social justice and social transformation for the betterment of Vanuatu, Melanesia, and the world."

To be clear, we do not mean to say that outsiders held no influence over the ni-Vanuatu youth in Nesar Studio. Tension often existed because Nesar Studio's productions are sometimes requested and designed by outside sources. Given that the majority of the media production activities at Nesar Studio are commissioned by "clients" (other NGOs, government departments, and aid agencies), young producers have been constrained in their creative freedom, bound by the obligation to, as Niki said, "satisfy the ideas of others." In this regard, we acknowledge the limits of ni-Vanuatu screen sovereignty, if not recognize that the commercial realm of multimedia has yet to be fully controlled by the youth. There is just not enough time or resources for crew members to work solely on personal ideas, so paid work is prioritized. For some, this can seem as an insurmountable barrier as they struggle to understand and meet the expectations of the clients, particularly clients who are unfamiliar with Nesar Studio and its foremost status as a learning and development collective. Roselyn disclosed her concern about one project she was asked to work on: "If it was just me making the film for myself, then it would probably be different. I'm worried that they'll watch it and won't like it." Roselyn's vulnerability is palpable. Her anxiety about what the client wanted to see in the film revealed the tensions between her aspirations to tell her own stories and the imperative to earn from commissioned work—two powerful forces at play in screen sovereignty. She expressed this in relation to the fact that if it was her decision alone, she would make a completely different film.

Despite these challenges, the young media producers affirmed that every opportunity had strengthened their technical competency and advanced their career potential. Andrew understood his work as mutually beneficial: "I see it as an exchange. I contribute something that is needed by others while at the same time I gain through learning." Project work can even improve personal development and self-confidence. A series of video productions commissioned by UNICEF and UN Women to document children's and women's stories, respectively, after the devastating impact of Tropical Cyclone Pam in 2015 provided an opportunity for the crew to interact with diverse groups in a post-disaster context. As a result, Roselyn stated that she developed confidence in her ability to elicit stories from people of all different ages.

Receiving payment through their media work is also a liberating outcome for young members, who otherwise would not have a source of income. Nesar Studio emphasizes the importance of fair remuneration to acknowledge their work and encourages them to do what they want. Thus, media crew members hang around and request more work and even invest their earnings to purchase their own production equipment. Furthermore, simple media platforms and technologies such as online videos, social media, and Bluetooth transfer enable anyone to circulate messages and media without having to write it in words. The members of Nesar Studio often focus on expressing ideas related to freedom. This is usually framed as something that Vanuatu has achieved, being an independent republic since 1980, and understood in relation to places such as West Papua—the western half of the island of Papua New Guinea that is currently occupied by Indonesia—and Kanaky.

In fact, the ni-Vanuatu youth of Port Vila also proved to be a resilient group in the aftermath of a natural disaster. In March 2015, Tropical Cyclone Pam inflicted much devastation in Vanuatu and impacted Further Arts and Nesar Studio, destroying the physical office and studio spaces. The studio was limited in its capacity to provide media training to more than fifteen members at a time, resulting in a significant proportion of the membership without access. Conversely, the impact of the cyclone generated new opportunities for Nesar Studio to continue operating and even advance the technical skills of core crew members. For instance, we partnered Further Arts and Nesar Studio with Komuniti Akses Media (KAM) TV, a local television station. KAM TV provided a space for the office and studio in return for Nesar Studio offering regular content to the station. The core media crew began producing two television programs, *Storian Blong Yumi*, about sociocultural happenings in Vanuatu, and *Lokol Mix*, about local music and musicians. *Lokol Mix*, in particular, has been a standout as it provided insight into the vibrant creativity and the economic marginalization of the music industry in Vanuatu. The crew members, some of them musicians themselves, wanted this show to go beyond the glossed-over, mainstream media perspective. That is, they *rimix*ed the reality of the industry and gave credence to musicians through a platform other than a festival stage to tell their stories and express what motivates them. The show has also sparked interest in the Fest'Napuan music festival and was used to promote the festival and its musicians in the lead up to the twentieth anniversary edition in October 2015.

Despite the devastation wrought by Tropical Cyclone Pam, the youth media crew found ways to engage multimedia production. With the support of Nesar Studio and Further Arts, the young media producers created the "space," both physically and conceptually, via several methods: asserting normative principles and a philosophy steeped in the valuing of youth participation; enabling autonomy in decision-making; providing and managing a physical space; and following operational structures to shape and maintain that space. The studio members, too, as we have discussed, were integral in the genesis of Nesar Studio, and therefore, its existence can be said to be codependent: the young producers and the institutional support fostered the environment for the constant energy and activity that appear to organize itself.

CONCLUSION

In urban Port Vila, media is increasingly exploited as a tool for local and national economic, political, social, and spiritual life. While traditional media sources are embedded in the values of Vanuatu as a collectivist society, focusing on distinct physical communities and places, new media technologies enable ni-Vanuatu to create and engage with new platforms and alternative communities not spatially bound by a geographical location or a shared familial or cultural identity. For urban youth with abundant ideas and energy, the ease of engagement with new media technologies has positively influenced their lifestyle choices and social relationships.

Despite the challenges of governmental censorship, commercial interests, and natural disasters, the young producers at Nesar Studio asserted the importance, and indeed their ownership, of the structure and its organizational relationships—in particular with Further Arts. For young urban ni-Vanuatu, born after Independence, their practice of screen sovereignty has partly derived from the forces of decolonization and self-determination. But it is the emphasis on the "post" in postcolonial that inflected their reality in different ways. Vanuatu as a sovereign Indigenous nation provides a different context in relation to the "disappearances" and "erasures" manifested by settler cities where Indigenous peoples are governed by the descendants of colonizers. As Kepa 'Ōkusitino Maumau, Moana 'Ulu'ave-Hafoka, and Lea Lani Kinikini have shown in chapter 2, Salt Lake City, Utah, created a moral panic about "Tongan gang members" in the 1990s, thereby attempting to marginalize the Tongan diasporic community in Utah. But unlike the Tongan men who faced criminal charges in a settler court not of their own making, the ni-Vanuatu youth reside in their sovereign and postcolonial state.

At the same time, the Melanesians of Bougainville, Kanaky (New Caledonia), and West Papua live much more in a colonial present than in a postcolonial future. Australia, France, Indonesia, the United States, and other countries continue to directly or indirectly claim sovereignty over the resources of these Indigenous communities, and Vanuatu is no exception. Clearly, Vanuatu is independent, but independence does not necessarily entail the decolonization of everyday life. Although Nesar Studio and Further Arts have supported the youth and the wider community, the radio stations play more international content than domestic, and the government continues to view young people as a threat to the social order. But as we have emphasized in this chapter, the youth have begun to express their forms of screen sovereignty by way of media production and story-telling. As Marcel says, "Vanuatu people have an oral culture, we are story-telling people." The ni-Vanuatu youth have also been demanding more guidance, training, and education in the creative industries. When support has not been available, they have co-opted resources to express their identities and produce media about their own lives and the lives of the people who are important to them.

As we have found, the youth have been developing both individual and collective forms of digital media. Their notion of screen sovereignty has thus been shaped by their proximity to Port Vila, an urban and settler city, and by their *rimix* of new technologies, creative support from Further Arts and other organizations, older notions of *kastom*, and even contemporary forms of African American and Black diasporic traditions. Their access to and partial ownership of media has helped them to navigate the creative, spatial, and virtual worlds of Port Vila, Vanuatu, and beyond.

NOTES

This research was partially supported by the Australian government through the Australian Research Council's Linkage Projects funding scheme (project LP150100973). We also thank the Australian Research Council for partially funding our research in Vanuatu.

1   Katherine Irwin and Karen Umemoto, *Jacked Up and Unjust: Pacific Islander Teens Confront Violent Legacies* (Oakland: University of California Press, 2016).

2   Linda Tuhiwai Smith, *Decolonizing Methodologies: Research and Indigenous Peoples* (London: Zed Books, 1999).

3   Dwayne Donald and Mandy Krahn, "Abandoning Pathologization: Conceptualizing Indigenous Youth Identity as Flowing from Communitarian Understandings," in *Critical Youth Studies Reader*, ed. Awad Ibrahim and Shirley R. Steinberg (New York: Peter Lang, 2014), 114–29.

4   Karyn Recollet, "Gesturing Indigenous Futurities through the Remix," *Dance Research Journal* 48, no. 1 (2016): 91–105; and Grace L. Dillon, *Walking the Clouds: An Anthology of Indigenous Science Fiction* (Tucson: University of Arizona Press, 2012).

5   Jolene Rickard, "Sovereignty: A Line in the Sand," *Aperture*, no. 139 (1995): 50–59; and Michelle H. Raheja, "Visual Sovereignty," in *Native Studies Keywords*, ed. Stephanie Nohelani Teves, Andrea Smith, and Michelle H. Raheja (Tucson: University of Arizona Press, 2015), 25–34.

6   Kristin L. Dowell, *Sovereign Screens: Aboriginal Media on the Canadian West Coast* (Lincoln: University of Nebraska Press, 2013); and Faye Ginsburg, "Indigenous Media from U-Matic to YouTube: Media Sovereignty in the Digital Age," *Sociologia and Antropologia* 6, no. 3 (2016): 581–99.

7 Gregory Rawlings, "Foundations of Urbanisation: Port Vila Town and Pango Village, Vanuatu," *Oceania* 70, no. 1 (1999): 72–86.

8 Daniela Kraemer, "Planting Roots, Making Place: An Ethnography of Young Men in Port Vila, Vanuatu" (PhD diss., London School of Economics and Political Science, 2013).

9 Andrew Ala, "Mango Urban Settlement, Luganville, Vanuatu," in *In Search of a Home*, ed. Leonard Mason and Pat Hereniko (Suva, Fiji: Institute of Pacific Studies, University of the South Pacific, 1987), 203.

10 Daniela Kraemer, "'Do you have a mobile?': Mobile Phone Practices and the Refashioning of Social Relationships in Port Vila Town," *Australian Journal of Anthropology* 28, no. 1 (2017): 39–55.

11 Kraemer, "Planting Roots, Making Place," 229.

12 Godwin Ligo, "Youth Gang Crackdown," *Vanuatu Daily Post* (Port Vila), August 24, 2017, https://dailypost.vu/news/youth-gang-crackdown/article _7b4b5752-de71-50a0-9e6a-b7c2fcf24d02.html.

13 Ligo, "Youth Gang Crackdown."

14 Kraemer, "Planting Roots, Making Place," 34.

15 Kraemer, "Planting Roots, Making Place," 35.

16 Lissant Bolton, *Unfolding the Moon: Enacting Women's* Kastom *in Vanuatu* (Honolulu: University of Hawai'i Press, 2003), xiii.

17 Marcel Meltherorong, personal communication with Thomas Dick, October 2018.

18 Haidy Geismar, "Copyright in Context: Carvings, Carvers, and Commodities in Vanuatu," *American Ethnologist* 32, no. 3 (2005): 437–59; and Margaret Jolly, "Custom and the Way of the Land: Past and Present in Vanuatu and Fiji," *Oceania* 62, no. 4 (1992): 330–54.

19 Michelle H. Raheja, *Reservation Reelism: Redfacing, Visual Sovereignty, and Representations of Native Americans in Film* (Lincoln: University of Nebraska Press, 2010).

20 Raheja, "Visual Sovereignty," 27.

21 Homi K. Bhabha, *The Location of Culture* (London: Routledge, 1994), 1–2.

22 Delly Roy, Cristina Panicali, Sarah Doyle, and Thomas Dick, "Songs and Stories of Biocultural Diversity: Gender and Creativity in Northern Vanuatu," *Langscape* 4, no. 1 (2015): 73–77.

23 Judy Iseke and Sylvia Moore, "Community-Based Indigenous Digital Storytelling with Elders and Youth," *American Indian Culture and Research Journal* 35, no. 4 (2011): 19–38.

CHAPTER 5

"HOLLA MAI! TONGAN 4 LIFE!"

Transnational Citizenship, Youth Style,
and Mediated Interaction through
Online Social Networking Communities

MARY K. GOOD

WHEN I ARRIVED IN THE CAPITAL CITY OF TONGA IN JANUARY 2008, it seemed as if the number of internet cafés had skyrocketed in the urban center since my previous visit in 2004.[1] Older-model desktop computer towers and bulky monitors filled the small, dark shops. Before and after school, students crammed the cafés, looking at page after page of multicolored screens filled with photos. It wasn't long before I struck up a conversation with two students who asked me enthusiastically, "Do you have a Bebo?" They quickly taught me the basics of Bebo, an online social networking website, and how to start a profile page of my own. On the site, a variety of colorful media greeted users, and Tongan youth encouraged others to "Holla mai!"—a combination of "Holla," a global slang rooted in African American hip hop, as in to "holler" or call friends, with the Tongan deictic "mai," a direct action in the direction of the speaker. In other words, "Holla mai!" meant "Come, interact with me!" By the time I reached the outer island of 'Eua, I was prepared for the "Bebo fever" that captivated many youth: any time I snapped a picture with my digital camera, there would be pleas to post it to the photo subject's page. I then accumulated a growing number of online "friends." It appeared that Tongan youth eagerly, if somewhat precariously, settled into an online life in the digital age. But how did this virtual, and physical, process happen so quickly? Why were students so excited about this new trend in technology that they would gladly spend any pocket money they had to get online?

Far from being merely a passing fad, Tongan youths' fascination with the social networking website Bebo revealed a deep attachment to core Tongan values even as it catapulted its users into processes of global modernity, entwining them in the fringes of techno-capital. Within the context of a country where it is estimated that the population of 110,000 is roughly the same size as the number of ethnic Tongans living abroad, the connections made and questions raised regarding one's place in multiple sites within the transnational field take on new significance. Online social networking communities make ideal proving grounds for engaging with transnational identity and citizenship, as they exemplify Sarah Mahler and Patricia Pessar's notion of "transnational social spaces—spaces that are anchored in, but extend beyond, borders of any one nation-state."[2] The ways local Tongan youth created online identities within the public sphere of the virtual world and made connections to others provide the ideal venue for an ethnographic analysis of their cultural meanings about transnational practices and their movements of people, ideas, capital, and things.[3] An examination of Tongan youths' activities on the Bebo site shows how they developed a sense of transnational citizenship and explored orientations to global modernity while balancing traditional notions of gender, kinship, and age-appropriate behavior on their home island of 'Eua.

While the young people with whom I worked did not, by and large, orient to this new online space as a site for developing a political consciousness, they did use Bebo to present themselves as global actors in ways that might translate into forms of critical awareness later in life. For youth living within the island nation of Tonga or in diasporic enclaves in Aotearoa New Zealand, Australia, and the United States, online social networking websites like Bebo represented exciting ways to communicate with friends and relatives through a novel form of mediated interaction. In this way, the early forms of social networking that I observed among Tongan youth could be framed in a manner that resonates with Awad Ibrahim's characterization of youth "as action; as a performative category; as an identity that is both produced through and is producing our sense of self; as an agentive, ambiguous, fluid, shifting, multiple, complex, stylized, and forever becoming category."[4]

In this chapter, I explore how youth on the island of 'Eua in Tonga cre-ated, interpreted, and engaged with ideas of transnational identity and citizenship through mediated face-to-face interactions in the online social network of Bebo at a very early stage of social media in Tonga. Now defunct, Bebo allowed users with relatively low computer literacy skills to craft a unique profile page or pages in order to interact with others through a variety of media experiences, including personal messages, photos, song clips, and video. At a time when ideas about what it means to be a Tongan circulate within the nation and abroad, Bebo showed how the youth could invest in and critically examine this aspect of their lives, whether they were able to physically and virtually move through transnational circuits or only digitally imagine doing so.

In order to fully understand the choices Tongan youth from 'Eua make in the construction of their profile pages, it is first necessary to understand the physical world that makes Tongan online networks possible.[5] After giving some background context for online social life in Tonga, I will also highlight Tongan youths' and adults' perceptions of online social network-ing. As with other processes of global modernity and adoptions of new digital media, Tongans view online social networking with some ambiva-lence, recognizing its potential benefits and dangers along moral, social, economic, and other fault lines.[6] Tongans have participated in global modernity in a number of different ways, and many people in Tonga have self-consciously crafted "modern" and "cosmopolitan" selves[7]; the creative practices young men and women utilized on their Bebo pages present an additional aspect of a range of local-global articulations. I will then ana-lyze specific profiles from Tongan youth to shed light on the ways new forms of identity encompass traditional culture and enable transnational connections. Emphasizing Jannis Androutsopoulos's argument that a "multimodal" analysis of digital media allows researchers to better under-stand how typography, graphics, and other resources bolster linguistic dimensions of media to form a coherent, recognizable style, I will show the ways various elements build a clear presence and style for this particular group of users.[8]

My main data set is a collection of Bebo profile pages, understood as digital "texts" or "cultural spaces" in online media.[9] Comparably, in chap-ter 2, Kepa 'Ōkusitino Maumau, Moana 'Uluʻave-Hafoka, and Lea Lani Kinikini examine how legal texts produced the "fiction" of Tongan youth gangs in Salt Lake City. In chapter 7, Alika Bourgette analyzes Native mas-culinities in early-twentieth-century Honolulu. In each case, these authors also understand and theorize ideologies as the ways in which people constitute, interpret, and address the semiotic meaning and impact of signs in everyday life.[10] Rather than only embrace one national identity, affiliate with only one Pacific city or homeland, or reject older forms of cultural belonging, I argue that the Tongan youth developed new transnational identities and forms of citizenship by using multimodal semiotic and linguistic forms in the online platform of Bebo.

The use of Bebo by Tongan youth from the island of 'Eua shows a remarkable engagement with online spaces that incorporates the digital realm into the Tongan understanding of tā-vā, theorized by 'Ōkusitino Māhina and Tēvita Ka'ili as the marking of social relations across time and space.[11] Within the framework of tā-vā relations, Ka'ili emphasizes the critical aspect of caring for one another and "maintaining beautiful relations."[12] The practices employed by youth to communicate with friends and relatives while extending their social reach on Bebo can be interpreted as another dimension of this critical aspect of Tongan life: the maintenance of social relationships through time and (here, transnational and virtual) space. Using this novel form of digital communication, youth nevertheless practiced long-standing forms of talanoa, or storytelling, that symmetrically intertwined orality, time, and space.[13] Bebo, and the use of social networking sites that follow, created a virtual tā-vā in new media.

RESEARCH METHODS

Drawing on tools from linguistic anthropology, cultural anthropology, and cultural studies, I investigate the ways that specific choices are made in the selection of typography, photos and graphic images, and other stylistic elements that act as semiotic vehicles for global hip hop, African American culture, and other markers of "coolness." In this manner, my chapter grows out of a continued research interest in Tongans' engagement with processes of global modernity.[14] I examined approximately sixty profile pages from Tongans living in Tonga, New Zealand, and the United States that were actively maintained between 2008 and 2011. The Bebo users in this sample spanned from thirteen years of age into their mid-thirties and represented a wide range of computer literacy and frequency of use. Young women also maintained roughly two-thirds of the pages, reflecting the general state of internet use among youth at the time of my research.

Tongan gender ideologies cast women as more inclined to indoor activities requiring stillness, obedience, concentration, and, to some extent, creativity. These skills appear in their traditional crafts like weaving fine mats or, in the case of young women, in performing well in school tasks. Men, however, are viewed as suited for outdoor, active, and physical pursuits.[15] The youth with whom I worked were highly attuned to these cultural understandings of gender roles, and thus fewer young men spent as much time as young women in the careful maintenance of online social networking pages in the early days of internet use described here. Over time, however, and particularly when greater numbers of young men were exposed to the internet and Bebo while in school computing classes or in youth skills workshops, they enthusiastically began to use social media tools. The introduction of smartphones and cellular data services in more recent years drastically changed the ways both young men and women accessed and interacted with online social media. This chapter deals specifically with the understudied period of time, and the undertheorized role of Tongan youth identities, before cell phones made the internet more available and widespread.

In keeping with the ways online "friends" spread organically, the research participant group was not a random sample. Instead, I began with friends I met during my fieldwork on the island of 'Eua and expanded these networks with trips to the main island of Tongatapu, which, in turn, grew with visits from Tongan relatives and stretched outward across the Tongan diaspora. Unlike the use of social networking sites by many users in the United States in the first decade of the twenty-first century, Tongans' requests for and acceptance of new friends on Bebo was fluid, incorporating friends of friends, extended family one might not have met in person, and strangers. These practices parallel ways of making friends in face-to-face contexts, which I address in the following section.

TONGANS ON THE INTERNET

Although regular use of the internet in general, and online social networking websites in particular, is relatively new to Tongan youth, internet access has been available to Tongans at home and abroad for a fairly long time. Regular internet service became available to the public in Tonga in 1997 in the form of Kalianet, named for the double-hulled canoes of early Tongan seafaring explorers. However, even before this web portal had sailed into view in the homeland, Tongans working and studying overseas had begun to explore the internet. Tongans began immigrating to various locations for work, education, and other opportunities in large numbers beginning in the 1970s, and since that time, the material, financial, social, and intellectual contributions of Tongans living abroad have been an essential aspect of cultural life in Tonga.[16] This tradition of far-reaching Tongan travel paved the way for contemporary actions in the online world and in the creation of transnational identities not based in one "homeland."

In 1995, among a flurry of internet projects designed to preserve the cultural heritage of Pacific Islanders while making their presence more widely known through public relations campaigns, a Tongan studying in the United States developed the "kava bowl" online forum. The site, organized as a bulletin board with multiple topics available for users' discussion, was intended to mimic the free-flowing conversations that occurred in "real life" around the carved wooden bowls filled with kava. In Tonga, kava is a drink made out of pounded *piper methysticum* pepper root and mixed with water.[17] However, unlike in-person gatherings, the online forum welcomed Tongans of all ages, genders, and statuses, and the contributors judged to have the most reasoned opinion or "the last word" on a given topic were not always the highest-ranking men in the group.

The kava bowl forum included some users from Tonga, but most contributors described themselves as Tongan immigrants living in the United States, New Zealand, or Australia.[18] It is likely that internet use from within Tonga was relatively low in the 1990s and the following decade due to the high costs of installing the service in one's home and the even larger amounts of capital necessary to start up an internet café. Additionally, a lack of computer literacy kept interest in visiting the new internet cafés to a minimum for the first few years of service. The highly cultivated Tongan values of shame (*mā*) and the fervent desire not to be seen as attempting to know too much or rise above one's place (*fiepoto, fielahi*) likewise contributed to the initial Tongan aversion to the internet cafés.

Then, in the early twenty-first century, several changes occurred that led to crowded internet cafés full of eager young computer users. Through partnerships with the American, Australian, and Japanese volunteer aid organizations in Tonga and donations from these and other nations, courses in computer skills became more widely available in high schools. Changes in requirements for work visas in New Zealand (and, to a lesser extent, in Australia and the United States) increased the number of Tongan circular migrants going overseas for employment. At the same time, Tongan adults sent their children abroad for varying amounts of time, either for extended holidays or to live with relatives for some of their primary school education. As increasing numbers of Tongans went overseas, the numbers of people whose curiosity was piqued by computers and the internet grew as well, and more Tongans began to acquire the resources to explore this interest. As Linea, a thirteen-year-old girl, explained to me, "we [Linea and her older brother] went on holiday to see our Aunty last year in New Zealand. Me and [her young cousins] would all go to the library when it rained and play on the computers there. One of the librarians was a kind lady, and she showed us how to play games. Then Finau [an older male cousin] showed us how to go on Bebo, and we had fun."[19] As with many forms of knowledge acquired by young people,[20] online social networking abilities were passed through peer circles and seen as play or ways to escape boredom.

According to my research participants, Bebo was introduced to Tonga somewhere around 2005 or 2006, mainly through networks of overseas relatives, as in the case of Linea, or through expatriate aid workers in Tonga. At that time, enough young people had the necessary skills to jump into the online world and share the network with their friends and relatives. By 2009, there were few high school–aged youth in the area of my research that did not have at least some online experience. Hina, a young woman in her twenties who worked at a combination DVD rental shop and online access point in the town of 'Ohonua, laughingly commented on the Bebo trend to me one evening. As I chatted with her while playing on the computers with a group of young teenaged women, she remarked, "The kids, all they do is come in and Bebo, Bebo, Bebo!" Rolling her eyes, Hina continued, "They beg their parents, 'please can I go to the shop to use the computer, it's for a school project,' but really all they do is play on the Bebo! A waste of time, a waste of money!" Yet Hina also kept up her own Bebo profile page, begrudgingly admitting it was fun to connect with overseas relatives and make new friends in Tonga and elsewhere.

BEBO IN TONGA (AND BEYOND)

Bebo was launched in 2005 as a platform similar to early online social networks like Friendster and MySpace. According to its Wikipedia entry, Bebo was extremely popular in Ireland and the United Kingdom in 2006 to 2007, overtaking other social networking sites in number of users. People on 'Eua began to use Bebo on computers in the local internet cafés after hearing about the site and developing profiles with relatives in the Tongan capital city of Nuku'alofa or while visiting family overseas. As I observed, the site was relatively easy to navigate, and the creation of a personal profile page only required a user to supply an email address and a password. The lack of a usable email address did not necessarily stop young people from using the site, however. For example, one afternoon in early 2008 while visiting an internet café, I watched as two young women helped each other to create Bebo profiles. When it came time to supply an email address, the older of the two showed the other young woman how to fill in the form with "just anything." The former then instructed the new user how to create a recognizable fake email address, a string of characters ending in "@gmail.com." In this way, Tongan youth with limited computer skills circumvented the barriers to access placed on the site.

In using Bebo to connect with other users, Tongan youth initially mapped their understandings of social connections in the physical world onto the online platform. They then slowly transformed their understandings to extend the reach of their virtual connections. At the time of my research on the island of 'Eua in 2008 to 2009, most Tongan teens and young adults lived relatively circumscribed lives, with what might be characterized as a careful, loving supervision of their activities through close-knit communities. The town of 'Ohonua, where I spent the most time, had grown over its history so that one's neighbors were often one's extended family and also corresponded to one's church congregation. The social circles of youth resembled a set of concentric circles, with the most time spent among siblings and close relatives, then peer groups based on church affiliation, extended kin who might live in a different area of the small town, and then schoolmates.

Much to my surprise, most youth described themselves as having "no friends" when asked or, conversely, listed all the youth in their school as being their friends. Discussions of friends in the lived social worlds of Tongan youth were further complicated because most young people were familiar with the English word *friend*. But no real, direct equivalent exists in the Tongan language, and the English *friend* is often applied only to romantic partners. Instead, youth recalled churchgoers, same-sex peers, schoolmates, or teammates. Young people also spent most of their time in single-gender groups and, to some extent, in mixed-age groups, with older children looking after younger ones.[21] For most youth, the only times they might encounter people whom they have never met, then, is on trips to other islands in Tonga to see relatives, longer trips overseas, or during school and church events that bring together multiple institutions. For this reason, the annual sports competition held in Teufaiva Stadium in

Nuku'alofa is particularly exciting to high school youth, as it brings students from all over the country to interact with one another.

When building networks of online affiliations, youth tended to follow similar patterns of connections but also explored the new possibilities afforded by digital technologies. The young men and women whom I observed interacting with Bebo often made "friend" links with their relatives first, then schoolmates and neighborhood friends. While the number of Tongan young people who used Bebo regularly was higher than that of other age groups, many middle-aged Tongans also had profiles, especially those living overseas. Youth regularly included them in their online connections. Beyond this, however, Tongan youth also "added" friends of friends, even those they did not know personally but were tagged by name in photos on friends' profiles. Many young women I talked to found these online affiliations an exciting means of meeting new people without the possibility of feeling shamed (*mā*), as with physical in-person encounters that normally require the rules of brother-sister respect (*faka'apa'apa*).

Notably, in conversations with elders and family members of young people, very few adults expressed concern about the possibility of youth interacting with strangers and non-kin online. One older man simply stated, "Ah, it's just playing around. It's just kids' stuff. And they are learning from the computers." Because children and young adults often fall under the loving supervision of their older relatives, people on 'Eua did not develop the "stranger danger" culture known to most mainstream Americans from the early 1980s onward. Children and youth frequently did manage to escape the watchful eyes of their elders and engage in unsanctioned activities that ranged from swimming in the ocean to drinking alcohol with friends. In fact, some youth arranged secret rendezvous with romantic partners they met online. The majority of Bebo users did not arouse suspicion or evoke concern among adults. A woman in her sixties who had spent all of her life on 'Eua, including raising her own (now adult) children there, explained to me that she thought children were much safer in contemporary times than when she was a teenager. "We used to be so naughty!" she laughed, recounting times that she and her friends would sneak out at night to meet their boyfriends. "Now, the kids have school, they have church group, they have homework, they can play on the computer. Things have changed for the better. They aren't so disobedient now." While the possibility of "risky" behavior online existed for youth on 'Eua, many adults and youth saw the rise of Bebo and the internet as no more threatening than the everyday challenges present in the physical world.

"SKINS," SITES, AND SHOUT-OUTS: CREATING A WORLD ONLINE

Within this fairly short period in the development of youth interest in online social networking, a number of practices sprouted that signaled new ways of thinking about the place and identity of youth in Tonga, in the diaspora, and transnationally. The communicative practices used on Bebo for social networking had their roots in cultural norms for face-to-face interaction; they also resonated with long-standing practices of letter writing between relatives "at home" and "overseas" and with brief telephone conversations to keep in contact with relatives and close friends abroad.[22] Youth had ample time at school, in church groups, and during free time to engage in conversations with age-mates and other peers in face-to-face, physical contexts as described above. Prior to the arrival of the internet, people in Tonga would send and receive letters in the mail when relatives went overseas. High school–aged youth and those in their early twenties indicated that before easy access to the internet and cell phone text messaging, sweethearts exchanged love notes to show their romantic devotion. "You would have a code," one nineteen-year-old young man expressed, "like writing in red pen for love and blue pen for other things. You would ask a schoolmate to take the letter to her [the romantic interest] so that no one would know it was from you." Love letters acted as material manifestations of emotional engagement. As a volunteer at the local high school on 'Eua, I also saw same-gender friends occasionally pass notes to one another in class, again signaling their desire to maintain their communication. As I argue, these types of face-to-face practices transferred to the online space, where the physical and virtual links between the Tongan youth grew by way of written messages, photos, and other images on their Bebo profile pages.

To a social media novice, the world of Bebo at first appeared as a multisensory onslaught of sound, moving pictures and graphics, and multicolored text demanding one's attention. Members of the network personalized their profile pages in a number of ways, including "skins," or graphics that served as the background wallpaper for the page (see below for further analysis of one of these skins). Users also incorporated animated dancing babies, smiling faces, and leaping animals on the top of their profile pages or in a format that appeared to trickle down when a user scrolled through their pages; embedded YouTube videos and/or audio tracks that played when a user visited their pages; and added photo albums, Twitter feeds, and links to other websites. Tongan youth used all of these resources to create multimodal, polysemiotic representations of identity, utilizing multiple sensory domains to express themselves. Thus, in a way, a person's digital profile similarly presented the self of the physical world, where one's clothing, hairstyle, language, and movements combined to form a self-representation. I will thus examine how all of the "pieces" of Bebo profiles coalesced in order to understand the ways in which Tongan youth constituted their online subjectivities in 'Eua and elsewhere.

First, I turn to language as a semiotic marker of style. Use of multiple languages represents one of the most pervasive and visible expressions of Tongan identity in Tonga and outside the country. Although Tongan is the first language of most Indigenous people born in Tonga, English is also recognized as an official language of government, and secondary schools use English as the primary language of instruction. However, most high school students, along with other community members, do not often use spoken English for communication unless talking to a non-Tongan. At the time of my research, even in cases such as the arrival in Tonga of extended family who had been born and raised elsewhere, the primary mode of address was in Tongan. The ability to speak Tongan is viewed as fundamental to what it means to be Tongan.

On Bebo profile pages, however, young people used a mix of English and Tongan in speaking with their friends and displayed a variety of styles. Early Tongan adopters of Bebo might have felt inclined to write in English at least some of the time on their profile pages for a few reasons linked to the perceived context. For example, the Bebo platform's main instructional and setup text was in English, which allowed users to respond with English in their audio and graphic additions to their pages; moreover, in the time period when youth used Bebo most frequently, computer equipment was associated with schools and internet cafés, both sites that were indexically and ideologically linked to English use. When I asked some of the young women that I accompanied to the internet café why they chose to write in English, they politely dodged the question or answered "because it's fun" or "it looks nice." On more than one occasion, I received responses that jokingly quoted schoolteachers who exhorted their students to "speak in English to get a good future." While these answers did not always provide clarity in interpreting English use, it did appear as if the young women I talked to connected English language use on their pages to a global, future-oriented perspective.[23] On the profile pages I examined, users did occasionally write in Tongan or switch between Tongan and English, and Tongan language was sometimes used in other elements on the page. However, Tongan youth chose English as a language of communication far more often when online social networking than when speaking to friends face-to-face.

The way that Tongan youth employed English on the Bebo site differed from how English was used in the classroom, revealing youth agency in crafting style and identity. Casual Tongan and Tongan-English youth slang that indexed familiarity with a "cool" style was combined with formal or polite speech, as when spoken to slightly older family members. Particularly in the sections of the profile entitled "Tagline," where a user could include a quote or a short description, and "Me, Myself, and I," where users were encouraged to describe themselves in detail, English was used in a stylized way that integrated keyboard elements for ornamentation. For example, a female user going by "Broken Gurl" employed different aspects of the English and Tongan languages to create an online identity using the following text:

Tagline
"bRoKeN GurL>>..telnE H@l@ki-um@t@!!!
Me, Myself, and I
Me, My Life and I......☺☺☺☺☺☺... I'm a sigle girl wif a fresh
brain........ Mah name is Miss.V@!@g!n! and i was born in the
beautiful island of 'Eu@ and mah mum from Ha'apai and mah dad from
the Fug@fonu@ and I'm staying at the Fug@fonu@..... So if u wana know
about me just add me, leave a comment or mail on mah page an hey here's
my number if u wana give me a call 8891733 an hey by the way feel free to
al me for being a frens!.....ok.......... ...:b :b :b:b :b :b:b :b :b:b

In the user's tagline "bRoKeN GurL>>..telnE H@l@ki-um@t@!!!," she used both lowercase and uppercase letters as well as the non-alphabetic keyboard characters ">," "@," and ".." to add character and ornamentation rather than referential meaning to the text. She, like many others, employed a variety of English in her self-description marked with orthographical representations of characteristic Polynesian phonology, such as reduced consonant clusters (e.g., [f] for "th" at the end of a word, as in "wif" for "with"). The user also told me that she made these choices for fun and as "just a remix," a phrase youth used to indicate the mixing of Tongan and English. They also considered this linguistic and online process as stylish play. The idea of a language "remix" came from popular songs circulating on the radio and on Bebo pages at the time, where Tongan artists "remixed" a popular American hip hop or R&B hit song with English and Tongan verses. The Tongan youth notion of remix was influenced by African American hip hop culture.

Tongan youth also juxtaposed elements of "home" and "overseas" to add to the transnational identities crafted on their pages. "Skins" decorated users' pages and added flare to the default black backgrounds of their Bebo pages. These skins were designed by users and individuals who sold skins and other elements for profit through the Bebo platform. When setting up their pages, users selected from a number of templates, including those that other users had crafted and then "made public" to circulate their designs more widely. For this chapter, I specifically analyze two of these shared skins, first to address the ways in which youth from 'Eua called attention to place and, later, to explore their online affiliation with gang culture.

In one example of a skin, the user calls attention to 'Eua by invoking a common nickname, "Fungafonua," which means "the top of the world." 'Eua boasts the highest elevation in the Kingdom of Tonga, with dramatic cliffs plunging down to the ocean on one side of the island. In this skin, the nickname can be seen at the top of the banner, which would sit at the very top of a profile page, and is repeated again at the bottom along with "The Beauty of 'Eua" written in English. In the center of the skin, several different iconic geographic landmarks are depicted, including the high sea cliffs, the main port in the island's main town of 'Ohonua, and an archway that, according to Tongan oral histories, the demigod Maui created. Notably, the traditional fale-style entryway at the front of 'Eua High School is positioned in the center of the image, which would be recognizable to people from 'Eua and other Tongan users.[24] A scarlet macaw is then depicted in the bottom-left corner of the image, which is likely meant to represent the far more rare *Koki*, or red shining-parrot, native to 'Eua. Youth from 'Eua regularly used such skins to show their pride in and affiliation with their island home, even for those youth who had spent considerable time overseas. Quite frequently, they made skins representing 'Eua, a particular region of the island, or a school sports team to show their deep attachment to the land (*fonua*), which many Tongans consider a familial and sacred tradition.

These online skins took on new meaning, rooting youth to a homeland as they moved through geographical and virtual spaces. These affect-laden graphical attachments to a home island were juxtaposed with representations of mobility and cosmopolitan worldliness, as illustrated in a photo that the same user included in her photo album "My Summer 2009–2010." In this photo, the user and a group of her friends strike poses in front of the obelisk at One Tree Hill in Auckland, New Zealand. Many youth would recognize the landmark, given that many people from 'Eua have spent time in a suburb of Auckland or have ties to extended kin there. One Tree Hill, a popular tourist spot for sightseeing, often serves as a favorite attraction for visiting relatives, as with this young woman on her summer holiday. Taken together, the photos of her summer holiday in New Zealand and the banner proclaiming attachment to 'Eua craft a particular kind of identity for the young woman. It is particularly remarkable that this user and many of her friends with similar elements in their profiles were in their teens when they affiliated with multiple global sites on their user profiles.

Finally, Bebo users also called upon specific iconic styles that resonated with global youth culture and African American hip hop culture to create transnational identities online. The underlying interpretations of these symbolic elements present a complex picture that throws the transnational place of Tongan youth into high relief. For instance, Tongan youth commonly used skins and other stylistic elements that aligned themselves with gang culture. In one such skin, a cartoon drawing of a young Tongan man wearing a red hoodie, jeans, and sneakers stares from the center of the page, with Tongan flags and designs taken from traditional *tapa* bark cloth in the background. With two Tongan flags flanking the boy, the phrases "Tongan Souljah" and "Siana—Datz How We Do" appear in cursive across the page. The bottom of the picture gives the designer's name, "Tapu mo Tonga Skins." This skin first appeared around the same time that the popular single "Crank That (Soulja Boy)" by African American artist Soulja Boy Tell'em circulated among the youth in Tonga (the song was originally released in the United States in 2007). *Siana* is a casual, somewhat slang-type term in Tongan for "man," similar to "guy" or "dude" in colloquial English. While this particular skin was taken from the profile page of a young woman, the image itself indexed a style of masculinity associated with gang culture. This young Tongan user appropriated elements of African American hip hop and gangster culture, informing complex ideas about youth culture as well as gender roles in Tonga.

"Gangster" slang, hip hop, and rap from the United States were very popular among Tongan youth at the time of Bebo's introduction to Tonga and remain popular to this day. The youth culture in Tonga likewise draws upon the long-standing tradition of hip hop, reggae, and associated musical styles that emerged from Aotearoa, the Cook Islands, Hawaiʻi, and other islands across the Pacific. Almost from its very beginnings, African American hip hop reached Aotearoa and other parts of the Pacific through radio airplay, mixtapes sent by overseas relatives, and US military personnel and quickly caught on among Pacific Islanders. In particular, groups from Aotearoa attempted to emulate the new style in the 1980s while adding in elements specific to the Indigenous sounds of the Pacific.[25]

American rap, hip hop, and R&B continue to exert considerable hegemonic influence across the Pacific and globally.[26] Groups of Māori, Sāmoan, Tongan, and other youth have also made a niche in performing tracks with their island styles. Tony Mitchell has suggested that the types of vocal stylings found in hip hop and rap parallel traditional a cappella forms already found in the music of Pacific Islanders.[27] Given that the indigenous Māori and Pacific Islander immigrants of Aotearoa were in the midst of an emergent political struggle against racial discrimination at roughly the same time as the birth of American hip hop and rap music, many youth in the Pacific shared an affinity with the struggle against oppression reflected in this music and in the Black Power movement more generally.[28] In subsequent years, gang culture emerged in the Pacific as an amalgamation of African American music and politics and more Indigenous-specific movements.

In terms of Tongan perspectives on gang culture, the picture becomes even more complicated. Although Tongans have become involved in gangs in the diaspora, and mainstream discourses accuse deportees from the United States of bringing criminal gang activity into Tonga itself, most Tongans think of "gang members," or "kau kengi," as groups of boys affiliated with one of the large boys-only high schools located in Nukuʻalofa. These two schools just happen to distinguish between themselves with the colors red and blue, associated with the well-known US-based gangs Bloods and Crips, respectively. They are colors that also carry strong national significance: red is the main color of the nation's flag and associated with royalty (and the national rugby team, near-royalty themselves), and blue is the color associated with the Wesleyan Methodist Church, which carries a strong religious and social presence within Tonga. Along with the students of these schools, many other youth choose one of the schools to "affiliate" with, based sometimes on the matriculation of friends or relatives. The schools are likewise well known for "gang activity," including large fights at sports events. Alumni or ex-students of the schools would occasionally get into fights at bars as well because of their strong ties to the institutions. Considering this, then, it is important to recognize that although Tongan youth associated gang culture with hip hop culture in ways that reflect the global circulation of US-based Black culture,[29] the underlying meaning of "gangster" style as it is juxtaposed with Tongan elements in profile page skins needs to be read from a culturally specific perspective. Tongan youth integrated "gangster style" in the Bebo platform as a means of signaling transnational ideas of coolness, loyalty, and toughness that reflected elements of Tongan culture.

Following from this, the Bebo group page "Katifonia," created by young men living in Aotearoa, used a variety of markers in language and other choices to claim transnational identity. On its profile page, the group used a photo of a small house on short stilts and covered in a colorful mural. Palm trees, tropical plants, and a view of the ocean appear in the background of the photo. The page also includes several tough-sounding slogans, such as "LIVE FOR NOTHING DIE FOR SOMYTHING [*sic*]." The group claims in its "Me, Myself, and I" description to be "For Thaa People Hu Straight be Repping KAtifonia Forever, ForAlways And For All them ones Who went to K.K.C [local school] . . . Remember To Be Repping That Katifonia Stylah..!!" (text reproduced with original spelling and capitalization). Across the profile page, a banner also reproduced additional gang-like slogans in the type of font often associated with graffiti. The group claimed residence in or loyalty to the Aotearoa city of Katikati, near Tauranga on the North Island. Yet this group also boldly asserted familiarity with and influence from two other sites as well.

With the picture of an iconic Tongan boys' hut and the use of both Tongan and English slang, Katifonia represented first a Tongan identity. These huts dot housing compounds throughout the island of 'Eua and across the Tongan archipelago. During adolescence, Tongan boys begin to interact with other young men, forming homosocial bonds in addition to observing the traditional rules of brother-sister respect, or *fakaʻapaʻapa*.[30] In the physical world, the "hut" is a quintessentially male space where young men hang out, play cards, and watch movies. They also occasionally engage in illicit activities within the confines of the hut, such as drinking alcohol and viewing pornography. The photo of the iconic hut on this profile page thus acted as a powerful symbol that tied the users in Aotearoa to traditional and potentially rebellious notions of Tongan masculinity.

At the same time, the use of "Katifonia" evoked a second site of the Tongan diaspora, California, as well as symbolized a transnational hip hop culture through its spelling and the graffiti-like typography used on the page.[31] Transliterated for the Tongan alphabet and linguistic structure, "California" becomes "Kalifonia" with a "k" and no "r"; recall, as well, that this group was based in Katikati, so "Kalifonia" becomes "Katifonia" to invoke the local city's name. Thus, calling a social group Katifonia played on place names and tied this virtual community based in Aotearoa not only to its Tongan roots but also to California as part of the transnational sphere of Tongan youth. California also loomed large in the geographical understandings of Tongan youth both for its global reputation as a site of music and film transmission and for its large diasporic community of Tongans in Los Angeles and Oakland.

CONCLUSION

What signals a comfort in local, global, and transnational spaces also indicates a shift in ways of thinking about Tongan-ness and identity. Whereas earlier generations of Tongans remained firmly grounded in nationalist thinking and rooted to Tongan citizenship in the homeland, the aspects of identity emphasized by the youth in their Bebo profiles imply a movement toward thinking of Tongan-ness as an ethnic, digital, and transnational identity instead of simply a nationalist one. As I have shown, this virtual process alters citizenship claims to Tonga and expresses a more transnationally oriented citizenship instead. I use the term *ethnic identity* rather than racial identity to differentiate this idea of how Tongan youth perceive themselves in the world from a purely nationalist-traditional identity, on the one hand, and from the ways "Pacific Islander" and "Pasifika" might be conceived of as pan-racial identities, on the other. For most of my research participants in 'Eua, "Tongan" represented a more relevant identity than "Pacific Islander" in the United States and "Pasifika" in Aotearoa and even Australia. For them, Tongan was based in language, values, and practices.

Future research about the rise and spread of virtual Tongan youth identities might reveal how Tongans in the diaspora and the Kingdom of Tonga strategically employ Tongan, Pacific Islander, and Pasifika transnational citizenships and identities to their own ends. For now, Tongan youth navigating the early Bebo context from 'Eua or Aotearoa claimed transnational spaces that were materially different from the proudly Tongan ethos of their parents and grandparents but were also marked by specific Tongan roots that have not been fully addressed by their Pacific Islander and Pasifika identities. The transnational identities youth portray are *Tongan* transnational identities, working along a continuum of local specificity and global engagement.

The virtual exchanges of Tongan youth examined here also corresponded to their physical realities across time and space and the wider *tā-vā* relations of Tongans. The Bebo community did not operate in a vacuum—other cultural, economic, and political processes both facilitated and threatened the worlds created online. A variety of resources were also required to initiate and maintain an online presence as well as to produce the activities captured in profile photos and discussed in wall comments. For each profile displayed online, one must consider the various familial connections and national transactions that made it possible for that young person to know how to use a computer, have the equipment or money to do so, and have the opportunity to travel across the Tongan diaspora or to imagine such travel. In some ways, the Tongan youth in the online social worlds of Bebo embraced the rhetoric of neoliberal citizenship while at the same time repudiating it, maintaining a firm grounding in extended kin networks and the realities of social life. As I have argued, at the same time that Tongan youth created new forms of online presence, they relied on and advanced a longer history of African American music traditions as well as Tongan gender norms, kinship ties, and transnational movement.

In light of the Arab Spring events in the Middle East in 2010 that linked massive political uprisings through new media such as Facebook and Twitter, some could argue that the friendly conversations, acts of social surveillance and admonishment, and other performances of cultural identity and transnational citizenship described here appear frivolous or, at best, overstretch definitions of "citizenship." However, among Tongans themselves, the use of social networking websites and other resources on the internet is no less fraught with significance for the political future of their nation and for their ties with other countries. Like many aspects of global modernity discussed elsewhere,[32] Tongans view internet usage with ambivalence. The youth acknowledged its benefits in communicating information about their identities, relations, and travels, yet adults and youth alike have increasingly recognized the internet's ability to strain the boundaries of their culturally constructed moral frameworks. Nevertheless, at its onset, Bebo allowed the youth to expand their relationships and identities in multiple ways. In so doing, they experienced new forms of transnational citizenship unavailable to them—or anyone else, for that matter—in the "real world."

Bebo profiles also allowed Tongan youth to expand their spatial existence, creating virtual relationships and maintaining bonds with friends and kin in faraway places. Along with this spatial extension, the youth drew out relationships temporally, evoking memories of past events by way of posted graphics and photos and publicly commenting on possibilities for future activities and "real world," in-person meetings. Through this navigation across significant geographical space using specific semiotic resources, including language, photos, graphics, and media, Tongan youth constructed identities as transnational citizens across Aotearoa, the Kingdom of Tonga, and the United States. Rather than personify a credible "traditional" identity to satisfy those in the homeland or accommodate a singular mainstream culture, they claimed identities that encompassed several places at once—including virtual spaces. In a heavily stratified society governed by strict hierarchies of age, gender, and status, participation in political and civic life in Tonga was clearly limited for the young people on Bebo at the time of this research. However, their "playful" engagements with social media could position them to gain political capital and social influence in a future marked by transnational forms of identity and citizenship, virtual processes that have shaped and have been shaped by their worlds of culture and kin.

NOTES

1   I wish to thank the Government of the Kingdom of Tonga for allowing me to conduct this research, especially the staff of the Prime Minister's Office and the Ministry of Education for their helpful guidance. This research could not have been completed without the generosity and kind cooperation of the people of 'Eua, Tonga, and I am forever in their debt.

2   Sarah J. Mahler and Patricia R. Pessar, "Gendered Geographies of Power: Analyzing Gender across Transnational Spaces," *Identities: Global Studies in Culture and Power* 7, no. 4 (2001): 441–59.

3   Aihwa Ong, *Flexible Citizenship: The Cultural Logics of Transnationality* (Durham, NC: Duke University Press, 1999).

4   Awad Ibrahim, "Critical Youth Studies: An Introduction," in *Critical Youth Studies Reader*, ed. Awad Ibrahim and Shirley R. Steinberg, with a preface by Paul Willis (New York: Peter Lang, 2014), xvi.

5   I use "physical world" here rather than "IRL" or "in real life" to underscore the idea that online activity for Tongan youth represents an extension of their everyday life.

6   Mary K. Good, "Modern Moralities, Moral Modernities: Ambivalence and Change among Youth in Tonga" (PhD diss., University of Arizona, 2012).

7   Niko Besnier, *On the Edge of the Global: Modern Anxieties in a Pacific Island Nation* (Stanford, CA: Stanford University Press, 2011); and Good, "Modern Moralities, Moral Modernities."

8   Jannis Androutsopoulos, "Typography as a Resource of Media Style: Cases from Music Youth Culture," in *Proceedings of the 1st International Conference on Typography and Visual Communication* (Thessaloniki: University of Macedonia Press, 2009); and Dick Hebdige, *Subculture: The Meaning of Style* (London: Routledge, 1979).

9   Angela McRobbie, *Feminism and Youth Culture* (New York: Routledge, 2000).

10 Webb Keane, "Semiotics and the Social Analysis of Material Things," *Language and Communication* 23, nos. 3–4 (2003): 409–25; and Webb Keane, "On Semiotic Ideology," *Signs and Society* 6, no. 1 (2018): 64–87.

11 'Ōkusitino Māhina, "From *Vale,* Ignorance, to '*Ilo,* Knowledge, to *Poto,* Skill, the Tongan Theory of Ako, Education: Theorizing Old Problems Anew," *AlterNative: An International Journal of Indigenous Scholarship* 4, no. 1 (2008): 67–96; and Tēvita O. Ka'ili, *Marking Indigeneity: The Tongan Art of Sociospatial Relations* (Tucson: University of Arizona Press, 2017).

12 Ka'ili, *Marking Indigeneity.*

13 Ka'ili, *Marking Indigeneity,* 20. See also Arcia Tecun (Daniel Hernandez), 'Inoke Hafoka, Lavinia 'Ulu'ave, and Moana 'Ulu'ave-Hafoka, "Talanoa: Tongan Epistemology and Indigenous Research Method," *AlterNative* 14, no. 2 (2018): 156–63.

14 Good, "Modern Moralities, Moral Modernities."

15 Helen Morton, *Becoming Tongan: An Ethnography of Childhood* (Honolulu: University of Hawai'i Press, 1996); and Susan Philips, "The Organization of Ideological Diversity in Discourse: Modern and Neotraditional Visions of the Tongan State," *American Ethnologist* 31, no. 2 (2003): 231–50.

16 Helen Morton Lee, *Tongans Overseas: Between Two Shores* (Honolulu: University of Hawai'i Press, 2003); and Helen Lee and Steve Tupai Francis, eds., *Migration and Transnationalism: Pacific Perspectives* (Canberra: Australian National University Press, 2009).

17 Helen Morton, "Islanders in Space: Tongans Online," in *Small Worlds, Global Lives: Islands and Migration,* ed. Russell King and John Connell (London: Pinter, 1999). See also chapter 9 in this volume.

18 Morton, "Islanders in Space."

19 All names appearing in this chapter are pseudonyms. All quotations and materials are used with consent from the speakers and creators.

20 Morton, *Becoming Tongan.*

21 Morton, *Becoming Tongan.*

22 Niko Besnier, *Literacy, Emotion, and Authority: Reading and Writing on a Polynesian Atoll* (Cambridge: Cambridge University Press, 1995).

23 For a similar trend among Sāmoan transnational Facebook use, see Tiresa Po'e, "Facebook and Fa'a Samoa: Exploring the Expression of Samoan Identity Online" (master's thesis, University of Auckland, 2017).

24 In the Tongan language, "fale" means "house."

25 Tony Mitchell, ed., *Global Noise: Rap and Hip Hop Outside the USA* (Middletown, CT: Wesleyan University Press, 2001); and Kirsten Zemke-White, "Keeping It Real (Indigenous): Hip Hop in Aotearoa as Community, Culture and Consciousness," in *Cultural Studies in Aotearoa New Zealand: Identity, Space and Place*, ed. Claudia Bell and Steve Matthewman (Melbourne: Oxford University Press, 2004), 205–28.

26 Mitchell, *Global Noise*.

27 Mitchell, *Global Noise*.

28 See also Moses Ma'alo Faleolo's analysis of gangs in chapter 8.

29 H. Samy Alim, "Straight Outta Compton, Straight *aus München*: Global Linguistic Flows, Identities, and the Politics of Language in a Global Hip Hop Nation," in *Global Linguistic Flows: Hip Hop Cultures, Youth Identities, and the Politics of Language*, ed. H. Samy Alim, Awad Ibrahim, and Alastair Pennycook (New York: Routledge, 2009), 1–22.

30 Morton, *Becoming Tongan*.

31 Androutsopoulos, "Typography as a Resource."

32 Besnier, *On the Edge*; and Good, "Modern Moralities."

CHAPTER 6

MAKING WAVES

Marshallese Youth Culture, "Minor Songs," and Major Challenges

JESSICA A. SCHWARTZ

MARSHALLESE ELDERS AND YOUTH ALIKE EXPLAIN A CERTAIN feeling when it comes to Americanization. The feeling can best be described as "emakūt" (moving), or the cultural destabilization associated with the US militarization and modernization of the Marshall Islands. As a result, some Marshallese have tense relationships with the United States, a country that has failed to abide by its Cold War promises of nuclear remediation. For the United States not only subjected the Marshallese to nuclear violence, scientific testing, and land displacement from the 1940s to the 1980s but also offered white, patriarchal, and mainstream pathways for employment and security. The Marshallese now rely on the United States for resources, with the US military being one of its largest employers. This dependency did not arbitrarily arise as the United States strategically created the Marshall Islands into a socioeconomically minoritized country. Whenever the Marshallese express emakūt, they often refer to these fraught histories of disenfranchisement while they simultaneously seek to foster geopolitical relationships with the United States and the wider international community. Their feeling thus subscribes to a "major mode" of engagement with the United States and the world; it is a feeling of cultural destabilization, strategic dependency, and futuristic representation. It is also a feeling by which major countries make their polices and songs heard and known.

If emakūt reflects a Marshallese feeling of cultural loss, measured optimism, and political anxiety in the major mode of geopolitics and sound, then what constitutes their "minor" counterparts? In this chapter, I share how Marshallese youth creatively repurpose the tropes and positionalities of (the) "minor mode" in hip-hop songs, rap vocal techniques, and slam poetry. In contrast to the militarized futures proposed by the United States and the alarmist cries of "disappearing lands" that paint the future of the Marshall Islands as one underwater, the Marshallese youth use their expressions to intimate alternative Indigenous futurities that connect with other anti-colonial and marginalized groups. Their creative dissent rejects a future in which they are assimilated or erased, offsetting the temporal logic that everyone unites in modern time and listens to major sounds. As Mark Rifkin contends, Native temporalities are related to struggles for and reciprocal relations with the lands and ancestors in ways that cannot be reduced to settler time.[1]

Music is a moral code, and what I am referring to as "minor songs" have been judged as being about sex, romantic desires, and bodily movements that are not in line with religious moral codes. Moreover, the minor mode was conventionally associated with the devil in Western moral history. Marshallese were also viewed as "heathens" by the Congregationalist missionaries; later, when the United States staged Marshallese in nuclear newsreels, they were called "savages." Today, Marshallese youth, who live across the diaspora and have varying degrees of knowledge about their culture and history, draw from Black diasporic culture to express different modalities of togetherness about motherly and brotherly love. For example, the late American rapper and poet Tupac Shakur composed songs titled "Keep Ya Head Up" (1993) and "Dear Mama" (1995) that spoke about the closeness of his fraternal crew. As the Marshallese youth reveal, they turn to Tupac's music to similarly invoke his tenderness and affection as well as his street reporting of police brutality and gang violence. In chapter 9, Arcia Tecun, Edmond Fehoko, and 'Inoke Hafoka examine Tupac Shakur and faikava in comparable terms. For the Marshallese youth, then, the minor songs of hip hop, rap, and spoken word emphasize belonging, love, resistance, and more. Together, they produce a distinctive voice and an idiosyncratic timbre about the emergent Marshallese nation-state.

In what follows, I show how minor songs shift the "major" issues from the legal, scientific, and masculine military domains to the affective dimensions of feeling manifested by Indigenous matrilineal futurities. While I read the gendered aspects of hip hop and rap music performed by male youth and slam poetry performed by female youth, there is power in recognizing the gender discrepancies while still reading them in complementary formation. That is to say, their music reverberates with the vocal empowerment of their mothers and grandmothers. As I show, the minor songs of the Marshallese youth cull from their mothers' strength. They also advance Marshallese outreach and solidarity; address the challenges of their community, as with climate change; and underscore the powerful role of matrilineality in diasporic networks that resound the percussive call to listen in Arkansas, Majuro, and elsewhere.

Toward these efforts, I develop a tripartite framework—cultural, historical, and theoretical—to analyze how hip-hop artists F.O.B and Flavah C, rap artist YastaMan, and slam poet Kathy Jetñil-Kijiner emphasize poetics through their own voices and "rep" the Marshall Islands in ways that draw on the strength of women. By adopting the framework of "minor transnationalism," I show how they uphold Marshallese values of belonging, performance, and spirituality that exceed the white, masculine, and national representations of their society.[2] In their conceptualization of minor transnationalism, the literary critics Françoise Lionnet and Shu-mei Shih argue that we tend to forget the robust interconnections between minorities and the vibrant composites or "creolized identities" of other communities, be it through in-person collaborations or mediated influences.[3] In this way, even the globalized impress of media can become part of a scrapped history, one that is critically affixed in a bricolage of histories. By highlighting the acoustic and geopolitical engagements of the Marshallese youth, we can then understand how and why their music partly emerged from and radically countered the challenges of US militarization and modernization. They creatively emphasize "the minor's inherent complexity and multiplicity" despite the dominant US nation-state's efforts to diminish their agency.[4] This strength-based approach foregrounds their competencies in music and protest as well as unsettles the more paternalistic and punitive models of adult discipline in Oceania.[5]

In this chapter, I thus use the multivalent term *minor songs* from my translation of the Marshallese phrase *al in maina* (songs of minor), possibly referring to key. In this regard, al in maina depicts the popularity of Marshallese "love songs," a Marshallese appropriation of sounds originally associated with the American pop market of the 1950s. Separated into four sections, I first survey the missionization and militarization of the

Marshall Islands and discuss the musical productions therein. The second section then examines the contributions of F.O.B, Flavah C, and YastaMan at the May Day celebrations in Springdale, Arkansas, in 2013. In the third part, I focus on Kathy Jetñil-Kijiner's performance at the United Nations (UN) Climate Summit Opening Ceremony in New York City in 2014. The conclusion ruminates on the different scales through which minor songs resonate with gender complementarity in local festivals and geopolitical arenas. Throughout these examples, I show how the discursive-material constructs of the matriline offer a complex foray into entertainment and transnational spaces in which the "minor" is repositioned to grapple with the "major" challenges of the Marshall Islands. Overall, I argue that Marshallese youth culture draws on the skills of Marshallese mothers, women, and values of the "feminine voice" in the verbal arts by amplifying the sounds of their nation. Such critical positioning creates new relational modes of becoming, as with the making of Marshallese youth musicians, poets, and rappers.

THE MINOR SONGS OF THE MARSHALL ISLANDS

The Marshall Islands has been subject to 150 years of US colonialism since nineteenth-century American missionaries first arrived on Ebon from Boston via Hawai'i in 1857. German colonial authority arrived shortly thereafter (1885) and were replaced by a twentieth-century Japanese civilian administration that shifted to military rule during World War II. After the United States claimed victory over Japan, following intensive Asia-Pacific theaters, they governed the islands through the UN-mandated Trust Territory of the Pacific Islands (TTPI, 1947–1986). From 1946 to 1958, the United States also violently tested its most powerful atomic and thermonuclear devices on the islands, irradiating and studying Marshallese communities. As Keith L. Camacho, Elizabeth DeLoughrey, Teresia K. Teaiwa, and other Pacific scholars have shown, the militarization of the Pacific is a highly gendered process, with high enlistments of mainly male youth. In the Marshall Islands, for instance, Indigenous youth are taught US militarism and patriotism by way of K–12 schooling and now enlist at nearly twice the rate per capita of US citizens.[6]

Constitutional independence in 1979, coupled with the Compact of Free Association (COFA) agreement signed with the United States in 1986, not only officially recognized the Republic of the Marshall Islands (RMI, or Majol in Marshallese) as a nation-state but also created the conditions in which Marshallese youth have become politicized. Following its independence, the COFA also allowed the nation to engage the international community within the legal constraints of the U.S. military's control of their lands, seas, and skies. Additionally, the COFA compensates some Marshallese families for nuclear damages as well as pays for land leased by US military. The US base in Kwajalein, a key site of the Strategic Defense Initiative or "Star Wars" during the Cold War, is one such site. In return, the COFA enables the Marshallese to live, work, and travel between the United States and the RMI without visas.[7] Today, approximately 25,000 Marshallese reside in the United States, especially in the Midwest where their community is growing.[8]

Within this context, Marshallese youth music education and musical diplomacy, which originated in the missionary period, has continued through the neocolonial period. Conventionally, the idea of harmony is taught by teachers, preachers, and other intermediaries of the church and the state. In the Marshall Islands, this person is called a "rikaki," or somebody who determines the key, or metaphorical keynote. The key is the foundation of tonal harmony; it establishes the first tone of a scale, or tonic. Over the course of the harmonic progression, there is an affective pull toward "home" or the tonic. As voices harmonize, they move in what is represented laterally, producing vertical alignments that resound chordal harmony. The metaphor of musical harmony, in terms of diplomacy, is a particularly powerful construct that can represent "consonance" or the "majority" position and "dissonance"; musical harmony can likewise connote the "minority" position in the arrangement of concord-agreement and discord-disagreement. It is interesting that al in maina, that is, love songs, or songs that follow the lyrical content of many popular US songs, also retain references to Marshallese nonhuman movements, such as typhoon imagery and oceanic movements. The missionaries taught hymns, widely using the major key. Marshallese songs with lyrical themes concerning love, romantic/physical relationships, and "secular" matters (along with the minor key) were marginalized. Perhaps the missionaries instilled a mistrust of Marshallese love because al in maina refers to both human-human and human-ancestral land relations, each of which refer to the throat or the soul. They also invoke emotion and not the moral constraint required of Christianity. Perhaps al in maina can now redraw the boundaries of morality and decolonize the ways in which the missionaries have debased Marshallese relations to their ancestors, lands, and partners.

Church commentary on musical modes has historically linked the major mode with appeal to a higher power. The minor mode was even labeled "devil music." The moral classification of musical harmony has been a way to associate racialized bodies with non-normative behavior or rebellion, per the postwar phenomenon in which "sinners" made, listened to, and crucially danced to rock 'n' roll. Rock 'n' roll can be classified as love songs or pop songs with themes of love, romance, or sex. The lyrics often spoke about the love of cars, money, partying, dancing, and given the domestication of the military, even the sounds of war. Marshallese minor songs, then, can be aligned with the US minor songs that actually speak to major issues that have been provincialized under the missionaries' teachings. As a Protestant Christian community, many Marshallese now embody the conservative culture of these religious edicts and songs.

How harmony and musical diplomacy was first taught to the Marshallese emphasizes the importance of a Marshallese youth culture that creates minor transnationalisms by focusing on the matrilineal strength and power in transnational interconnections. To foreground Protestant music in ways that could similarly efface roro (customary incantations) and alin mur (steering songs, navigational battle songs), the American missionaries targeted the youth as well as adults. Within months of having arrived on Ebon, missionaries established schools. They separated the youth from their families and, in some instances, took them to boarding schools on islands where they shared classrooms with youth from Kiribati, formerly known as the Gilbert Islands. At schools, rikaki would quell the "sounds of Marshallese" in their interconnections with the land and lineage and thus the matriline. The missionaries then redirected Marshallese singing toward vertical power relations (God, the colonial state, and chiefly authority) or major harmonies as matters of diplomacy for the Germans and Marshallese chiefs (men) who worked with German political authorities. In these ways, missionaries upheld major mode songs to maintain their power. Youth, as a culture of becoming, have therefore been central to and targeted in the colonial overhaul of Marshallese culture in ways that removed children from intergenerational knowledge of their community. These anti-matrilineal practices even opened Marshallese lands for US seizure.[9]

Focusing solely on the major harmonies as power, as with the predominance of Protestant Christian (gospel) songs in the Marshall Islands and the diaspora, can subsequently overdetermine what becomes heard in music scholarship, particularly with youth songs of resistance. Indeed, nation-building under the COFA, the ongoing US militarization of the Marshall Islands, and the transnational movement of families have complicated the custodial roles of women, their kinship networks, and their cosmological mother-son relationships. For instance, as their oral histories illustrate, Marshallese women took charge of drumming during battles. They listened, as well, to the rumblings of lands and other movements of the human warriors and nonhuman participants as they offered rhythmic, percussive patterns that shaped the warriors' actions. If they decided it best, the women employed dysrhythmia to throw the other side off. Such conflicts also often started with a woman's call to go to war; then at some point before the war caused too much pain, the men would call on the eldest sister to make peace, which she did.

When thinking about alternatives to US militarism and nuclearism, the Marshallese women and men have shown how their gendered, percussive, and vocal roles can complement each other. Minor musical diplomacy, or youth outreach that aims to impact international relations in domestic and transnational contexts, extends these genealogies of cooperation and resistance among minor groups. By minor groups, I refer to youth from different nation-states who collaborate with one another and women and youth from the Marshall Islands who have become minorities within their own family structures. This analysis demands an understanding of what Marshallese uphold as "harmony" (thus harmonic progressions) and how they relate to concepts of home. Namely, songs in the minor keys matter here—those that do not only sing the praises of the Christian Father but also highlight a return to one's mother, land, and lineage. Minor songs also bring the youth and their mothers to the body as site of feeling and movement. Their minor songs interlock, thereby allowing Marshallese youth to creatively and critically re-imagine their futures in excess of the white family and nation.

Transforming the sounds of Marshallese into structures that mediate contemporary social relations is a powerful way to materialize alternative futures to the "belittling discourse" to which Marshallese have been subject.[10] As one influential rapper, YastaMan, explained, many of his songs are al in maina, love songs or popular songs that he distinguishes from the "major key" of religious music. Throughout the chapter, I therefore thread several cultural, historical, and theoretical examples that counter vertical impositions of education that have diminished Marshallese voices. Reappropriating "Rep" from "Republic" is a way for the youth to mediate the gender, generational, and genre divisions that cut across their minor and major songs. As I have briefly shown, musical aesthetics and political organization are closely related in the Marshall Islands. The following sections discuss how Marshallese youth artists "make waves" or conduct Island-style outreach in local festivals and geopolitical arenas.

ISLAND RHYTHMS AND REPPIN' MAJOL

One maker of waves, the Marshallese group Island Rhythm, uses the polysemic, homonymic word *mayday* or *May Day* at the end of a verse in the song "Bikini Atoll" (ca. 2004). Specifically, they describe how the United States offered the Marshallese the heads of dead presidents like Abraham Lincoln and George Washington, a symbolic reference to the US compensation for irradiating Bikini Atoll. But even with such monetary redress, Island Rhythm asserts that the United States will never repay the Marshallese for the US crimes of nuclear testing and scientific experimentation, hence the music group's invocation of May Day. Mayday, which replaced the Morse code SOS, is the international distress signal for life-threatening emergencies in the two-way radio communications of aircrafts and ships. Mayday calls, as "voice procedures," elicit responses to the emergencies. International Workers' Day, celebrated on May 1, is also called May Day; significantly, the singers of "Bikini Atoll" refer to this commemoration by reflecting on the uncompensated labor of the Marshallese men and women who died of radiation. For the RMI, May Day also represents a national holiday called Jemenei or Constitution Day; it celebrates Marshallese constitutional independence in 1979. Still, under the COFA, the United States maintains a "principal" position to the RMI "associate," which votes in line with the superpower at the UN and must maintain its strategic interests per the COFA. This is the representative voice of the RMI.

However, May Day offers minor alternatives to this major voice. Every year, to commemorate Marshallese independence, the RMI holds parades, potlucks, worship services, music and dancing, sporting, and other celebratory festivities for all ages. These May Day events are held in Majuro, the political capital of the RMI, and among large Marshallese diasporic communities in the United States. Around 8,000 to 10,000 Marshallese reside in Springdale, Arkansas, which RMI Ambassador Charles Paul often referred to as "HQ," or headquarters, in 2013. Chad Blair, the author of *Honolulu Civil Beat*'s seven-part series called "The Micronesians," wrote, "Springdale is as close to a model as there is for Micronesian integration and assimilation."[11]

A few Marshallese migrated to the Midwest in the 1970s, while the Marshall Islands was still part of the TTPI, to attend private, religious colleges, where some had been offered scholarships. After the COFA went into effect, the Marshallese began migrating to the United States to access health care, educational, and employment opportunities. By the 1980s, some Marshallese had made their way to Springdale, Arkansas, to work in the poultry plants there. Tyson Foods, in particular, began actively recruiting Marshallese workers in the 1990s due to their legal status under the COFA. The relatively low cost of living, compared to Hawai'i and California, where many of the first migrants from the Marshall Islands had settled, was also a draw to the region. In 2009, due to the growing population in Springdale, the RMI government established a consulate there to serve the needs of Marshallese residents. Consequently, the consul general organized Constitution Day festivities that mirrored activities in the RMI and that welcomed Marshallese from across the United States. In recent years, dance competitions, a Ms. Jemenei Day pageant, and Battle of the Bands public concerts have also emerged and attracted many families.

To be clear, the term *minor* need not be overdetermined by vertical power structures, such as majority/minority or hegemony/minority. It is positively reappropriated, as with the hip-hop group F.O.B and their usage of the phrase "fresh off the boat" to challenge the stereotypes of recent Asian and Pacific Islander immigrants. As a term of empowerment and endearment, F.O.B also stands for "Family of Brothers."[12] Two members are from the Marshall Islands, and one member is from the Philippines. The description from their *ReverbNation* website speaks to their notion of "reppin'," which is a place-based and party-feel space for camaraderie and struggle:

> F.O.B means a Family of Brothers. These three artists, each bring their trademark flavors to the group, which has been meshing Hip-Hop, R&B and Reggae for the last 7 years. Flip (representing the Philippines), King Darius and Yungstar (both representing the Marshall Islands), have been close-knit brothers since their high-school years. With their abiity [sic] to create music that is unique and yet relevant, it is only a matter of time before the music gets into the right hands. Whether it's the party-feel or the honoring of the struglgles [sic] of their people, F.O.B is a group of regular brothers with real talent and relatability [sic].[13]

Marshallese youth, which I define here as a flexible category of ages ranging from the early teens to late twenties, have developed a transnational culture that includes hip hop, poetry, singing, and spoken word/slam poetry. Their topics range from romantic relationships to nuclear testing, articulations of which are vital components of the health of the nation and its people. They also express familial togetherness and community.

The majority of Pacific Islanders in Springdale are Marshallese.[14] In 2013, I visited Springdale for the May Day celebrations. In addition to the official festivities, community members from Bikini Atoll decided to host a two-day Battle of the Bands competition. And two of the biggest names in Marshallese hip-hop music, F.O.B and Flavah C, hosted a separate concert, for which YastaMan, credited as the first Marshallese rapper, was the emcee (figure 6.1).[15] A few months earlier, F.O.B even served as the opening act for the popular and world-renowned African American rap group Bone Thugs-n-Harmony at a concert in Oregon. I asked Howie, one of the members of F.O.B, about the experience, and he said that he received "advice" and "learned" from the members of the famous rap crew about how to build community. In their mid- to late twenties, Flavah C and F.O.B now graced the audiences of Arkansas after coming from Oregon, where they currently reside. And YastaMan had traveled from Arizona. While I was in Majuro conducting ethnographic work between 2008 and 2010, I had seen Flavah C perform in a venue more modest than Springdale's civic center. At the latter location, advance tickets for the concert cost $20 (children under five were admitted for free), and the venue was packed. Artists sang and rapped primarily in the Marshallese language and were often accompanied by teams of dancers who moved to the Marshallese hip-hop flows and rhythms that had been in the making since the early 1990s when substantial numbers of Marshallese families began to relocate to Hawai'i and then the continental United States.

As already noted, the Marshallese also express tense feelings about an Americanization premised on Anglo-American Protestantism and state-based culture. That Marshallese youth and their music have endured these oppressive systems is a matter worth hearing. That, plainly, matters. "I love [making music]," Flavah C, with his eyes lit up, recalled. He then described the Marshallese rock bands, like Chaninway, that inspired him to play keyboards, sing, and write songs (figure 6.2).[16] "And also we're from the tiniest place in this whole world and," he paused with an emphatic sincerity. As he began to gesture in broad strokes with his arms, he announced, "I wanna *rep'* the Marshall Islands and to show everybody in the world who we are and what we can do as far as music." As he spoke, the others nodded their heads in agreement and maintained solemn expressions reflecting the

FIGURE 6.1. YastaMan, considered the first Marshallese rapper, emcees the F.O.B and Flavah C concert in Springdale, Arkansas, 2013. (Photo credit: April L. Brown)

FIGURE 6.2. Howie, YastaMan, and Flavah C, left to right, during an interview with the author in Springdale, Arkansas, 2013. (Photo credit: April L. Brown)

seriousness of the statement. He then spoke about the artists' hard work that goes into the successes they have had. For example, they sold out shows in other islands like Pohnpei and in Marshallese diasporic locales like Springdale. "I really want [audiences around the world] to be like 'man, they're really talented and they're from *the Marshall Islands.*' Like nobody knows where that is. That's why we're all doing this. [He points to his shirt.] You see our shirts—'Rep Majol'—you know, the RMI, and this is what we're doing. For me it's all about reppin' where we're from."

Flavah C, YastaMan, and Howie's music have cultivated hip hop, which constitute what can be considered minor songs in today's Marshallese youth culture, or al in maina. Local, now transnational, festivals like May Day have elevated their music and messages to new heights, enabling them to distribute their music to Marshallese audiences throughout the diaspora and to non-Marshallese more generally. In contrast to the music education that aimed to rid them of their expressive means, these youth artists have begun to challenge this moral code, itself a "eugenics of the tongue," that sought to make them *sound like* the American missionaries.[17] When I was in the Marshall Islands, non-Marshallese teachers and Marshallese teaching assistants would scold children, mostly those in the younger grades who were learning English, for talking during lessons. "Jab ke roro!" they would snap. Although "stop chatting" meant the quelling of noisy nonsense or trivial talk, "jab ke roro" can also refer to its literal meaning: "stop making incantations." And incantations, roro more specifically, recall the ongoing human spirit. Part of the youth's refusal to strictly adhere to the religious hymns of major songs therefore concerns the elevation of their technique.

An example of embodied resistance is YastaMan's rap style. He demonstrated how he learned to "rep" the Marshall Islands. As the scholar Raphael Travis Jr., notes, this rapping exemplified the cognitive and the "physical body as much as it is an outpouring of skill. It is practiced, but it is also improvisational at its core."[18] Some Marshallese rappers even likened their art forms to roro, which is an incantation as well as the plural human classifier. To repeat a word in Marshallese is to temporally extend its material existence and denote an ongoing activity. Although speculative, roro could refer to the spiritual animations through which the many Marshallese humans and their spirited energies endure in ongoing activities in the atollscape, landscape, and seascape.

When American Board of Commissioners for Foreign Missions missionaries from Boston arrived in the Marshall Islands in 1857, they heard roro as ancestral worship and believed that the only ancestor worth worshipping was the Christian God. Marshallese "chants" were to be banned, which meant that Marshallese were to be disenchanted in ways that "humanized" or "civilized" them. Particularly important was excising roro and with it Marshallese spirits through the Bible and the hymnbook, *Bok in Al Kab Tun Ko*, or the Book of Songs with Tunes. But what the missionaries failed to appreciate is that the Marshallese language and reverence for their ancestors was not going to easily become silenced; roro remain in Marshallese music, as with hip hop. They wove antiphonal cues for roro in the melodies of hymn-sounding songs. To the untrained ear, there is a flattening of the melody. But to Marshallese who can perceive the invitation, this is a call for an improvisational response in which a person can run up behind the singer and riff excitedly, conjoining and repairing the spiritual entwinement. In this regard, hip hop, reggae, and spoken word all coalesce as part of the Marshallese repertoire to resist mainstream silence when it comes to their atolls.

Take, for instance, the "Introduction" about Kwajalein Atoll in the F.O.B segment of the 2013 Springdale concert. Currently, the United States leases eleven of the ninety-seven islands, including the main island of Kwajalein, as part of the Ronald Reagan Ballistic Missile Defense Test Site.[19] F.O.B member Les, being from the nearby island of Ebeye, was inspired to compose a musical bricolage of news reporters discussing the militarization of Kwajalein and Ebeye and the lack of material resources on Ebeye. Addressing his music of resistance, Howie explained that Les "loves where he's from. He started taking samples from interviews from reporters that did documentaries on how small [Ebeye] the island and how they had limited resource[s]. If you could hear throughout the songs, he took samples of the statements and issues that are actually important and needed to help with the situation there, since he grew up there."

Howie stressed that because these issues are not discussed enough outside the RMI, Les appropriated the major media and gave a voice to this "Family of Brothers." Additionally, Flavah C mentioned that their music is about "social relationships but also about the islands, the Marshall Islands, like where it's located, the population, not enough resources" because they want "people to know and think about it." And, he said, they create music "because we miss it [Marshall Islands]." YastaMan chimed in, saying, "how we can make it [our hip hop] better. We're musicians, we're just trying to do what we do best and through that be proud of and REP Marshall Islands, you know? And [learn] how we can do better." The topic of "doing better" permeated the interview and reflected the healing elements of hip hop. As several chapters in this volume similarly demonstrate, Marshallese and Pacific Islander hip hop now play vital roles in global hip-hop culture.

When speaking about gender, one of the Marshallese rap taglines has become "baby girl." On the one hand, the Marshallese youth grapple with the complexity of such statements that echo the male-dominated art form of rap in ways that can be taken as pejorative. On the other, a tagline like "baby girl" can be placed in dialogue with other references to women and the importance of upholding Marshallese matrilineal culture. When I spoke with YastaMan about his influences, he referenced Shaggy, the Jamaican reggae singer, DJ, and a former United States Marine recruit.[20] YastaMan explained that his favorite song by Shaggy is called "Strength of a Woman." He relayed a sentiment held by many Marshallese about the importance of recognizing the power of women and mothers as the foundations of the islands. YastaMan then sang a few of the lyrics from "Strength of a Woman" that he felt "repped" Marshallese culture. In doing so, he highlighted Shaggy's deep appreciation for his mother who birthed him as well as speculated on the possibility that God is a woman who brings life to the world. Moreover, YastaMan closely identified with Shaggy's powerful metaphors of the mother, the canoe, and the ocean in this song, illustrating how Black and Marshallese sensibilities inform YastaMan's music.[21]

The lyrics from "Strength of a Woman" can thus refer to the Marshallese cosmological figures of Loktannuur and Jebro, the mother-son duo who make up the template for the ideal relationship, which is evoked politically. Marshallese attach importance to the figure of Jebro as he embodies their political ideal of carrying the weight of one's mother (in a positive way). In brief, Loktannuur, a primal matriarch of the atolls, had twelve sons who once raced canoes across a lagoon to become chief.[22] She asked each son if they would carry her and her bundle with them. One by one, they declined because they thought she would weigh them down. Finally, her youngest son, Jebro, agreed. When Loktannur unfurled her bundle, it was the first sail that she had woven. Indeed, Marshallese women are valued for their weaving; their word for "health" is weaving life. With the canoe sail, Jebro was able to "weave life" by capturing the strength of his mother through the winds and the waves. He won the race and became chief. As a chief, he was entrusted with guiding his people and leading them in health, so they could continue on. Today, the Marshallese youth harness the wind by way of roro, hip hop, reggae, rap, and other verbal arts in which Marshallese bodies persist through the shaping and sharing of their sounds.

SLAMMING HISTORIES: MOTHERS AND SONS (AND DAUGHTERS)

As the Marshallese male artists reveal, US radioactive colonialism and militarism continue to impact their lives at home and in the diaspora. In fact, such state violence has disproportionately impacted women; it has also ignored Indigenous knowledge and healing practices that challenge the colonialist and masculinist terms of scientific research. International media subtends these institutions, which often pose Marshallese women and children near flooded areas in photos and television. The news reports likewise tell the same threat-based stories of climate change, fixing Marshallese as "victims" and "exiles" in harm's way.[23] Such staging is part of the "universalizing representational practices" identified by Liisa Malkki that lump "womenandchildren" as part of the larger military culture in ways that deprecate them as needing help from their own precarity.[24]

Although the major codes, policies, and sounds of the United States have minoritized Marshallese women, the grandmothers, mothers, aunties, and sisters continue to enact their relations and vocal means of empowerment. In the 1980s, for instance, the late Darlene Keju began Youth to Youth in Health, which offered a place for youth to learn about the pressing issues of the day. Moreover, the women most injured by the nuclear weapons tests collectivized as Iju in Eañ, the Northern Star, to represent themselves as guides and to call on the Northern Star, or their atoll, Rongelap. They also participate in the Majuro-based women's organization Women United Together Marshall Islands. Unlike the missionary harmonies of domesticity and passive reverence, the Marshallese women make their cultural strengths and injuries heard. Women's calls for an invigorated, healthy, and educated community have also become the stuff of transnational Marshallese youth culture, as with Kathy Jetñil-Kijiner.

As a spoken word poet, Kathy Jetñil-Kijiner created a nonprofit, Jo-Jikum, in 2012 (figure 6.3). She then trained Marshallese youth as "earth champions" to respond to climate change, a base that she would utilize in future work with youth. At a youth arts camp in Majuro, one participant

FIGURE 6.3. Kathy Jetñil-Kijiner speaks at a youth event in Springdale, Arkansas, May 2019. (Photo credit: April L. Brown)

even drew a picture of the RMI's capitol building underwater. Art and poetry produced by youth, Jetñil-Kijiner explained, "comes out of fear of losing their culture and their island. They don't know how to use that fear." "That's why," she said, "we're trying to empower them. They shouldn't just be seen as victims."[25] For her work in raising awareness of climate change's effects and the urgency to act, *Vogue Magazine* named her as one of thirteen climate warriors in 2015.[26] As her celebrity increased, so did Jetñil-Kijiner's media presence and global reach. She joined other organizations that focused on grassroots, youth-centered, and educational movements, including 350 Pacific Climate Warriors and the Pacific Storytellers Cooperative of Pacific Resources for Education and Learning.[27] In her performance art, she moves from the abrupt and roro-like cadence of slam poetry to media-rich versions of storytelling, or bwebwenato.

One such production, titled "Rise," produced by 350.org in 2018, features Jetñil-Kijiner and Greenland Indigenous poet Aka Niviâna, who share shells and rocks, respectively, from their ancestral homelands. The video, filmed on-site in both countries, juxtaposes the lands of the two women, one from low-lying atolls in the Pacific and the other from mountains and snow, as they describe stories about the lagoons and glaciers in their homelands. Jetñil-Kijiner speaks of two sisters from Wotje Atoll, one who turned to stone and her sister who chose to stay by her side and can still be seen by onlookers on the reef.[28] The end credits encourage viewers to divest from fossil fuels.

A second video highlighted on Jetñil-Kijiner's website, titled "Anointed," follows the poet as she sails on a canoe to Enewetak Atoll, the once testing site of US nuclear weapons and the current resting place of Runit Dome. This eighteen-inch-thick, now cracked, concrete cap covers tons of contaminated waste deposited into a test crater and is popularly referred to as the "tomb." Here she recites a poem that details the story of L'Etao and his mother, a turtle goddess, who gifted part of her shell to her son.[29] With the power to transform, L'Etao, the trickster, turned himself into the first fire, gave this fire to a young boy, and laughed as the fire almost burned down the village of the young boy. Images of Marshallese who suffer from disabilities and birth defects are interspersed with footage of nuclear explosions as Jetñil-Kijiner relays how her people have been told that the illnesses they suffer are normal. In one scene, she stands atop Runit Dome with an alele, a Marshallese basket filled with important items that link a person and their community to their lands and matrilineal lineages. By merging the stories of L'Etao's fire, US nuclear violence, and matrilineal life, Jetñil-Kijiner provocatively questions the ethics of people who view themselves as the tricksters with the power to burn and to kill.

In 2014, Jetñil-Kijiner, now a global figure of Marshallese women's agency, spoke to the UN Climate Summit Opening Ceremony in New York City. She opened her poem with a reference to the figure of Jebro. The moral of the story, she explained, "is to honor your mother and [the] challenges that life brings." She said, "We look at our children and wonder how they will know themselves or their culture, should we lose our islands. . . . The people who support this movement are Indigenous mothers like me, families like mine, and millions more, standing up for the changes needed, and working to make them happen."[30] Twenty-six years old at the time of the UN summit, Jetñil-Kijiner, a young mother, represented the strength of an intergenerational matriline. Her work complemented that of the aforementioned rappers given their transnationally inspired urban arts; she likewise invested in critical international dialogue with the media, shifting the major, mainstream to the minor, transnational.

The poem Jetñil-Kijiner presented at the UN is titled "Dear Matefele Peinam"; it was addressed to and named after the poet's seven-month-old daughter. Dressed in traditional clothing, Jetñil-Kijiner recited the rhythmic poem—a blend of resolve and protest. A video played behind her on a large screen. Footage of her daughter and of walks with her along the beach was intermixed with video of flooding in the Marshall Islands, industrial polluters, and activist marches. The video also included a clip from the Peoples' Climate March in New York City that occurred just two days prior. The march drew over 300,000 people to the streets and brought considerable attention for its size and protesting youth. Within this context, Jetñil-Kijiner spoke in complex tropes of ambiguity—in which her daughter did not stand for the future (as in Western conceptualizations of youth) but represented a powerful symbol of intergenerational strength.

Throughout the presentation, Jetñil-Kijiner's voice was expressive, with pauses and loud crescendos, as she described the damages inflicted upon Marshallese lands. This poetic pace connected with the slow, quiet, measured sequences when she spoke of or to her daughter. A piano and stringed instruments then swelled to a crescendo toward the end of the poem. On the official UN website and video link, only the first 25 seconds of the 3-minute, 18-second video is shown; gone are the images of industrial polluters, effigies of politicians, and individuals whose nations are recognizable on the YouTube version. On the UN rendering, the camera pans away from the poet long enough to show the RMI contingent, the male presiding UN officials nodding, and two blonde women from Sweden, one of whom leans slightly forward and appears to evince a look of concern.

Eighty percent of the audience is male, and yet Jetñil-Kijiner was chosen to represent civil society, or one of three representative groups at the UN. The others included representatives of governments and the corporate sector. Civil society is made up mostly of NGOs, Indigenous groups, and activists who vie for consultant status to UN officials. As such, Jetñil-Kijiner officially represented global citizenry, centering the RMI and the Pacific Islands through her voice that directed the matrilineal winds and waves—not those that engulf her and her daughter but rather those that rock the heteropatriarchy of environmental racism and sexism:

> men say that one day
> that lagoon will devour you
> . . . .
> they say you, your daughter, and your granddaughter too

will wander, rootless

with only a passport to call home

. . . .

mommy promises you

no one

will come and devour you

no greedy whale of a company

sharking through political seas

no backwater bullying of businesses with broken morals

no blindfolded bureaucracies gonna push

this *mother ocean* over

the edge . . .

because baby we are going to fight

your mommy daddy

bubu jimma your country and your president too

we will all fight

and even though there are those

hidden behind platinum titles

who like to pretend

that we don't exist

that the Marshall Islands

. . . .

still

there are those

who see us

hands reaching out

fists raising up

banners unfurling

megaphones booming

and we are

canoes blocking coal ships[31]

Focusing on a maternal line against what "men" say, Jetñil-Kijiner's words respond to the deleterious effects of imperial and capitalist violence. Different histories and genealogies arise when we listen globally to Jetñil-Kijiner's protest. Each word evokes the "mother ocean," the small infant, and the teaming airwaves that carry voices "chanting for change NOW."[32] Her spoken word poems draw from a vernacular that uses Marshallese poetics, sound symbolism, and the animating force of roro that crescendo upward in pitch and volume. As with hip hop, roro make space for others to join in and express their energies; roro are minor harmonies articulating in multidirectional registers.

Following Jetñil-Kijiner's performance, her husband and daughter came on stage. The attending members at the UN Assembly then gave a standing ovation, one that Jetñil-Kijiner noted was rare.[33] *Slate*, a daily magazine and blog network, published the next day how Jetñil-Kijiner's poem had brought "world leaders to tears."[34] The *Huffington Post* also praised the twenty-six-year-old poet, describing her as having "recently demonstrated the impact a poem can have."[35] Years later, *Grist* identified Jetñil-Kijiner as a leading millennial voice of the 1.5 degrees C movement that began in New York and carried onto Paris and beyond. "Seemingly through the force of persuasion, her pledge and thousands of others like hers worked."[36] Yet most Western media—that is, the major sounds of journalism—focused on the speech by Hollywood celebrity Leonardo DiCaprio and the US and China's pledge to cut emissions in the future.[37]

At the Paris Summit in 2015, the Marshall Islands delegation included Jetñil-Kijiner, who also accompanied and led poets from around the world for the organization Global Call for Climate Action, created to inspire youth to act through art. Standing in front of a model of the Eiffel Tower, Jetñil-Kijiner performed "Tell Them," a poem she had written in 2011 that references a traditional alele or a Marshallese basket of great significance. The poem ends with the urgency to "tell them about the water; how we have seen it rising" and how "most importantly, you tell them that we don't want to leave, we've never wanted to leave, and that we are nothing without our islands."[38]

Three years after her presentation at the UN, Jetñil-Kijiner came out with a written collection of poems, *Iep Jāltok: Poems from a Marshallese Daughter*, in which she positions herself as a "daughter" and returns again to the alele. In some Pacific matrilineal societies like the Marshallese, there is a saying about families with girl children: "in her position she represents a basket whose contents are available to you." *Iep jaltok* literally means "a basket whose opening is facing the speaker" and *iep jaltok ajri ne*, "You are fortunate to have a girl child." She thus shares her value, her daughter's value, and her mother's value within the lineage. Her mother, President Hilda Heine, was also the first female president of the RMI, elected in 2016, and all of Micronesia. As Jetñil-Kijiner writes in the dedication, "This book is dedicated to my mother, my first and most infinite source of inspiration."

CONCLUSION

By retooling modern technologies and major sounds, the Marshallese youth of local festivals and geopolitical arenas situate themselves in transnational movements through collective-personal aural skills training, which has been radio and internet based. They register the rumbles of the ancestral, living lands and contour their art forms with knowledge learned from breathing the oceanic air and tracing patterns of amimono (handicraft). By harnessing the power of aelōñ kein (Indigenous name for the Marshall Islands), their minor songs express their love for land and family, ippān doon (togetherness), and political and social justice. Whereas Yasta-Man practices his rap-reggae technique as a way to resist the severance of his voice, Flavah C's melodic hip hop grounds his commitment to "Rep Majol," and Kathy Jetñil-Kijiner has become a new voice, mother, poet, and celebrity of climate change. "Rep Majol" now makes up their minor songs, namely, the hip hop, rap, and slam poetry circulations that draw on and contribute to the anti-colonial bricolage of Black and Marshallese diasporic futurities. Collectively, they struggle against the major challenges and sounds of racism, police and military brutality, and environmental injustice and climate change. Their songs are also mobile and portable and can be listened to on a personal device, a minor transnationalism that similarly resonates with Mary K. Good's analysis of the Bebo platform in chapter 5.

By stressing this repertoire as minor, I have critically utilized the term *minor*, as in juvenile, minor mode, and minor transnationalisms. I have also proposed a minor for Western media that often posits women and children as being in need of saving by the masculine military. The minor formation of "representation" or what I called "reppin'" or "rep" refers to the non-spacing interval in harmony, the feeling and vibrational movements of love and family, of homeland and place that moves the voices of these artists. They are the resonances of the visceral drumbeat percussion of women, of mothers harnessing inspiration for war, for peace, for conflict resolution. To imagine Marshallese youth, then, is to foreground their deep love for their Marshallese families from May Day to International Workers' Day to the UN and Indigenous Peoples' Day. All Pacific youth cultures must be heard within this multitudinal rumbling.

NOTES

1 Mark Rifkin, *Beyond Settler Time: Temporal Sovereignty and Indigenous Self-Determination* (Durham, NC: Duke University Press, 2017).

2 Françoise Lionnet and Shu-mei Shih, eds., *Minor Transnationalism* (Durham, NC: Duke University Press, 2005).

3 See Édouard Glissant, *Poetics of Relation*, trans. Betsy Wing (Ann Arbor: University of Michigan Press, 1997).

4 Lionnet and Shih, *Minor Transnationalism*, 8.

5 Katherine Irwin and Karen Umemoto, *Jacked Up and Unjust: Pacific Islander Teens Confront Violent Legacies* (Oakland: University of California Press, 2016), 107.

6 Gregory Dvorak, "'The Martial Islands': Making Marshallese Masculinities between American and Japanese Militarism," *Contemporary Pacific* 20, no. 1 (2008): 55–86; and Danny Leffler, "On an Island Halfway around the World, Locals Enlist to Fight and Die for the United States," *Task and Purpose*, October 12, 2017, https://taskandpurpose.com/island-soldier-nathan-fitch -enlist-military.

7 See Holly M. Barker's influential *Bravo for the Marshallese: Regaining Control in a Post-nuclear, Post-colonial World*, 2nd ed. (Belmont, CA: Wadsworth, Cengage Learning, 2013).

8 See the Marshallese Educational Initiative website, www.mei.ngo/marshallese -in-arkansas.

9 See Jessica A. Schwartz, "Between Death and Life: Mobility, War, and Marshallese Women's Songs of Survival," *Women and Music* 16, no. 1 (2012): 23–56.

10 See Epeli Hauʻofa, "Our Sea of Islands," in *A New Oceania: Rediscovering Our Sea of Islands*, ed. Eric Waddell, Vijay Naidu, and Epeli Hauʻofa (Suva, Fiji: School of Social and Economic Development, University of the South Pacific, 1993), 2–16.

11 Chad Blair, "The New Kids on the Block: A 'Hidden Minority,'" *Honolulu Civil Beat*, October 2015, www.civilbeat.org/2015/10/the-new-kids-on-the-block-a -hidden-minority.

12 F.O.B (Family of Brothas [*sic*]), ReverbNation, accessed January 11, 2019, www .reverbnation.com/fob2215.

13 "About the Artist," F.O.B (Family of Brothas [*sic*]), ReverbNation.

14 On early Marshallese migration to the midwestern United States, refer to Jessica A. Schwartz, "Marshallese Cultural Diplomacy in Arkansas," *American Quarterly* 67, no. 3 (September 2015): 781–812.

15 Flavah C and F.O.B did not label their music as hip hop or identify their music as part of any particular genre; the description here is the author's. Flavah C, YastaMan, and F.O.B interview with the author, May 29, 2013, Springdale, Arkansas.

16 Flavah C, YastaMan, and F.O.B interview with the author. All subsequent quotations from the artists are from this interview.

17 Ana María Ochoa Gautier, *Aurality: Listening and Knowledge in Nineteenth-Century Colombia* (Durham, NC: Duke University Press, 2014).

18 Raphael Travis Jr., *The Healing Power of Hip-Hop* (Santa Barbara: Praeger, 2016), 7.

19 On the US militarization of Kwajalein, refer to Giff Johnson, *Collision Course at Kwajalein: Marshall Islanders in the Shadow of the Bomb* (Honolulu: Pacific Concerns Resource Centre, 1984).

20 It seemed to me that YastaMan also shared with Shaggy the culture of enlistment, since Shaggy was in the US Marines and Pacific Islanders often enroll in rates that exceed those of the US continent. Space constraints here do not allow focus on this subject.

21 See Shaggy, "Strength of a Woman," on *Lucky Day*, Genius Media Group, 2019, accessed March 1, 2019, https://genius.com/Shaggy-strength-of-a-woman-lyrics.

22 Phillip H. McArthur, "Ambivalent Fantasies: Local Prehistories and Global Dramas in the Marshall Islands," *Journal of Folklore Research* 45, no. 3 (2008): 263–98.

23 CNN's *Two Degrees* newsletter, by John D. Sutter, is a prime example of sensationalist journalism; see "You're Making This Island Disappear," accessed February 26, 2019, www.cnn.com/interactive/2015/06/opinions/sutter-two-degrees-marshall-islands.

24 Liisa H. Malkki, *Purity and Exile: Violence, Memory, and National Cosmology among Hutu Refugees in Tanzania* (Chicago: University of Chicago Press, 1995), 11. For a discussion of the larger military culture, see Cynthia H. Enloe, *Bananas, Beaches and Bases: Making Feminist Sense of International Politics* (London: Pandora, 1989).

25 Lauri Goering, "Interview: Pacific Island Poet Marshals Youth against Climate Threats," Thomson Reuters Foundation, November 18, 2016, http://news.trust.org/item/20161118225353-skupz/?source=spotlight.

26 "About," Kathy Jetñil-Kijiner website, accessed October 15, 2019, www.kathyjetnilkijiner.com/author-bio. See also Kathy Jetñil-Kijiner, "Iep Jaltok: A History of Marshallese Literature" (master's portfolio, University of Hawai'i, Mānoa, 2014); and Kathy Jetñil-Kijiner, *Iep Jaltok: Poems from a Marshallese Daughter* (Tucson: University of Arizona Press, 2017).

27 "Community," Kathy Jetñil-Kijiner website, accessed October 15, 2019, www.kathyjetnilkijiner.com/community.

28 "Rise: From One Island to Another," poem by Kathy Jetñil-Kijiner and Aka Niviâna on 350.org, produced by Dan Lin Media, 2018, https://350.org/rise-from-one-island-to-another.

29 "Anointed," poem by Kathy Jetñil-Kijiner, Pacific Resources for Education and Learning, 2018, www.kathyjetnilkijiner.com/videos-featuring-kathy.

30 Kathy Jetnil-Kijiner, "Statement by Ms. Kathy Jetnil-Kijiner, Civil Society Representative from the Marshall Islands at the opening of the United Nations Climate Summit 2014," YouTube video, 6:50, posted by "United Nations," September 23, 2014, www.youtube.com/watch?v=mc_IgE7TBSY.

31 Kathy Jetñil-Kijiner, "Dear Matefele Peinam," YouTube video, posted by "Kathy Jetñil-Kijiner," September 23, 2014, www.youtube.com/watch?v=DJuRjy9k7GA.

32 See Katherine Brooks, "Young Poet Kathy Jetnil-Kijiner Explains the Essence of Climate Change at UN Summit," *Huffington Post*, September 23, 2014, www .huffpost.com/entry/kathy-jetnil-kijiner_n_5870194; and Eric Holthaus, "The 1.5 Generation," *Grist*, August 22, 2018, https://grist.org/article/courage-and -bolt-cutters-meet-the-next-generation-of-climate-activists.

33 Conversation with Jetñil-Kijiner, Springdale, Arkansas, May 25, 2019.

34 Eric Holthaus, "This Climate Change Poem Moved World Leaders to Tears Today," *Slate*, September 23, 2014, https://slate.com/technology/2014/09/kathy -jetnil-kijiner-solastalgia-marshall-islander-s-poem-moves-u-n-climate -summit-to-tears.html.

35 Brooks, "Young Poet."

36 Holthaus, "1.5 Generation."

37 Holthaus, "This Climate Change Poem."

38 "Marshall Islands Poet to the U.N. Climate Summit: 'Tell Them We Are Nothing without Our Islands,'" *Democracy Now*, December 2, 2015, www .democracynow.org/2015/12/2/marshall_islands_poet_to_the_un.

PART III

INDIGENOUS MASCULINITIES

CHAPTER 7

KANAKA WAIKĪKĪ

The Stonewall Gang and Beachboys of O'ahu, 1916–1954

ALIKA BOURGETTE

NATIVE HAWAIIAN MEN AND WOMEN, THROUGH HAOLE-dominated print culture and tourist narratives, have often been depicted as sexualized bodies. In service to the burgeoning tourist industry, haole journalists and travel writers painted the young Native Hawaiian men of Waikīkī as "the perfect servants" or "drunken derelicts" to draw lines of distinction between the two racial groups.[1] Their depictions of Native Hawaiian inferiority aimed to idealize white rationality, underscoring the latter group's purported position at the apex of Native Hawaiian society. By privileging the oral accounts of Native Hawaiian men who grew up in Waikīkī over the racist accounts offered by print media, in this chapter, I show how Native Hawaiian boys transitioned from "beachboys" and "gang" members to tour guides of the wealthy in early-twentieth-century Honolulu. In this manner, Native Hawaiian boys and young men appropriated, resisted, and upheld the increasingly dominant heteronormative codes of Honolulu as a tourist destination.

Over the course of the chapter, I follow the stories of two residents from the Hamohamo neighborhood of Waikīkī, Lemon "Rusty" Holt and Joe Akana, from their childhood to their young adulthood. I analyze their humor about and horseplay with business owners, Japanese neighbors, and tourists as well as examine their membership in neighborhood "gangs" and how they perceived sexual access to "their" girls. In contrast to the feminized depictions they received in the press, I show how these Native Hawaiian men transformed from neighborhood pranksters into members of the Hui Nalu Surf Club and "beachboys" who made their living as cultural and sexual liaisons and professional tour guides for wealthy tourists. Hui Nalu, an organization for Native Hawaiian surfers founded in 1908, receives recognition today as a surf-oriented extension of resistance movements born out of anti-annexation sentiments in the wake of the January 17, 1893, overthrow of the Hawaiian monarchy.[2] I also demonstrate how a closer reading of beachboys' personal accounts reveals more about their gender than their description as "ladies' men . . . during a time when American miscegenation laws prohibited men of color from marrying white women," as described by the scholar Isaiah Helekunihi Walker.[3] Relations between beachboys and their wealthy clients sometimes transgressed heteronormative as well as racial norms with wealthy men. The Maharaja of Indore, one such patron examined in this chapter, lavished gifts and companion travel to the mainland for the beachboys' exemplary service. In this way, some wealthy men made souvenirs of the beachboys' bodies, displaying their favorite island experiences at public events back home.

As their narratives reveal, Native Hawaiian youth resisted colonial structures in an urbanizing Waikīkī and found ways to confront racism, sexism, and poverty. Native Hawaiian boys in particular understood their dispossession as an ongoing form of abuse by colonial power. As such, they cultivated violent reputations as a way to respond to abuse and punish those who would seek to take advantage of them.[4] Participation in sports and brawls provided recognition from and masculine agency with their peers. Their efforts also reflected a strategic desire to avoid placement at the bottom of the colonial and racial structure in Honolulu, as with the mischievous pranks enacted by Rusty Holt and Joe Akana against their neighbors and tourists.

Tourist images casted Native Hawaiians as savage, infantile, or otherwise backwards in order to delineate ways colonized people may interact within the racial state. As Adria L. Imada has shown, the Hawaiian and US states mobilized the practice of hula as a source of identity that both resisted and reinforced colonial relationships of paternalism.[5] Although sanctioned by the Hawaiian Kingdom as a form cultural diplomacy, traveling hula circuits nevertheless reinforced gendered and racialized conceptions of Native savagery abroad.[6] In these ways, as Ty P. Kāwika Tengan has argued, the tourist exhibitions of Native Hawaiian boys and men paralleled their "loss of land, tradition, authenticity, culture, and power."[7] A 1926 issue of *Vogue*, a popular periodical of cosmopolitan fashion, captured these depictions of Native Hawaiian young men, stating that they were "magnificently built, bronzed young athletes, who lounge on the sands in bathing-suits, have no visible means of support, but are always willing to paddle an outrigger canoe or to sing and strum for the toss of a coin."[8]

How did these gendered processes of colonial and Indigenous representation and resistance unfold in the Waikīkī area of Honolulu, one of the oldest cities in Oceania? In this chapter, I also examine how Native Hawaiian boys responded to colonial heteropatriarchy through homosocial understandings of girls and women as sexual partners warranting protection rather than engagement as social equals. These dynamics shaped the way Waikīkī boys grouped together as "gangs."[9] By perceiving and excluding girls as fragile and sexualized, Hawaiian boys reaffirmed their own masculine dominance and often reinforced heterosexual norms. However, a few boys and young men in Waikīkī may have wielded multiple masculinities beyond the heteronormative model perpetuated by colonial heteropatriarchy.[10]

The University of Hawai'i Center for Oral History, part of the College of Social Sciences and Social Sciences Research Institute, has recorded the recollections of the people of Hawai'i, including men like Joe Akana. Since its establishment in 1976, the Center for Oral History has interviewed over eight hundred individuals, resulting in over 36,000 transcript pages archived.[11] Among those, the fifty-one interviews that comprise the collection entitled *Waikīkī, 1900–1985: Oral Histories* provide much context to this chapter.[12] Indeed, oral histories illuminate new details about historical events that are missed or misrepresented in materials produced by hegemonic influences. However, as stories told through the lens of one's memory, oral histories can also obscure elements of the recent and distant past. By prioritizing the oral accounts of beachboys and Native Hawaiian men, my chapter subsequently but not intentionally reinscribes the absence of Native Hawaiian girls and women in these oral histories of Waikīkī. When asked directly about his own sisters' and mother's participation in Waikīkī social life, for instance, Rusty Holt responded, "Nothing . . . I don't remember them doing very much."[13] As his comment illustrates, the oral histories of Native Hawaiian men also reflected misogynistic understandings of girls and women. Whether by way of Indigenous rituals, political representation, or religious authority, the exclusion of Indigenous girls and women from the male-dominated spaces of Hawai'i and wider Oceania persist. In chapter 9, Arcia Tecun, Edmond Fehoko, and 'Inoke Hafoka similarly struggle with this predicament as they explore the making of diasporic kava circles for young Tongan men in Aotearoa and Utah. In light of these limitations, I pair these oral histories with other print sources, such as advertisements and newspaper articles of the early twentieth century. By reading them "against the grain" of heteronormativity in these oral histories and related texts, I show how Native Hawaiian boys and young men created narratives of homoerotic and homosocial desire and resistance in Waikīkī.

RASCALS OF WAIKĪKĪ AND THE STONEWALL GANG

Local rascals Rusty Holt and Joe Akana gave color to the Hamohamo neighborhood, pulling pranks on the neighborhood shop owners and joining the ranks of the Waikīkī beachboys. Of Native Hawaiian descent, their stories recorded the daily lives of Hawaiian families residing near Hamohamo, capturing family members' occupations, personal memories, and social gatherings from the turn of the twentieth century through the 1930s. Rusty Holt, born into the prominent Lemon family on September 22, 1904, recalled his family's ties to royalty through Queen Lili'uokalani and Prince Kuhio. Growing up on the Lemon estate, Rusty lived adjacent to the Queen's Hamohamo residence and recounted his multiple encounters with her. Joe Akana, son of a Chinese immigrant to Hawai'i, lived across the Kukaunahi Stream from the Lemon property. As childhood friends, Rusty and Joe caused mischief together. As they grew older, they participated as members of the Stonewall Gang, a group of neighborhood boys who played sports and brawled with other Honolulu gangs (figure 7.1). When on their home turf, sitting on the eponymous Stonewall on the Lē'ahi (Diamond Head) end of Waikīkī Beach, the Stonewall Gang passed the time by entertaining tourists, diving for coins to catch fish, and singing songs for money.

Rusty Holt experienced Waikīkī's early transitions firsthand. The third child of seven born to Augusta Helen Lemon Holt and Edward Holt, Rusty had Hawaiian ancestry through his mother's side. In the 1890s through the turn of the century, Rusty's maternal grandmother, Mary Ann Wond, headed the Kapi'olani Maternity Home for women of Hawaiian descent at the behest of Queen Kapi'olani.[14] The Lemon family's close connection to royalty allowed them to buy property adjacent to Queen Lili'uokalani's Hamohamo property. The one-acre estate shared street boundaries with Kalakaua, Paoakalani, and Kapahulu Avenues and Lemon Road, which

FIGURE 7.1. Native Hawaiian boys, ca. 1900. (Photo credit: Audrey Judy private collection)

still today bears the family's name. Rusty's memories of entertaining royalty hinted to his family's importance. Queen Liliʻuokalani occasionally visited his grandmother, the two having been classmates at the Royal School.[15] Rusty recalled the Queen's preference for haohao (soft and young) coconuts, small fish, and other reef edibles:

> Also, I had to go out to the stone wall, in the front of the stonewall [at Kuhio Beach], dive and catch three or four, or five, or six manini (convict tang fish). She liked manini. She ate them raw. I also had to go out to near Queen's Surf and dive for wana (sea urchin), plenty of wana there, bring that home then go back out to Queen's Surf and dive for lipoa, limu (two types of seaweed). She liked lipoa! And my grandmother, in the meantime, would be cooking Hawaiian stew. And that's what she had, whenever she came.[16]

The stone beach wall defined the geography of Waikīkī Beach, forming the terminus of the beach on its Lēʻahi (Diamond Head) end. The wall formed a groin protecting Kuhio Beach from oncoming surf. The calmness of this portion of the beach made it an ideal swimming spot and gathering place for neighborhood children. Rusty remembered that in the mid-1920s, he and other members of the Stonewall Gang would spend their days in the waters by the wall "diving for nickels" from the tourists:

> When the tourists came, we would take off our tights, dive into the water, and come up with manini, one or two manini, showing the tourists that we were catching the fish with our tights. We'd hold it up, and if the tourists dropped a nickel, we turned around, we didn't have any tights on and we showed them our 'okoles (behinds). When they dropped a quarter, we thanked them and did not show them our 'okoles. That, we did right along all (the) time. Those were the days of "dive for nickels," they call it.[17]

The arrival of tourists from the steamships *Claudine*, *Lurline*, and *Matsonia* provided Rusty and his friends with targets for their shenanigans. Their behavior exhibited a willingness to take advantage of tourist imaginations of the local children as helpful yet economically disadvantaged (figure 7.2). Showing rudeness to the white newcomers allowed Native

FIGURE 7.2. Diving boys, Honolulu Harbor, 1916. (Photo credit: Audrey Judy private collection)

Hawaiian children the opportunity to up-end racial stratification, exerting their place ahead of the haole tourists.

Coin divers, like Rusty Holt, hailed from each of Honolulu's working-class neighborhoods. Native Hawaiian boys demonstrated their aquatic prowess, making up to $3 a day chasing nickels through the water as new arrivals dropped them from the decks of arriving steamships.[18] Kaka'ako resident Sam Kapu spoke to oral interviewer Perry Nakayama about the territoriality each neighborhood had regarding diving spots, that each neighborhood had its own turf. Kapu's neighborhood, Kaka'ako, held sway over Piers Two through Ten at Honolulu Harbor. Boys from each neighborhood enforced their territorial rights to coin diving spots by punishing trespassers. Describing the process of protecting one's turf, Kapu stated,

> NAKAYAMA: Supposing someone from, say, Palama came into your folks' district?
> KAPU: You know what they find? Their clothes "chewed beef."
> NAKAYAMA: What?
> KAPU: Chew beef, tied 'em up. We tie up their clothes and shishi (urinate) on 'em.[19]

Kapu explained that the offending boys finding chewed beef where they had left their clothes dissuaded repeated offenses. The smell of urine lingered in the boys' clothes, shaming them for the rest of the day. When asked if girls dove for coins alongside boys from their neighborhood, Kapu found the question difficult to answer:

> NAKAYAMA: What about wahine (women)? Any wahine divers?
> KAPU: No. Those days were, well, they never have too much wahines like now. I guess the ratio was about four to one with girls.
> NAKAYAMA: Oh, but there would be some?
> KAPU: Yeah, but they know they're, you know . . .[20]

Kapu then trailed off and began talking about the steamships on which he used to work. His reluctance to respond to the interviewer's question upheld the heteronormative norms of the media and tourism. At the same time, Kapu's inability to describe the non-male divers in familiar terms suggests that nonbinary Native Hawaiian youths may have dived for coins as well.[21]

Pulling pranks allowed Native Hawaiian boys to exhibit their masculinity and to establish their social dominance over both haole tourists and nonwhite neighbors. Rusty Holt's memories of playing tricks on the local Japanese shopkeepers provided a clear image of the racial and physical layout of the Hamohamo neighborhood. He recalled that the intersection of Paoakalani and Kalakaua Avenues formed the nucleus of the commercial district. His uncle, Jimmy Lemon, operated a beer shop there adjacent to the Aoki Store, owned by Japanese immigrants. Rusty remembered working for the store and maintaining close relations with the Aoki family and other neighboring business owners. In particular, Rusty had fond memories of a first-generation Chinese man he called "Old Man Tailor" who provided laundry service for the linens from the Moana and Seaside hotels. Rusty, famous for his mischievous pranks, recalled Old Man Tailor as the only Waikīkī shop owner who treated him kindly. One prank involving both the Aoki Store and Old Man Tailor, however, left Holt feeling guilty.

In preparation for when he might need to punish someone who had crossed him, Rusty collected duck eggs from his neighbors' ponds and buried them in his yard for months, letting them rot in their shells. One day, Mrs. Aoki had warranted Rusty's wrath:

> Well, about that time Mrs. Aoki was giving me a bad time. I wanted crack seed (Chinese dried fruit) and no way could I get it. Then I decided that, "All right, old lady, you're gonna get it this time." So I got a bunch of those eggs, ripe duck eggs, got on the streetcar and as we went past Aoki's, I started letting them go. Unfortunately, I missed Aoki's. I missed the barbershop, and the eggs went right into my good, good friend's laundry shop. It splattered rotten duck eggs all over the place. I don't know. I felt worse than anybody, I guess, because I had done something to a person who liked me and I liked him. So much for duck eggs.[22]

Rusty's actions underscored his perception of entitlement to service from Mrs. Aoki, which he enforced through mean-spirited pranks. For Native Hawaiian youth in Honolulu, marginalization wrought by colonial heteropatriarchy partly developed a masculinity premised on the enacting of punishment to correct perceived injustices. Where Rusty Holt could not target less tangible sources of inequity, such as the colonial state, he aimed his ire at immigrant neighbors whom he did not necessarily like. In this way, Rusty appropriated colonial sexual norms by targeting Mrs. Aoki, a Japanese woman, while befriending Old Man Tailor, a Chinese man.

Moreover, their relational experiences as people similarly marginalized by settler elites made Rusty's neighbors vulnerable to his frustrations.

Waikīkī residents also recalled the importance of belonging to a gang. Joe Akana and Louis Kahanamoku, members of the Stonewall and Kālia gangs, respectively, remembered sport and fighting as being organized along neighborhood lines. Of the Stonewall gang, Joe reflected, "Well, daytime, they were loafers. Lot of them were loafers, but lot of them worked. They hanged out on the Stonewall at night just because of music. And then, there were fights. You see, there were gangs in the different districts. Palama gang . . . And then, School Street gang. They were toughies. And Kaka'ako gang. They were another bunch of toughies. Each one of these places I named, districts, had football teams, too. But barefoot teams. They had different leagues with different weights."[23] Representing your neighborhood carried significance for the young men who participated in gangs. While some neighborhoods focused on organized sports as their primary social activity, gangs from working-class neighborhoods prided themselves on their ability to fight. Louis Kahanamoku, younger brother of famous Olympian and waterman Duke Kahanamoku, corroborated Joe's view of neighborhood sporting events devolving into fights: "We played a little baseball. You know, we choose up [sides]. Get different districts. Kālia, you go out and played that bunch, the Stonewall Gang. And then we had another bunch go play the gang up in Kalihi. But us, we want to play the tough guys. Kalihi and Kaka'ako, guarantee going to be a fight, so we want to get in it."[24]

Gang members also had the responsibility of protecting their home turf from outsiders. For members of the Stonewall Gang, fighting drunken soldiers from nearby Fort DeRussy proved an important task. They saw the service members who frequented Waikīkī bars as threats who "sometimes got nasty with our girls."[25] Rooted in hypermasculine views of women as both sexual conquests and objects needing protection, tensions between soldiers and Waikīkī locals resulted in physical altercations. A May 1915 *Hawaiian Gazette* article reported that the Honolulu mayor spoke at Fort DeRussy after soldiers interrupted a luau he had hosted in Kapi'olani Park in an incident that resulted in fighting.[26] In response to army officials' objection to the use of police force in this incident, the mayor stated, "There was widespread curiosity about the luau and even after the courses had been served, I knew we ran the danger of being overrun by the whole town if a line was not drawn and the police given orders to see that it was not overstepped."[27] Even the city mayor noted animosity between Waikīkī's

Hawaiian and military populations when he made provisions to host a luau honoring notable Hawaiian residents. While police authorities in the aforementioned incident favored local Hawaiians over haole new arrivals, typical media views of Hawaiian youths adopted negative connotations.

The *Honolulu Star-Bulletin* first recorded gang activity on Waikīkī Beach in 1916, citing an altercation between Waikīkī local Archie Boyd and tavern manager George H. Willey that went to trial. The article pointed to the defendant's character flaws, cursing in the presence of women and breaking his drinking glass at the bar when the altercation occurred, to incite moral panic in their haole elite readership. Although Waikīkī residents did admit to participating in gang fights, the newspaper account exaggerated the situation, linking one instance of public drunkenness to broader "gang" phenomena. In a statement following the trial's guilty verdict, Prosecuting Attorney Frank Thompson rebuked the rise of violence on the beachfront, stating, "New York has the Bowery; Chicago, Detroit, San Francisco, all have their tough places, and that's what a certain gang is trying to make out of Waikīkī Beach. There is a bunch of drunken derelicts like 'Steamboat Bill' and 'Tough Bill' that needs cleaning out. Their very names suggest their character."[28]

The prosecuting attorney was referring to brothers Daniel and George Keaweamahi, who were known as "Steamboat Bill" and "Tough Bill," respectively. Multiple oral history accounts from Waikīkī residents recounted fond memories of the two men.[29] Known for their large stature and kindness, the Keaweamahi brothers served as lifeguards, beachboys, and founding members of the Hui Nalu Surf Club. A 1918 *Hawaiian Gazette* article entitled "Keaweamahi Adds to His Collection of Lives Saved at Beach" praised Steamboat Bill for saving the life of a nineteen-year-old young man caught in dangerous surf.[30] Kālia resident Mary Clarke also recalled community fishing trips where her brother and Tough Bill caught fish and distributed them to families.[31] The depiction of the Keaweamahi brothers in the *Honolulu Star-Bulletin* did not match their likeness according to their closest friends and neighbors, suggesting sensational coverage of Waikīkī beachboys in the local press. Interestingly, Archie Boyd, the original subject of the newspaper article and a defendant in the Waikīkī assault case, did not appear in any of the fifty-one oral history accounts of early-twentieth-century Waikīkī. Linking an isolated case of violence to character attacks against the Keaweamahi brothers affirmed the prosecuting attorney's negative view of beachboys and Hamohamo residents like Joe Akana of the Stonewall Gang.

Born on May 4, 1907, in his family's home on ʻOhua Lane, Joseph Yim Kaʻimuʻiole Akana grew up surrounded by members of the Stonewall Gang, participating in shenanigans with his friend Rusty Holt.[32] Similar to his friend, Joe had Hawaiian ancestry through his mother, Martha Akeo Nawahine of Waiheʻe, Maui. His parents met on Maui where his father, first-generation Chinese immigrant Yim Kung Akana, worked on a sugar plantation for the Baldwin family. The youngest of eight children, Joe lived in a busy house. In his interview with ʻIwalani Hodges, he recalled how his home lent itself to being a social center for the community. The place had a wraparound lanai that extended thirty feet in the back. His older brothers invited their friends from the Stonewall Gang for evening dances on Saturday nights: "When they [Joe Akana's brothers] grew older, you know, they used to go to dances and things like that, but they decided they want to have dances at home. They had a gang in Waikīkī. The Holt Brothers—Melvin, Elmer—and Leslie Lemon. Boys that hung out at Stonewall at night. They used to hire orchestras, you know. . . . So they hired the orchestras, their gang, and they had dances. Almost every Saturday night in the summer! Oh, God, these guys."[33]

Music played an important role in the image of the Stonewall Gang. Younger than the core group that made up the gang, Joe did not consider himself a full member, but he recalled many of the group's songs, of which he performed his own renditions during his beachboy days.[34] His home sat at the intersection of Kalakaua Avenue and ʻOhua Lane, where Joe recalled living behind the Aoki Store. A stream also separated his house from the Lemon estate. Both Joe and Rusty had memories of a particular Chinese dim sum vendor who used to walk through the area, selling his food. Joe mentioned how he enjoyed eating the manapua (Hawaiian-style pork buns) the vendor sold. Rusty then explained how they acquired them: "[The vendor] carried two baskets on a stick in the middle—one basket in the front and also a can, a five-gallon or ten-gallon can. In those containers, there was black sugar manapua, hash, and one or two other items. Joe [Akana] would talk to him and point to the front basket. While the old man was talking to Joe about the front basket, I would be in the back helping myself and stuffing things, all I could stuff, into my pockets."[35] The merchants and street vendors of Kalakaua Avenue provided Rusty and Joe with ample opportunities for pranks and entertainment. Although Rusty moved from Waikīkī shortly after finishing high school, Joe built on his childhood experiences with the Stonewall Gang as a successful beachboy and member of the Hui Nalu Surf Club. Joe's remembrances highlighted the beachboy's multifaceted role as an emerging entertainer, local liaison, and tour guide.

Firsthand accounts gleaned from Joe Akana, Rusty Holt, and other members of the Stonewall Gang developed a view of the diverse masculinities in the youth male culture of Waikīkī. By playing pranks on haole visitors and Asian immigrant neighbors, Rusty Holt resisted notions of racial stratification that would marginalize him. Within circles of same-age peers, Waikīkī boys also organized themselves into gangs, vying for superiority through sports and fighting. But as youth like Joe Akana, Louis Kahanamoku, and "Tough Bill" Keaweamahi aged, their affiliations transitioned from gangs to the Hui Nalu Surf Club. Hui Nalu sought to protect Native Hawaiian interests on the waves against the encroachment of the whites-only Outrigger Canoe Club and also organized beach concessions for the hotels along Waikīkī Beach. In the next section, I discuss how the surf instructors, musicians, and guides of Hui Nalu served as the first beachboys of Waikīkī.

HUI NALU, BEACHBOYS, AND SEX APPEAL

In their resistance to white hegemony, Native Hawaiians formed organizations that promoted their rights and interests, as with Hui Aloha ʻĀina and Hui Kalaiʻāina.[36] Much like how these two organizations petitioned against the US annexation of Hawaiʻi, Hui Nalu similarly protested white encroachment by protecting Native Hawaiian access to the shore and surf of Waikīkī Beach. As Walker has highlighted, Hui Nalu also represented their men as ideal models of masculinity, successful in their sexual pursuit of wealthy white women on the beach.[37] Coining the phrase "ka poʻina nalu" for the surf zone, Walker looked at the space as a cultural "boarderland" where Native Hawaiian masculinities surpassed those of haole men.[38] In this section, I will investigate the sexual success of Hui Nalu's beachboys in further depth, exposing that contrary to Walker's sole portrayal of heteronormative Native Hawaiian men, a few beachboys may have wielded multiple sexualities in Waikīkī.

Joe Akana began making money on the beach at the age of fourteen. He chose not to complete high school due to playing hooky on days he knew the steamships would sail in. He noted that tourists paid money for every display of talent. Just as Rusty Holt dove for nickels, Joe performed for tourists as well. Climbing coconut trees and providing swimming lessons brought in modest money, but Joe recalled that taking tourists out on the water in an outrigger canoe brought in the best money:

> Could make as much as five dollars a day . . . Because in those days, it was a dollar a passenger for a canoe ride. We go out and catch three waves. But we fill the boat up with as much as six paying customers. Six dollars. The house was [Edward] "Dudi" Miller, the owner of the canoe. He had his cut. And the captain out of six passengers, he got dollar and a half; and the second captain got dollar and a half. When I first started, I was second captain. That meant two boys—two skilled boys—went in the canoe with six paying passengers.

Acting as the "house," Dudi Miller managed passengers and recruited other beachboys, such as Joe Akana, to work as his crew. The formula of two beachboys guiding a crew of haole tourists over the waves proved a consistent and successful one. In a 1920 *Los Angeles Times* piece on Waikīkī, a journalist recounted his experience outrigger canoeing: "There is a native in the prow to paddle and another in the stern to steer and when they get the canoe about half way over to San Francisco, suddenly they decide to turn around and let the sportive billows play tag with helpless you. From long years of experience these natives know just when and where to make this turn, and best of all, they know how to do it."[39] The author's language revealed his paternal fascination with "native" culture. The travel writer imagined his beachboy guides living idyllic lives spent honing their canoeing skills. However, for Joe, giving canoe tours represented a quick way to make a dollar while skipping class. As the hotel scene in Waikīkī developed into the 1930s, young men like him shifted their attention from participating in neighborhood fights to becoming professional entertainers.

The life of a Waikīkī beachboy required showmanship as well as skills on the water. As such, the Hui Nalu Surf Club formed to protect Native Hawaiian and other nonwhite locals' interests on the beach. Developing their business skills as tourism bloomed in the late 1920s and into the 1930s, Hui Nalu members soon provided more expensive tour experiences. Louis Kahanamoku recalled that the hustle began before the new arrivals even made it to the beach: "Us boys would go down the ship. And we'd buy leis for them. Was thirty-five cents a lei or fifty cents. But we just buy 'em. We come out with arms full of leis, and we put 'em on the tourists that hang around the hotel beaches. We come out of there, twenty, thirty, forty bucks by the time we got out, put [chuckles] leis on."[40] Buying flower leis for the new arrivals not only netted a large profit for the beachboys up front but allowed them to identify wealthy potential patrons based on the amount they tipped and the level of interest they had in the locals' services. From their clubhouse on the beachfront of the Moana Hotel, Hui Nalu members attracted the attention of their patrons.

In most cases, individual beachboys offered their services to entire families. Joe Akana remembered working for the Honeyman family every summer for five years in the 1930s. Robert Honeyman Jr., an affluent mechanical engineer, lived with his family in San Juan Capistrano, California. His wife, who appeared in the press as "Mrs. Robert Honeyman," had inherited a large fortune from her father, John K. Steward of Chicago, the inventor of the speedometer.[41] Joe recalled that the Honeymans would ship over two Cadillacs for their use while on the island. Joe had the clearest memory of Bob, the oldest son, with whom he spent the most time. Of the son, Joe stated, "He went out with me. He'd come down with two Cadillacs every year. Two Cadillacs. And I used one. Just he and I. And the father, and the wife, and the daughter used the other one. But Bob and I used one Cadillac for just he and I." In these ways, Joe served as a skilled water guide and mentor for the teenaged boy.

Beachboys also shared varied recollections of sexual encounters with their clients. Multiple beachboys recounted that wealthy clients often hired them to entertain their daughters.[42] Beachboy recollections differed, however, on memories of sexual activity with the women they entertained. On one extreme, Louis Kahanamoku insisted that sexual intercourse proved central to his interactions with haole women. On the other, Joe contended that he gained his clients' trust by establishing a policy of "No rough stuff."[43] Having different interviewers could account for how the two men admitted to sexual activity with their clients. Louis Kahanamoku, for instance, could have felt more comfortable revealing, or even bragging about, his experiences to his male interviewer, Warren Nishimoto. But Joe may have felt the need for humility when discussing his relations with 'Iwalani Hodges, a woman. In either case, sexual attraction helped sell sexualized images of the Native Hawaiian beachboy to willing clients.

To improve their sexual appeal to tourists, members of Hui Nalu even performed on- and offstage as actors and musicians. In February 1914, a *Honolulu Star-Bulletin* theater critic reviewed a burlesque variety show casted by Hui Nalu beachboys in conjunction with the Kilohana Art

League in Waikīkī.[44] The club staged the show in order to raise funds to build their first clubhouse on Waikīkī Beach. Consisting of four acts, the play featured beachboy legends Edward "Dudi" Miller, George "Tough Bill" Keaweamahi, and then-famous Duke Kahanamoku "dressed—or undressed" in fanciful costumes, displaying their athletic prowess and showmanship in various bits requiring their ability to sing, dance, and even dive into an onstage pool.[45] The reviewer gave surprising praise that the ensemble of champion swimmers and watermen proved to have decent voices and acting skills. The show elicited a provocative response in the critic, who omitted a full description of the show's racier scenes but alluded to such content in a subsequent scene that featured "a bevy of pretty and handsomely dressed girls and correct young men in evening clothes."[46] While the author did not explicitly disclose cross-dressing among Hui Nalu members, the men may have engaged non-normative gender play and transgressions.

With Hui Nalu drawing its ranks from the aforementioned Kālia and Stonewall gangs, it followed that musical talent played a central role in the beachboy image. Joe Akana, later a Hui Nalu member himself, recalled that the founders of the club gathered every Sunday on the Moana Pier in the early 1920s to play music. Of the Sunday night jams, he recalled, "Oh, beautiful, beautiful. You know, when the moon was up and the pier music was going on, oh God. When the thing broke up at night, when it was all over, one beach boy, he went this way, one went this way with his wahine (woman), and they all go in their different directions."[47] Joe's remarks intertwined beachboy musicianship and sexuality. Whether on stage or on the beachfront, Hui Nalu members used their performance skills to attract women and men alike. Top performing beachboys also received the benefit of high-paying clients who rewarded their guides with lavish presents and trips to the US continent. Joe recounted one such case during his employment with the Maharaja of Indore as head beachboy and leader of Hui Nalu.

Perhaps Joe Akana's highest profile client, the Maharaja of Indore, took the beachboy into his confidence, impressed by his superior performance and business acumen. Sir Yeshwant Rao Holkar, the Maharaja of Indore and then the richest man in the world, set sail from Los Angeles for Honolulu on October 12, 1936, as part of a year-long tour of the United States.[48] A *Los Angeles Times* article announced his departure from San Pedro Harbor aboard Matson's *Lurline* steamer, waxing on his "smartly clad" figure and his "clipped, crisp Oxfordian accent."[49] As the ruler of a princely state in British India, the Maharaja finished his education at Christchurch, Oxford. Joe recalled that Bert Ogilvie, then the manager of the Royal Hawaiian Hotel, introduced him to the Maharaja shortly after the dignitary's arrival:

> Like the Maharajah of Indore, when he came with his party of seventeen, he didn't know who to select as a beach boy. So Bert Ogilvie who managed the Royal [Hawaiian Hotel] at that time, he called me.
>
> "Joe, you take care of the maharajah."
>
> There was seventeen in the party. I could only take care of he and his wife. But I picked certain boys out of the [Hui Nalu] club to take care of his party. The maharani had her guests; he had his guests. And they had like his aide-de-camp and her lady-in-waiting, things like that, you knew, that made up the whole party.[50]

Joe had earned the trust of the manager of the Royal Hawaiian Hotel through his reputation as a first-class beachboy. As he did with the Honeyman family, Joe gave his highest-profile clients his complete attention, taking no other clients during the Maharaja's stay.

Using connections made through Bert Ogilvie, the beachboy set the itinerary for the Maharaja, his wife, and their retinue of servants and associates. Beyond providing the standard array of beach concessions, including surf lessons and outrigger canoe trips, Joe transported the Maharaja to Honolulu's restaurants and shops. The cashier's office at the Royal Hawaiian Hotel also gave Joe an open line of credit to ensure that the Maharaja and Maharani did not worry about any expenses until the conclusion of their stay. Of his time with the couple, Joe recounted, "I kept track of everything spent. I made his inter-island itinerary and things like that. They'd go to the different islands. I was the only guy who could ride the same automobile or ride the same elevator with them, the couple. The [Maharaja's] aide-de-camp and the secretary couldn't ride the same elevator with them."[51] His role as a tour guide gave Joe Akana exclusive access to the Maharaja and Maharani in ways that even their closest advisors lacked. The services Joe provided transcended those typically requested of beachboys at the time. The positive connection he formed with the Maharaja prompted the affluent ruler to request that Joe follow him on his return trip to Los Angeles as part of his tour party. Affluent clients often treated beachboys to overseas trips as a form of souvenir taking. Prized for their toned bodies and exotic features, beachboys like Joe Akana provided the parties of wealthy patrons a degree of social cachet.

No stranger to the press, the Maharaja collected new members of his retinue as he traveled to numerous locations as a means of attracting the public's attention. In the summer of 1933, for example, the Maharaja embarked on an official tour of Europe, leaving from Bombay for Trieste, Italy. *The Times of India* reported his departure from Ballard Pier with "fourteen pilgrims to Rome" in tow.[52] The party included ecclesiastic officials from Goa, including the vicar to the Bishop of Panjim. As part of his diplomatic training as a leading official in a British imperial princely state, the Maharaja made appearances alongside notable and diverse travelers to generate an affable persona. The Maharaja's adventures represented a continuous, movable festival, which Joe Akana joined in Waikīkī and followed to Los Angeles.

Joe's presence in the Maharaja's retinue demonstrated the Indian ruler's wealth and desire to surround himself with notable and intriguing people. The *Los Angeles Times* reported the Maharaja's return to Southern California in November 1936 after a month's stay at the Royal Hawaiian Hotel in Waikīkī.[53] However, his plans to visit San Diego and stay at the Hotel del Coronado came undone after he and his wife became ill. As a result, they remained in Los Angeles longer than expected, into December 1936. Joe recalled parts of the affair. In particular, he remembered the live-in nurse the Maharaja picked up during that trip, stating, "The maharajah was sick in L.A., and when they went to Miami, he took his nurse with him. Then from Miami they went to New York to meet their daughter who was only about five years old with her amah or whatever. From New York, they went to St. Moritz, Switzerland. All this time, his nurse was with them. But while they were in St. Moritz, [the Maharani] developed TB [tuberculosis] and she died there." In his interview, Joe noted that the ailing couple's nurse, Margaret Lawler, went on to marry the Maharaja two years after the Maharani's death.

Proximity to the Maharaja gave Joe Akana access to intimate details of the ruler's life and well-being. The beachboy shared information on the couple's health of which the press had only limited knowledge. The *Los Angeles Times* revealed only that the Maharaja was "ill with a cold" when he announced that he had canceled his plans to continue south to recuperate at the home of Hollywood actress Gail Patrick.[54] Through his proximity to the couple, Joe knew that their health suffered more than they revealed to outsiders. Joe's inclusion in his client's entourage even after the couple left Hawai'i followed the experiences had by other beachboys. In his own interviews, Alan "Turkey" Love similarly recalled the frequency with which he accompanied clients back to the hometowns on the US continent.

FROM STEAMSHIPS TO STRATOCRUISERS: BEACHBOY-CLIENT INTIMACIES TAKE FLIGHT

Junior to Joe Akana by twelve years, Alan "Turkey" Love recounted his frequent travel to the US continent as a perk for working as a beachboy. Love began his beachboy career in earnest upon his graduation from high school in 1938. Impacted by the cessation of civilian tourism with the onset of World War II, he did not see his most successful years as a beachboy until after the war.[55] But with the technological advancements in air travel, developed as a result of the war effort, an increasing number of tourists arrived in Hawai'i. Pan American Airways, in particular, utilized the Boeing 377 Stratocruisers to cut in half the eighteen-hour trans-Pacific flight from San Francisco and Los Angeles to Honolulu.[56] By 1949, Pan American provided fifteen weekly flights between the West Coast and Hawai'i. As the airport and the airplane replaced the harbor and the steamship as the sites of tourist arrivals and departures in Honolulu, Alan "Turkey" Love and other beachboys adjusted their approach to attracting clients.

Love recalled that the Hawaiian Town nightclub in the Pan Am Building near the old Honolulu Airport became the new sending off point for leaving tourists. He observed, "You know, the Pan American Building? After the ships were pau (after regular steamship service had ended), we used to go down to the airport, the old airport . . . Sure. I made about six trips by going down there. These people go downstairs, buy a ticket, I'm on my way to the Mainland. I made six, seven, eight trips like that."[57] By the early 1950s, air travel had not only increased the ease by which tourists could arrive, but it had also made it possible for the tourists to bring home a beachboy as a souvenir. Joe Akana's 1936 trip to Los Angeles as part of the Maharaja of Indore's entourage marked a unique experience at that time. Only patrons of immense wealth, such as the Maharaja, could afford companion travel for their favorite beachboys. For Alan "Turkey" Love, travel to the US continent required little more than having drinks with a wealthy client at the airport bar. After the first such trip, Love accounted for such spontaneity whenever he would take drinks at the Hawaiian Town nightclub, making sure he "had the right clothes on" for air travel.

For Love's clients, returning with a beachboy represented more than the opportunity to show off a living piece of vacation memorabilia to friends back home. The dark, toned, athletic bodies of the beachboys held their own appeal. Withholding the client's name, Love spoke of a particular tourist who would return to the mainland after his yearly trip to Waikīkī with a couple of beachboys and lavish them with gifts. Of the experience, Love revealed, "And every time we'd go, he would buy us clothes. [Chuckles] Got so every time we went, we'd go empty-handed. Really. Come back with plenty clothes." Fetishized views of the Native Hawaiian's body fueled the patron's interest in traveling with Love and a handful of other beachboys. In the same vein that heteronormative interactions fueled the sexual objectification of both Hawaiian men and women to opposite-sexed clients, Love's patron exhibited a homoerotic purview of the beachboy as a trophy to be clothed and displayed. Love and his friends received other gifts, including tickets to World Series games and travel between host cities.[58] As for Love, he consented to such exotification for his own benefit and material gains.

CONCLUSION

As exhibited bodies, fetishized companions, and musical performers, Native Hawaiian beachboys served as living souvenirs for affluent patrons on the US continent. Their masculinities took manifold iterations, often upholding and sometimes challenging the dominant heteronormative image of Waikīkī. Through Joe Akana and Alan "Turkey" Love's accounts, a more complex image of Waikīkī beachboys' masculinities emerges. Beyond the classical image of beachboys as temporary paramours to wealthy divorcées and daughters, the watermen offered masculine role models to tourists unsteady on the water. While evidence of explicit homosexual activities does not surface in the beachboys' accounts, homosocial desire fueled the interactions that brought Joe Akana and Alan "Turkey" Love to the mainland in the entourage of wealthy men.

Earlier accounts from Rusty Holt and Sam Kapu likewise reveal the homosocial organization of neighborhood gangs in the city of Honolulu. Through recollections of diving for coins and enforcing claims to turf, Native Hawaiian boys articulated injustices and resisted colonial heteropatriarchy by way of friendship, brawls, music, and pranks. And while they purposefully excluded Native Hawaiian girls in their narratives, they also inferred, when prodded, the possibility of nonbinary genders among their gang members. In these ways, the oral history records and print media of early-twentieth-century Waikīkī restrict our understanding of Native Hawaiian expressions of gender and sexuality as much as they enrich our knowledge of Native Hawaiian youth masculinity more generally. In each case, I found that Native Hawaiian boys and young men circumvented the colonial and racial organization of spaces normally reserved for haole elites in Hawai'i and elsewhere.

NOTES

1 Clayton Hamilton, "Honolulu Holds the Magic Mirror for Mankind," *Vogue*, January 1, 1924, 56; "Alleged 'Gang' Holds Sway at Waikiki Beach," *Honolulu Star-Bulletin*, June 1, 1916, 3.

2 Isaiah Helekunihi Walker, *Waves of Resistance: Surfing and History in Twentieth-Century Hawai'i* (Honolulu: University of Hawai'i Press, 2011), 5.

3 Walker, *Waves of Resistance*, 58.

4 Katherine Irwin and Karen Umemoto, *Jacked Up and Unjust: Pacific Islander Teens Confront Violent Legacies* (Oakland: University of California Press, 2016), 94.

5 Adria L. Imada, *Aloha America: Hula Circuits through the U.S. Empire* (Durham, NC: Duke University Press, 2012), 25.

6 Imada, *Aloha America*, 239.

7 Ty P. Kāwika Tengan, *Native Men Remade: Gender and Nation in Contemporary Hawai'i* (Durham, NC: Duke University Press, 2008), 8.

8 Rosemary Bevan Karelle, "Honolulu: This Hawaiian Paradise Bewitches the Visitor with Its Sea, Its Hills, and Its Magical Moon in a Tropical Night," *Vogue*, October 15, 1926, 136.

9 Karelle, "Honolulu," 151–52.

10 Kalissa Alexeyeff and Besnier Niko, "Gender on the Edge: Identities, Politics, Transformations," in *Gender on the Edge: Transgender, Gay, and Other Pacific Islanders*, ed. Niko Besnier and Kalissa Alexeyeff (Honolulu: University of Hawai'i Press, 2014), 10–11.

11 Michi Kodama-Nishimoto, Warren Nishimoto, and Cynthia A. Oshiro, *Talking Hawai'i's Story: Oral Histories of an Island People* (Honolulu: University of Hawai'i Press, 2009), xiii.

12 *Waikiki, 1900–1985: Oral Histories*, vols. 1–3 (Honolulu: Center for Oral History, Social Science Research Institute, University of Hawai'i, Mānoa, 1985–86).

13 Rusty Holt, oral history interview with Michi Kodama-Nishimoto, March 15, 1985, Wilhelmina Rise, Honolulu, in *Waikiki, 1900–1985*, 1:809.

14 Holt, oral history interview, 1:778.

15 Harold Morse, "Obituaries: Rusty Holt, 94, Avid Sportsman, Deep Local Roots," *Honolulu Star-Bulletin*, March 20, 1999.

16 Holt, oral history interview, 1:783.

17 Holt, oral history interview, 1:805.

18 Sam Kapu, oral history interview with Perry Nakayama, October 7, 1977, Ala Wai Golf Course, Honolulu, in *Remembering Kakaʻako, 1910–1950: Oral Histories*, 2 vols. (Honolulu: Center for Oral History, Social Science Research Institute, University of Hawaiʻi, Mānoa, 1978), 1:510.

19 Kapu, oral history interview, 1:512.

20 Kapu, oral history interview, 1:512.

21 Linda L. Ikeda, "Re-visioning Family: Māhūwahine and Male-to-Female Transgender in Contemporary Hawaiʻi," in Besnier and Alexeyeff, *Gender on the Edge*, 136.

22 Holt, oral history interview, 1:822.

23 Joe Akana, oral history interview with ʻIwalani Hodges and Michi Kodama-Nishimoto, March 8, 1985, Hawaiʻi Kai, Oʻahu, in *Waikiki, 1900–1985*, 1:10.

24 Louis Kahanamoku, oral history interview with Warren Nishimoto, May 20, 1985, Keauhou, Kona, Hawaiʻi, in *Waikiki, 1900–1985*, 1:857.

25 Akana, oral history interview, 1:11.

26 "Order of Mayor as to Soldiers Causes Trouble," *Hawaiian Gazette*, May 7, 1915, 8. Fort DeRussy was an army barracks on the Kālia end of Waikīkī at the time. The land remains part of the US Army recreation facility in Waikīkī.

27 "Order of Mayor," 8.

28 "Alleged 'Gang' Holds Sway," 3.

29 Ah Buck Yee, oral history interview with ʻIwalani Hodges, June 2, 1986, Waikīkī, Oʻahu, in *Waikiki, 1900–1985*, 1:1024; and Ernest Steiner, oral history interview with Michi Kodama-Nishimoto, March 5, 1985, Honolulu, Oʻahu, in *Waikiki, 1900–1985*, 1:85.

30 "Keaweamahi Adds to His Collection of Lives Saved at Beach," *Hawaiian Gazette*, July 2, 1918, 3.

31 Mary Paoa Clarke, oral history interview with Warren Nishimoto, May 20, 1985, Kailua, Kona, Hawaiʻi, in *Waikiki, 1900–1985*, 1:638.

32 Akana, oral history interview, 1:2.

33 Akana, oral history interview, 1:8.

34 See Akana, oral history interview, 1:49–57, for transcripts of songs he performed as a beachboy; Rusty Holt, only three years older than Joe Akana, considered himself one of the Stonewall Gang.

35 Holt, oral history interview, 1:789–90.

36 Noenoe K. Silva, *Aloha Betrayed: Native Hawaiian Resistance to American Colonialism* (Durham, NC: Duke University Press, 2004), 7.

37 Walker, *Waves of Resistance*, 5.

38 Walker, *Waves of Resistance*, 55.

39 "Truth about Waikiki Beach," *Los Angeles Times*, June 6, 1920, 32.

40 Kahanamoku, oral history interview, 1:871.

41   "Mrs. R. B. Honeyman Wins Estate Here," *New York Times*, January 17, 1922; and "Angelenos Attend Colorful Fresco Affair," *Los Angeles Times*, August 25, 1935.

42   Akana, oral history interview, 1:19; Kahanamoku, oral history interview, 1:872; Turkey Love, oral history interview with 'Iwalani Hodges, May 14, 1985, Hawai'i Kai, O'ahu, in *Waikiki, 1900–1985*, 1:1691.

43   Kahanamoku, oral history interview, 1:863; and Akana, oral history interview, 1:46.

44   "Hui Nalu Show Riotous Fun with Mirth, Music and Dancing," *Honolulu Star-Bulletin*, February 12, 1914, 5.

45   "Hui Nalu Show," 5.

46   "Hui Nalu Show," 5.

47   Akana, oral history interview, 1:20.

48   "Maharajah of Indore Sails for Honolulu," *Los Angeles Times*, October 12, 1936, A1.

49   "Maharajah of Indore."

50   Akana, oral history interview, 1:18.

51   Akana, oral history interview, 1:18.

52   "Maharaja of Indore Departure for Europe," *Times of India*, July 28, 1933.

53   "Maharajah Expected at San Diego," *Los Angeles Times*, November 9, 1936, A6.

54   "Cold Will Keep Maharajah Here Another Week," *Los Angeles Times*, November 22, 1936, A1.

55   Love, oral history interview, 1:1667–68.

56   "Pan American Adds New Flights to Honolulu," *Los Angeles Times*, May 15, 1949, A11.

57   Love, oral history interview, 1:1691.

58   Love, oral history interview, 1:1692.

CHAPTER 8

"STILL FEELING IT"

Addressing the Unresolved Grief among the Sāmoan
Bloods of Aotearoa New Zealand

MOSES MA'ALO FALEOLO

GRIEVING THE LOSS OF A LOVED ONE REPRESENTS BOTH A CHAL-
lenging and difficult time for many Sāmoan young people, with some
needing help to deal with their loss effectively. In some cases, parents may
not recognize this need and assume instead that children probably do not
understand the full emotional extent of what is going on and so do not talk
about it. Maybe over time, they will be able to understand the impact of
death and therefore be able to control any negative reactions. As a former
social worker, I find that it is often the case that unresolved grief in Sāmoan
young people is first made known through disclosure. By this time, the
trauma is deep rooted and entrenched and may motivate their association
with and participation in gangs. It is imperative that families spend time
with their teenage children and guide them through the grieving and
mourning process before, during, and after the death of a loved one, especially if they are very young. If this does not occur in families, it can lead to
problems during their lifetime. As a gang researcher and fellow Sāmoan, I
interviewed the young people in Auckland, Aotearoa New Zealand, who
were drawn to me as someone they could trust with their life histories.
Many broke down during our conversations, but at the same time they
were relieved to be free from this burden that weighed heavily on their

shoulders. It was a privilege to have supported the youths' coping mechanisms with grief, a process that occurred in Auckland and not in Apia, Sāmoa.

All the gang members I present in this chapter were "still feeling it." That is to say, they were still being affected by grief that, for them, became an important reason for joining a gang. These young men carried their unresolved grief and traumatic experiences into the gangs in the hope of getting some respite and support because other avenues were deemed ineffective. Hence, the gangs became a conduit where new gang members revealed their hurt and pain to older members who acted as counselors and mentors, supporting these new members toward some form of recovery. Importantly, gangs were already filled with members with similar backgrounds who were relatable, attentive, sympathetic, and from similar cultural backgrounds as the new members. As a result, these gang mentors became revered and respected for their advice more than families or professionals. Gang activities, which ushered in further traumatic experiences like physical fights, were regarded as beneficial because such experiences forced new members to be courageous, strong willed, and tough. Inasmuch as gangs help members deal with the traumatic experiences they brought with them, their gang membership also compounded their unresolved trauma. Despite multiple layers of trauma, the gang members presented in this chapter not only negotiated their grief and traumatic encounters. More vitally, they learned to thrive where most people would just give up.[1]

In this chapter, I highlight how gang members endure and address their unresolved grief as a result of losing a loved one. In the first section, I outline the significance of Auckland as a Māori, Pasifika, and Sāmoan city and as a backdrop in which the Sāmoan youth gangs grew up and were socialized.[2] In the second section, I describe the research design of the main study that led to the four life histories cited in this chapter, including a brief urban geography of four Sāmoan youth gang members. The third section then depicts their painful recollections of the passing of loved ones and other traumatic experiences, such as being abandoned in a foreign place, separated from siblings, and immersed in gang life. In the last section, I discuss several experiences of death and offer recommendations to help grieving families. As Stella Black, Jacquie Kidd, and Katey Thom demonstrate in their analysis of Māori youth justice in chapter 1 and as Vaoiva Ponton reveals in her assessment of Sāmoan youth education in chapter 3, Indigenous communities appreciate assistance from academics.

Receiving support from a Sāmoan gang researcher like me is no different. In this vein, I humbly share my insights with the families and scholars of Auckland and greater Oceania.

AUCKLAND, SĀMOAN GANGS, AND THE POLYNESIAN CAPITAL OF THE WORLD

Although Tāmaki Makaurau or Auckland is predominantly 59 percent Pākehā (New Zealand European), it is significant as a Māori, Pasifika, and Sāmoan city. At the start of the twentieth century, 85 percent of the Māori population lived in rural locations, and 15 percent resided in urban locations. By the turn of the twenty-first century, this trend had reversed with 85 percent of the Māori living in urban settings.[3] With widespread socio-economic, political, and cultural transformation in the region, Auckland became New Zealand's commercial and entrepreneurial capital and its largest and fastest growing city.[4] There is also great homogeneity among the Māori who live in Auckland, which has a higher concentration of Māori migrants from different tribal regions. Historically, the Māori have experienced the city as a colonial place, often feeling alien and powerless and with little or no control of their environment and their lives.

With a total population of 295,941, the experiences of Pasifika people are somewhat analogous to the Māori. About 67 percent or 194,958 of the Pacific population live in Auckland and make up 14.6 percent of the city's population.[5] Sāmoans are the largest of the Pacific ethnic groups, constituting nearly half of the total Pacific population living mostly in South Auckland, substantially New Zealand born and youthful.[6] In the 1950s, Pacific migrants, especially Polynesians, came to Auckland because jobs, schooling, and social services were plentiful.[7] They settled in the central city, but the industries that employed them were in South Auckland, such as Otara and Mangere. Early migrants faced new challenges in the unfamiliar urban environment. As a result, many Pacific people turned to their social networks—family, village, church, and even their homelands—to find homes and jobs, locate and obtain services, and deal with new institutions in English, their second or third language.

The relationships between Māori and Pacific people can be best described as complex. During the late 1960s and early 1970s, the central government opened its doors and welcomed immigration from the Pacific Islands to fill labor shortages in industrial, manufacturing, and commercial sectors. At the same time, many rural Māori moved to urban centers to also take advantage of employment, education, and housing opportunities. Instead, they competed with Pacific migrants for low wages. Subsequently, the relationships between Sāmoans, other Pacific people, and Māori became strained. For Pacific people, they often felt entitled to work in New Zealand. As one person noted, "Pacific Island people did not come here to hongi with Māori. We came here because the opportunities were here and, we thought, these came from Palangi [Whites], not Māori."[8] However, many Māori "regarded Pacific Islanders as uneducated, unsophisticated coconuts taking away resources that should have gone to Māori."[9] Although the first wave of migrants from the Pacific Islands who arrived in Aotearoa generally did not know about Māori and Te Tiriti of Waitangi (the Treaty of Waitangi), both Māori and Pacific peoples share similar kinship values and experiences of colonization. With the emergence of second- and third-generation Pacific peoples, they even found common ground in their socioeconomic gains and losses. At the same time, they often tested their relationships whenever the statuses of tangata whenua (Indigenous peoples of Aotearoa) and tauiwi (the first nations peoples from outside Aotearoa) became topics of debate.[10]

But from the mid-1980s onward, Māori and Pacific relationships greatly improved. Given their collective marginalization, they began to protest their low socioeconomic conditions.[11] They also found solidarity in their ancestral ties, common attitudes about indigeneity and the land, and support for working-class people, including Pākehā. As pan-ethnic communities, they worked together while experiencing discrimination, integration, and self-determination. Their struggle was at its most intense in the 1970s, a period when the government targeted, blamed, and arrested—all without due process—Pacific migrants for the downturn in economy. Known as the "dawn raids," immigration and police officials entered many Sāmoan and Tongan households throughout Auckland in the early morning hours, checked their residency statuses, and deported any unlawful residents back to their home countries in the Pacific.[12] After intense pressure from activist groups such as the Polynesian Panthers, the government's illegal invasion of Pacific homes stopped.[13]

By the 1990s, the Pacific people of Auckland had transformed various aspects of general society with their contributions in the arts, politics, and sports. They also developed youth gangs, a few of which, like the King Cobras, had formed in the 1950s.[14] As Pacific boys from various islands, they formed gangs to protect themselves, to feel good about themselves, and to access things not available from their families. The first emergence of Bloods gangs in Auckland occurred not long after the release of the movie *Colors* in 1988, in which an experienced cop and his rookie partner patrol the streets of East Los Angeles while trying to keep the gang violence under control.[15] The homeboy street gangs of Auckland then modeled after the Crips and the Bloods of Los Angeles.[16] The former represented Māori and Pacific communities, such as the Tongan Crip Gang, whereas Sāmoans often identified with the latter, as with the Sons of Sāmoa. Although they saw themselves as gangsters, they have been described as "wannabes" (not true youth gangs), been involved in petty crime, donned similar dress codes, and shared hand signals or chants. They are also territorial and dabble in opportunistic crime and are unaffiliated or affiliated with criminal gangs; a few even have biological relationships with adult gangs.[17] Gangs largely formed in South Auckland ethnoburbs.[18] Around seventy gangs now exist in Aotearoa.[19]

While the African American Crips and Bloods gangs of the 1990s appealed to Pasifika and Māori youth, the Sāmoan Bloods were unique for a number of reasons. They attracted, for instance, Sāmoan-born youth who were bullied in schools. Through their interaction with New Zealand–born members, they better acculturated to New Zealand's way of life. They also learned their fa'a Sāmoa or cultural identity and practiced their language. And some Sāmoan gangs only formed for protection and refrained from selling drugs and committing property crimes. The Sāmoan youth gang members who participated in this study originated in the ethnoburbs of Auckland. As with Honolulu and Salt Lake City examined in this volume, Auckland had poor-quality, high-density housing, run-down playgrounds, limited street lighting, poverty, community violence, and underground economies. Despite the presence of social services, education, and churches, these young men did not trust professionals, struggled with their schooling experiences, and only attended church to make their families happy. They are the young Sāmoan men of my chapter.

RESEARCH DESIGN AND LIFE HISTORY NARRATIVES

From 2012 to 2013, I spent eighteen months with four Sāmoan Bloods youth gangs in Auckland. Three gangs branched off one particular Sāmoan Bloods youth gang, Red Army (RA). The other was a stand-alone Sāmoan Bloods youth gang, Pearl Baker Stylez (PBS), who looked after a different territory than the RA's and was an ally. The RA and PBS emerged in 2001, with the RA forming to protect themselves from rival gangs. Of these gangs, only the RA sold drugs ("slanging") and committed aggravated robberies ("earns"), but both the RA and PBS hunted rival gang members for revenge ("marches"). The RA membership was also predominantly Sāmoan, but they had a few members representing other ethnicities. Depending on the territory they protected, some wore white with red colors, only red, or black and white with a bit of red. They attracted national news for participating in drive-by shootings, using a vehicle to mow down and kill a rival gang member, prostituting women, and running drugs for adult gangs.

With respect to the PBS gang, two best friends started it while attending their local church. They did so because they saw many Sāmoan youth (New Zealand born, Sāmoan born, and Sāmoans of mixed ethnicities) struggling to fit in with their families, neighborhoods, and schools. Their members were fairly educated, some were fluent in the Sāmoan language and aganu'u (Sāmoan cultural practices), and a few were working in paid jobs. To join this gang, one had to be a Sāmoan who wanted to learn fa'a Sāmoa. This membership criteria very much differed from the violence that gangs are typically known for. PBS even forbade its members from drug and alcohol consumption. Yet they still fought other gangs and became known and feared as ferocious fighters. In fact, they protected local retail outlets from being robbed and local parks and facilities from being vandalized by rival gangs. Given that the RA members respected them, the RA chose not to set up a branch where the PBS operated.

I selected the Sāmoan Bloods because their voices are rarely heard in the small but growing gang literature of Oceania.[20] Their main rival gangs, the Crips, also excluded Sāmoans and mainly welcomed Māori, Tongans, and other ethnicities, so I recruited from the Bloods. Another factor was trust given that I did not want to be seen as affiliated with rival gangs. A former police youth worker also introduced me to some of the gang members (RA and PBS) whom he worked with. Over a six-month period, I then fostered a relationship with them while observing their activities. As a Sāmoan, I gained their trust because I spoke the Sāmoan language (very convenient when meeting some of the members' parents), understood the Sāmoan way (fa'a Sāmoa), participated in Sāmoan activities like church and cultural events, and became a consistent presence all around. My work experiences and cultural background enabled me to explain the purpose of the study in ways that related easily to gang member participants. This context encouraged the Sāmoan youth to share their life histories and release their painful memories of stressful events. Thereafter, other gang members heard about my research and, like the gang members I first met, consented to participate. This snowball effect led to a total of twenty-five gang members in my study and over 250 hours of digital and audio recordings and data collection. In this chapter, I draw from the life history narratives of Syn, VDK, Young D, and Nero to show how they experienced unresolved grief in the Bloods. I use pseudonyms to honor their requests for anonymity. Their life stories reveal the intensity, frequency, and transference of unresolved grief before and/or during their time in the RA and PBS.

Indeed, grief is never fully completed for most people, especially children. As psychological and social work studies of grief illustrate, there are two easily distinguishable forms of uncomplicated or normal grief.[21] First, the uncomplicated grief that occurs immediately after a death can be intensely painful and is often characterized by behaviors that would be considered unusual in everyday life. These include sadness and crying, states of dissatisfaction and anxiety, preoccupation with thoughts and memories of the deceased person, and difficulty concentrating.[22] Second, the transition from uncomplicated to integrated grief usually begins within the first few months of the death when the emotional wounds begin to heal and the bereaved person finds his or her way back to a fulfilling life or normality. However, unresolved grief, the subject of my chapter, results from the failure to transition from uncomplicated to integrated grief.[23] As a result, unresolved grief is prolonged, perhaps indefinitely. Symptoms include separation distress, recurrent pangs of painful emotions, intense yearning for the deceased, and traumatic distress.[24]

In this regard, unresolved grief can leave Sāmoan children vulnerable to joining gangs. My investigation of the links between trauma, memory, and delinquency therefore becomes more salient when considering the life histories of young people.[25] Moreover, young people often use their gang membership as a coping strategy for negative emotions such as anger, frustration, and anxiety. When they think repetitively about something that has caused them distress, the gang also becomes an important means of emotional support and encouragement.[26] For Syn, VDK, Young D, and Nero, they carried unresolved grief into their gang and then accumulated other traumatic experiences, such as having to constantly prove oneself to the gang by way of fights. In turn, such violence desensitized these gang members and toughened them, making them feel impervious and apathetic. Thus, I trace each life history to understand how some Sāmoan boys, teenagers, and young adults come together, find comfort in their solidarity, and cope with unresolved grief.

Syn, a road worker, is in his early twenties, lives with his girlfriend in their own place, and is the oldest of the four participants. He and his siblings were separated from their biological parents when he was a child, and he was raised by his grandparents. VDK is the youngest Sāmoan participant in my study. He is sixteen years old and six feet tall. He lives with a stepbrother and attends a local high school. He was adopted as a baby and was raised by foster parents in a large family household where he had seven stepsiblings in their early twenties. He was very close to his foster mother and was spoiled by his older siblings when he was a child. Young D is seventeen years old and lives with his parents and siblings. He also is a casual part-timer for his parent's catering business and is the youngest child in his family. He looks up to his older sister and his fellow gang members (especially the older ones) rather than his parents. The fourth Sāmoan youth, Nero, at the time of the interview, was one month away from turning twenty years old. He is the oldest sibling in his family. He lives with his parents and was on home detention when I met him. Nero is really close to his younger brother and always looks out for him and tries to keep his brother from being interested in gangs.

SĀMOAN YOUTH EXPERIENCES AND PERSPECTIVES OF UNRESOLVED GRIEF

A common denominator running through each of the participants' life histories is unresolved grief. They also remembered someone close to them who died in their gang. The first account of unresolved grief in Syn's life history was the passing of his biological mother. Born in New Zealand, he recalled how he traveled with his mother from Australia to Sāmoa. He was left behind with his grandparents while his mother returned to Australia. Syn was also separated from his younger siblings and was raised in a country and family he was not familiar with. He felt abandoned and missed his mother greatly. Over time, Syn adjusted to his new life in Sāmoa, but he still yearned for his mother. When he was a teenager, he then learned that his mother passed away, and he never got over it. Given the life challenges that he faced, what is noteworthy is Syn's comment about his mother. If she was still alive, he said, she would have ensured that Syn kept away from gangs. The following exchange with Syn highlights his unresolved grief:

> SYN: When my mom passed away, I was five, cos she was sick aye, she came over from Australia and I stayed at Sāmoa with my

grandma. My mom was sick cos she had cancer so she came over to the islands just to do those fofos (therapeutic massage) and did that island medicine cos she was in pain and she couldn't like speak and she couldn't walk, but she was pretty young too, my mom was like in her forties going to fifties when she passed away . . .

MOSES: I wonder what you could have been feeling that day.

SYN: I knew it was going to happen . . . I just went to sleep that night and dreamt that there were heaps of cars in front of our house at the islands (Sāmoan Islands) and then that's all I remember was seeing a funeral car. I woke up and ran straight to my mom in the sitting room and she was all covered up. But yeah I knew it was going to happen cos the day before the whole family decided to turn take her IV off yeah cos she was on it for ages at home but before it happened she wanted all her sisters there and everyone just said their goodbyes to her and stuff and then they took that IV off and then next day she was, she left.

MOSES: But you got to experience the first five years of your life with her?

SYN: Not really that's why I wasn't really feeling the pain because my grandma wanted me so my grandma took me, I was born here (New Zealand) and we went over to Australia just me and my parents and then after that she got sick so we went over to the islands and then she went back to Australia and I stayed at the islands, there was three of us, I'm the oldest, and my bro and sis went to Australia with my parents.

MOSES: So your grandma became the mom?

SYN: Yeah I was the only child cos they (younger siblings) were all born in Australia; I didn't regret it though when my parents left me with my grandmother. One of my aunties went to Australia and stayed with my mom to look after her and then cos I didn't know anything back then but I think that's when something went down with um with her and my old man cos they split up coz of my aunty but my mom and dad split before my mom died.

MOSES: So do you think it affected you when you were a kid?

SYN: I reckon it still affects me now though cos I know if my mom was still alive I wouldn't be like this; it would've been a better

life for me cos the life that I'm living right now is just it's not a
life aye.

MOSES: And your father has never tried to make contact with you
since?

SYN: Nah, the stink thing is that I can't remember what he looks
like aye; I don't even have a photo.

It is clear from Syn's account that the gang he joined substituted for many things missing in his life growing up. Syn felt abandoned and lonely. His mother left him in Sāmoa, and he was separated from his siblings. He found out as he grew older probably from his grandparents that his mother was dying of cancer and that his parents split up because his father had an affair with his mother's sister. He didn't even know who his father was. Given these experiences, joining PBS made sense for Syn at the time, especially since they offered a sense of belonging. He also sought counsel from the older, like-minded Sāmoan members as if they were his elder brothers, if not father figures. PBS was not a typical gang.

VDK also lost his mom at a young age. In our conversation, he explored his grief, not knowing how to find forgiveness due to his previous actions that hurt his mom and wider family. Not being able to resolve his grief was a significant developmental challenge for VDK, whose self-blame had manifested as low self-esteem and depression. By speaking about losing his mom, he attempted to reconcile his feelings. I asked VDK about his (step)-mother's passing:

VDK: . . . when my mom passed away she had a stroke and I was
eleven . . . I was sleeping with my mom and dad in the garage
and there was something wrong with her she told me to go and
get my sister to massage her head and I went but I got distracted
and ended up watching TV so I forgot about it and then later I
went to get my bag in the garage and my mom was sleeping I
tried to wake her up cos she was sleeping in the toilet so I just
started crying and then I ran into the house and told my sister.
She came and then rang the ambulance cos she was still alive
but I think three weeks later she just passed away. [so very sad]

MOSES: How do you feel about that?

VDK: (long pause—silence) . . . feel stink cos it feels different with
her not at home.

MOSES: Did you blame yourself?

VDK: Yeah.

MOSES: Cos your mom was still alive for three weeks did you talk to her about it?

VDK: Yeah.

MOSES: You told her sorry?

VDK: I was pretty much crying but couldn't say anything cos she had an operation . . . she doesn't know anything like after her operation she didn't know us like the doctor said it'll take time for her to remember us like she didn't remember my dad's name and that, but I said sorry to her and I held her hand.

MOSES: Did you feel better after that?

VDK: Nah.

MOSES: Why not?

VDK: Cos she was still sick.

MOSES: To this day are you still hurting over it?

VDK: Just trying to forget about it.

MOSES: When was the last time you were hurting?

VDK: Probably last year.

MOSES: Need to let that go.

VDK: It feels different cos she was the only one that trusted me cos when there was money stolen that I stole she was the one that like nah he wouldn't steal it and stopped my brother and them from giving me a hiding but when she told me to do something and I didn't even listen . . . (tearful).

MOSES: But that's in the past now you need to let that go.

VDK: (Long pause . . . silence)

VDK's account is sad because one never knows when a friend or relative will depart. Many of us take life for granted. Like VDK, we often believe that those who love us will be around forever. In fact, he received much attention from his foster mother because an eleven-year age difference existed between his stepsiblings, all of whom did not develop a close relationship with him. VDK joined a gang, RA, which accepted him because of his height and intimidating features. But for VDK, the gang offered a place to address his self-blame and to meet other members who were like him. His life history of failing to do what his mother asked of him and preferring to watch television instead, a delayed response that led to his mother's coma and death, was laid bare to other gang members. They, too, shared similar pains, thus comforting and normalizing VDK's anxieties.

As with VDK's fond recollection of his mother, Young D's account of unresolved grief shows that even the toughest gang members can be emotionally hurt. Young D's life history demonstrated the difficulty of moving on because of regret and dejection. Sharing his memory of losing his grandfather caused him great discomfort. Like Syn, Young D's life history revealed multiple situations that cumulatively led to negative aspects of unresolved grief. These included not receiving further help from the hospital when his grandfather was dying, waiting on his loved one to pass, and not fulfilling his grandfather's dying wish. These events challenged mourners like Young D to function well with his family and others in Auckland. When I asked Young D about a negative childhood memory, he had this to say:

> YOUNG D: Think primary school days, a long time ago, my
>   grandpa he was dying and the hospital couldn't do anything
>   about it, so they just brought him home just to wait on his last
>   day. Our whole family was there and um my grandma asked
>   him what did he want to see before he goes (dies) and he said ah
>   to see me play rugby again, so that's why I want to play rugby
>   aye.
> MOSES: Your grandfather's still waiting for you to do that aye uso
>   (brother), he's basically up there in heaven going "when you're
>   ready son."
> YOUNG D: (silent and looking down)
> MOSES: You're going to make it happen ah uso?
> YOUNG D: (silent)
> MOSES: You really loved your grandfather aye?
> YOUNG D: (silent—teary eyed)
> MOSES: So that was a really important and a really exciting period
>   in your life aye?
> YOUNG D: (silent)
> MOSES: So every time you touch and you run that rugby ball up
>   aye you're thinking of your grandpa?
> YOUNG D: (crying)
> MOSES: Yeah bro think it's time aye, its time bro to let go, you've
>   achieved what your grandfather wanted: you were made captain
>   of an Auckland team, your rugby team went up there and won
>   the tournament, and those are one of the best days of your life.
> YOUNG D: (crying)

It took a few hours before Young D and I were able to continue our interview. He then related how his parents were too busy with the family catering business, and seldom did either give him any attention. According to Young D, his other sibling, an older sister, also did not care much about him. His grandfather was the only one who was there for him. When his grandfather departed, his group of friends became central in his life even though they were a gang. In fact, Syn introduced him to the PBS gang, and Young D joined. There was no initiation ritual. Syn became Young D's role model and counselor. Syn then channeled Young D's temper and grief through the punching of a body bag and through the teaching of self-control. Syn also taught Young D how to speak Sāmoan and aligned his lessons about discipline and love with fa'a Sāmoa. Young D felt that by learning more about his Sāmoan cultural identity he could be closer to his grandfather.

The final narrative of unresolved grief comes from Nero, whose painful reflections included feelings of worthlessness, self-blame, and multiple losses. Multiple losses can hinder the normal grieving process because those who experience them are overwhelmed from dealing with another death on top of the first. In Nero's case, he lost two younger brothers. He was still hurting and blaming himself for their deaths. One died in Sāmoa the day after White Sunday; this religious observation falls on a Sunday in October when children, young people, and teachers lead the worship activities. The other died in New Zealand while Nero was sleeping next to him. Nero claimed that if both his brothers were still alive, he would not have joined a gang. He would have had three brothers, and there would be no need to befriend other teenagers. Hence, the dialogue below reveals the significant difficulties Negro faced in grieving the loss of his two siblings as well as provides key lessons for professionals, social services, and policymakers who work with children.

MOSES: How do you feel about you, you know, you're telling me all this stuff? You know all this stuff starts bringing back memories now aye?

NERO: Yeah hard. It's like just good to talk to someone aye.

MOSES: Let it all out right?

NERO: Yeah hard and it's like . . . just different aye I never talked to anyone about all the stuff we get up to or we just get up to it and then not talk about it aye, and maybe that's why like we hold too much stuff in us.

MOSES: Do you have a childhood memory that still hurts? That you're carrying around.

NERO: Ah it's my little brother dying aye, yeah bro, he was four years old my first brother and passed away and I was about nine and we left Sāmoa because of that.

MOSES: How did he die?

NERO: Um meningococcal meningitis but they (the parents) were saying it was a ma'i (sickness) Sāmoa cos he died right after White Sunday, on the Monday . . . but yeah it just sucks losing someone, looking back now it still hurts me now when thinking back like what we would've been like if he was still here, like I see all of my other mates and I see them with all their brothers and that.

MOSES: Tell me about this hurt, what are you feeling when you're hurting, what do you feel?

NERO: I would've had like my gang you know my brothers and I would've probably lived another life cos if they're around I'll be like concentrating on them aye and like I'll be talking to them more than spending it and being in a gang. We would've had something better than what I'm doing now if he was still around, cos even my other little brother when he died here that just brought back pain for me in NZ.

MOSES: And how old was he when he died bro?

NERO: He was only like; he was only a toddler or maybe a baby. He was like, probably like four months old and seven weeks and my other brother who died in Sāmoa he was four years old and seven months, hard aye you know just thinking about it. (long pause)

MOSES: So you've had two brothers die aye bro?

NERO: Yeah hard.

MOSES: And have you had a chance to get over it man?

NERO: Actually I haven't talked to anyone about it.

MOSES: Is this the first time you've mentioned it?

NERO: Yeah and when my brother died here, I just got home too from the hood like I was and then my mom told me to look after him they were going to do a feau (run an errand) and I was like I haven't had sleep for ages so I was tired so I lay him next to me and then I just fell asleep next minute thing I remember I woke up my mom was trying to wake him up eh and they wouldn't tell me what happened . . . (long pause) . . . he died from cot death aye.

MOSES: Did you blame yourself bro?

NERO: Yeah hard, I was blaming myself, I still am blaming myself for that, nah it was me fuck if I had looked after my little baby brother properly he'd still be here if I wasn't out in the hood he'd still be here.

MOSES: I hope that one day you'll get over it cos it's probably one of those things you need to unlock and get over it soon or else it's going to eat away at you but you probably heard this all before aye from social workers and counselors.

NERO: I never told any of my social workers . . . (long pause, then starts crying).

Although Nero mentioned that if his brothers were alive, he would not have joined a gang, there were other moments when his social workers could have prevented him from joining a gang. At the time, Nero participated in the RA, one of the most notorious Bloods in Auckland, which led him to be on home detention and on court-imposed twenty-four-hour supervision. As he revealed, no social service professionals identified the unresolved grief he carried. Instead, he shared his grief and pain with me because I resembled his peers, that is, Sāmoan, male, relatable, and trustworthy. It was unfortunate that he joined the RAs, a gang often featured in national news for high-profile crimes. Sāmoan young people like Nero managed their unresolved grief by misusing substances and committing thefts, among other acts.

RESOLVING UNRESOLVED GRIEF: OBSERVATIONS AND RECOMMENDATIONS

What can we make of the unresolved grief of Syn, VDK, Young D, and Nero? We can begin with their similar and different forms of grief. For instance, the life histories about the passing of VDK's foster mother and Young D's grandfather showed how their elders lovingly raised them as if they were their actual sons. Indeed, they all experienced losing someone close to them. Syn dreamt of the impending death of his loved one; comparably, VDK's mother asked him to do something for him, but he stopped to watch television, and when he returned, she had died. Young D also witnessed his grandfather die on his bed in his family home. Nero was supposed to look after his baby brother but fell asleep, only to be awoken by his mother to discover the lifeless body of his younger sibling next to him. A crucial part of their unresolved pain is that these young men did not know how to forgive themselves. Were any of them at fault? Syn's mother passed away from cancer, VDK's stepmother died from a stroke, Young D's grandfather passed away from old age, and Nero's sibling in New Zealand died from Sudden Infant Death Syndrome. None of them are to blame. Yet they resorted to self-blame as a way to cope.

However, various differences also existed between them. Although it was not referred to by VDK, Young D, and Nero, Syn's account raised the issue of abandonment and how he was separated from his younger siblings and raised like an only child by extended family members. The death of his mother certainly intensified this feeling of abandonment. Young D also felt abandoned by the hospital that did not do much for his grandfather and caused undue stress for him. Futility and failure also arose in Nero's situation, but this young man experienced the loss of two close family members, whereas Syn, VDK, and Young D did not.

As illustrated in all four life histories, none of the gang members revealed how they and their families dealt with the loss of a loved one. Their Sāmoan families did not show them how to mourn, let alone explain why their loved ones died (especially at the time of the death), irrespective of the age of the youth. Without this guidance, children who witness death for the first time experience a life-changing event. Syn and Nero both claimed that if their loved ones had not died, they would not be gang members, while VDK still feels he is the reason why his mother died. And Young D is saddened that he did not have an opportunity to prove himself to his grandfather before he passed away. It also clear that these gang members did not fully grasp what death meant when they were children. Had their grief been addressed by their Sāmoan relatives, the gang members may have better managed their emotional loss and pain.

Based on this research, I offer three lessons for parents and professionals in Aotearoa New Zealand, Sāmoa, Oceania, and elsewhere. First, listen to young people and give them a chance to speak. This can be done by encouraging them to trust you without judging them and talking over them. It is vital that young people can turn to their parents and/or professionals for advice and guidance instead of turning to others who may not necessarily have the experience or expertise to address unresolved grief. The death of a loved one should be discussed openly and explored among family members as soon as possible. Children and young people should know what death is and why a death has occurred.[27]

Second, make space to talk about how the young person identified herself or himself with the deceased person in an appropriate manner. That is, the situation surrounding the deceased person should also be discussed so the young person does not dwell on feelings of regret and disappointment. Such conversations help them find ways to "let go," a refrain often compassionately shared by me and the Sāmoan youth in my study. The young person should also be informed of the funeral processes, what rituals will occur (e.g., what happens with the coffin and why adults often wail). Encourage, as well, the young person to write a letter to the deceased and to keep pictures of their happy times and places. Also, discuss when a cemetery visit might be planned, take the young person with you, and read the gravestone to them so they understand the meaning and remember their loved one. Otherwise, they will be "still feeling it," meaning their grief will be internalized and become unresolved.

Third, once children and young people know how to better cope with their grief, they should use their experiences to address other kinds of traumatic events. However, if they did not receive this support, they may be unable to deal with the loss of a loved one. Furthermore, they may not fully understand the breakdown of a personal relationship, surviving a motor vehicle accident, or receiving rejections after being interviewed for paid work opportunities due to a criminal record.[28] By addressing these recommendations, parents, families, and professionals can then be the first point of contact for emotional support and relief.

CONCLUDING REMARKS

Because grieving over the loss of a loved one can either be a successful transition to acceptance and forgiveness or not, it is difficult to gauge how Sāmoan young people fare. Growing up with rapid urban changes in ethnoburbs only adds to their existing pain, as with the Sāmoan youth gang members examined in this chapter. Nevertheless, I found that their accounts of unresolved grief and associated traumas reflected their survival skills, demonstrated how they managed conflict, and showed how they negotiated adversities. They may be "still feeling it"—that is, the hurt associated with losing a loved one—but they have begun to endure their loss, control the strains of other trauma, and build resoluteness and resiliency. As I have shown, Syn, VDK, Young D, and Nero also humbly taught me how their life histories can be therapeutic. If Aotearoa and other countries in Oceania and elsewhere around the world take the time to get to know these Sāmoan gang-involved young people, they will discover that they are admirable, inspirational, and intelligent. They are courageous, warrior-like Sāmoan males not because they are gang members but because they are like us. They are not criminal subcultures and deviant delinquents. They are survivors!

NOTES

1 Quinn, Katherine, Maria L. Pacella, Julia Dickson-Gomez, and Liesl A. Nydegger, "Childhood Adversity and the Continued Exposure to Trauma and Violence among Adolescent Gang Members," *American Journal of Community Psychology* 59, nos. 1–2 (2017): 36–49, https://doi.org/10.1002/ajcp.12123.

2 The term *Pasifika* originated in New Zealand to distinguish between two populations. One collective, known as Pacific peoples, was born in Oceania and migrated from their homelands to New Zealand to start a new life. The other group, Pasifika peoples, are the New Zealand–born children of Pacific peoples. Hence, the term *Pasifika* denotes New Zealand–born peoples, whereas the term *Pacific* refers to those born outside of New Zealand.

3 John Ryks, Amber L. Pearson, and Andrew Waa, "Mapping Urban Māori: A Population-Based Study of Māori Heterogeneity," *New Zealand Geographer* 72, no. 1 (2016): 28–40, https://doi.org/10.1111/nzg.12113.

4 Tahu Kukutai, "The Structure of Urban Māori Identities," in *Indigenous in the City: Contemporary Identities and Cultural Innovation*, ed. Evelyn Peters and Chris Andersen (Vancouver: University of British Columbia Press, 2014), 311–33.

5 Statistics New Zealand, *2013 Census QuickStats about Culture and Identity* (Wellington: New Zealand Government, 2014), http://archive.stats.govt.nz /Census/2013-census/profile-and-summary-reports/quickstats-culture -identity/pacific-peoples.aspx.

6 Auckland Council, *Pacific Peoples in Auckland: Results from the 2013 Census* (Auckland: Auckland Council, 2015).

7 Cluny Macpherson, "From Pacific Islanders to Pacific People and Beyond," in *Tangata Tangata: The Changing Ethnic Contours of New Zealand*, ed. Paul Spoonley, Cluny Macpherson, and David Pearson (Southbank, Victoria: Thomson Dunmore Press, 2004), 135–56; and Patrick Ongley, "Pacific Islands Migration and the New Zealand Labour Market," in *Nga Take: Ethnic Relations and Racism in Aotearoa/New Zealand*, ed. Paul Spoonley, David Pearson, Cluny Macpherson (Palmerston North, New Zealand: Dunmore Press, 1991), 17–36.

8 Sefita Hao'uli, "We Didn't Come to Hongi Māori," *Mana* 11 (Summer 1996): 38–39; and Tracey McIntosh, "Hibiscus in the Flax Bush: The Māori-Pacific Island Interface," in *Tangata o te moana nui: The Evolving Identities of Pacific Peoples in Aotearoa/New Zealand*, ed. Cluny Macpherson, Paul Spoonley, and Melani Anae (Palmerston North, New Zealand: Dunmore Press, 2001), 141–54.

9   Tapu Misa, "A Migrant Story," *Mana* 10 (1995): 14–17; and McIntosh, "Hibiscus in the Flax Bush."

10 Teresia Teaiwa and Sean Mallon, "Ambivalent Kinships? Pacific People in New Zealand," *In New Zealand Identities: Departures and Destinations*, ed. James H. Liu, Tim McCreanor, Tracey McIntosh, and Teresia Teaiwa (Wellington: Victoria University Press, 2005), 207–29.

11 Richard S. Hill, "Fitting Multiculturalism into Biculturalism: Māori-Pasifika Relations in New Zealand from the 1960s," *Ethnohistory* 57, no. 2 (2010): 291–319, https://doi.org/10.1215/00141801-2009-064.

12 Vasantha Krishnan, Penelope Schoeffel, and Julie Warren, *The Challenge of Change: Pacific Island Communities in New Zealand, 1986–1993* (Christchurch: Institute for Social Research and Development Limited, 1994); and Sarah Wright and Andrew Hornblow, "Emerging Needs, Evolving Services: The Health of Pacific Peoples in New Zealand," *Kotuitui: New Zealand Journal of Social Sciences Online* 3, no. 1 (2008): 21–33, https://doi.org/10.1080/1177083X .2008.9522430.

13 Melani Anae, *The Polynesian Panthers, 1971–1974: The Crucible Years* (Auckland: Reed Publishers, 2006).

14 Rāwiri Taonui and Greg Newbold, "Staunch: Māori Gangs in Urban New Zealand," in *Urban Social Capital: Civil Society and City Life*, ed. Joseph D. Lewandowski and Gregory W. Streich (Farnham, Surrey, UK: Ashgate, 2012), 159–76.

15 *Colors*, directed by Dennis Hopper (Los Angeles: Orion Pictures Production, 1988).

16 Erin J. Eggleston, "New Zealand Youth Gangs: Key Findings and Recommendations from an Urban Ethnography," *Social Policy Journal of New Zealand* 14 (2000): 148–63, www.msd.govt.nz/about-msd-and-our-work/publications -resources/journals-and-magazines/social-policy-journal/spj14/nz-youth -gangs-urban-ethnography.html.

17 Ministry of Social Development, *From Wannabes to Youth Offenders: Youth Gangs in Counties Manukau, Research Report* (Wellington: New Zealand Ministry of Social Development, 2006).

18 An "ethnoburb" is a suburban ethnic cluster of residential areas and business districts in a large metropolitan area that is a multiracial, multi-ethnic, and multicultural community where there is a large concentration of one ethnic minority but not the majority of the total population. See Wei Li, "Introduction: Asian Immigration and Community in the Pacific Rim," in *From Urban Enclave to Ethnic Suburb: New Asian Communities in Pacific Rim Countries*, ed. Wei Li (Honolulu: University of Hawai'i Press, 2006), 1–22.

19 Greg Newbold and Rāwiri Taonui, "Gangs—Māori Gangs and Pacific Youth Gangs," *Te Ara: The Encyclopedia of New Zealand*, accessed January 5, 2019, https://teara.govt.nz/en/gangs/page-3.

20 Moses Ma'alo Faleolo, "From the Street to the Village: The Transfer of NZ Youth Gang Culture to Sāmoa," *New Zealand Sociology* 31, no. 2 (2016): 48–73. Refer, as well, to Katherine Irwin and Karen Umemoto, *Jacked Up and Unjust:*

Pacific Islander Teens Confront Violent Legacies (Oakland: University of California Press, 2016).

21 Nina R. Jakoby, "Grief as a Social Emotion: Theoretical Perspectives," *Death Studies* 36, no. 8 (2012): 679–711, https://doi.org/10.1080/07481187.2011.584013; and Mark D. Miller, "Complicated Grief in Late Life," *Dialogues in Clinical Neuroscience* 14, no. 2 (2012): 195–202, www.ncbi.nlm.nih.gov/pmc/articles/PMC3384448.

22 Michelle Y. Pearlman, Karen D'Angelo Schwalbe, and Marylène Cloitre, eds., *Grief in Childhood: Fundamentals of Treatment in Clinical Practice* (Washington, DC: American Psychological Association, 2010); and Marion Katherine Shear and Elizabeth Mulhare, "Complicated Grief," *Psychiatric Annals* 38, no. 10 (2008): 662–70, https://doi.org/10.3928/00485713-20081001-10.

23 Holly B. Herberman Mash, Carol S. Fullerton, and Robert J. Ursano, "Complicated Grief and Bereavement in Young Adults Following Close Friend and Sibling Loss," *Depression and Anxiety* 30, no. 12 (2013): 1202–10, https://doi.org/10.1002/da.22068; and Alexander H. Jordan and Brett T. Litz, "Prolonged Grief Disorder: Diagnostic, Assessment, and Treatment Considerations," *Professional Psychology: Research and Practice* 45, no. 3 (2014): 180–87, https://doi.org/10.1037/a0036836.

24 Marion Katherine Shear, "Grief and Mourning Gone Awry: Pathway and Course Complicated Grief," *Dialogues in Clinical Neuroscience* 14, no. 2 (2012): 119–28, www.ncbi.nlm.nih.gov/pmc/articles/PMC3384440; and Marion Katherine Shear and Harry N. Shair, "Attachment, Loss, and Complicated Grief," *Developmental Psychobiology* 47, no. 3 (2005): 253–67, https://doi.org/10.1002/dev.20091.

25 Karen Treisman, *Working with Relational and Developmental Trauma in Children and Adolescents* (London: Routledge, 2016).

26 Terence P. Thornberry and Marvin D. Krohn, "The Development of Delinquency: An Interactional Perspective," in *Handbook of Youth and Justice*, ed. Susan O. White (New York: Plenum, 2001), 289–305, https://doi.org/10.1007/978-1-4615-1289-9_15; and Terence P. Thornberry, Marvin D. Krohn, Alan J. Lizotte, Carolyn A. Smith, and Kimberly Tobin, *Gangs and Delinquency in Developmental Perspective* (Cambridge: Cambridge University Press, 2003).

27 Byron Seiuli, "Uputaua: A Therapeutic Approach to Researching Sāmoan Communities," in "Ignored No Longer: Emerging Indigenous Researchers on Indigenous Psychologies," special issue, *Australian Community Psychologist* 24, no. 1 (2012): 24–37.

28 Patricia K. Kerig, Melissa Arnzen-Moeddel, and Stephen P. Becker, "Assessing the Sensitivity and Specificity of the MAYSI-2 for Detecting Trauma among Youth in Juvenile Detention," *Child and Youth Care Forum* 40, no. 5 (2011): 345–62, https://doi.org/10.1007/s10566-010-9124-4.

CHAPTER 9

FAIKAVA

A Philosophy of Diasporic Tongan Youth,
Hip Hop, and Urban Kava Circles

ARCIA TECUN, EDMOND FEHOKO,
AND 'INOKE HAFOKA

> I was looking for my culture and kava is where I found it.
>
> —TONGAN YOUTH

WE ARE A MIX OF DIASPORIC PEOPLES WHO HAVE LIVED WITH
Tongan communities in Aotearoa New Zealand and the United States.
Arcia Tecun is Wīnak (Mayan), and Edmond Fehoko and 'Inoke Hafoka
are Tongan. For this chapter, we weave our lived experiences, which
include over fifteen years in kava circles, alongside ethnographic and qualitative research over the last decade. We draw from this background to
theorize the expanding role of kava among many Tongan youth. Specifically, we focus on the usage of kava in diaspora settings. Kava is an ancestral drink used by the Indigenous peoples of Fiji, Hawai'i, Papua, Pohnpei,
Sāmoa, Tonga, Vanuatu, and other islands of the Moana, or Pacific Ocean.[1]
Kava traverses social, political, and religious spectra as well as various
social ranks. Kava is a soporific beverage; however, the effects depend on
how much kava is infused with water, the amount consumed, and the kind
of kava being used. The faikava (to have a kava gathering) is a Tongan

practice and social space where people sit around the kumete/tānoa/tāno'a (kava bowl) imbibing kava while engaging in talanoa (relationally mindful critical oratory).[2] In the Tongan language, faikava also means "to do/make kava" or "kava drinking event," hence our appreciation of faikava as an active process of reflection and performance by its participants. As we show in this chapter, faikava facilitates community camaraderie, the nurturing of social networks and relationships (tauhi vā), storytelling, the performance of song and comedy, the transmission of relevant knowledge, and the reflection of life experiences.[3]

Faikava is a complex and diverse practice that is also stigmatized for a variety of reasons, including but not limited to the gendered dynamics within communities. One issue concerns the accusation that some married men spend more time in faikava than with their nuclear families. The scholar Afu Taufa explains that the gendered imbalance in these relations would then make some women feel "underappreciated" by their spouses.[4] Another matter regards how courtship traditions that are usually relegated to young unmarried men get entangled with married participants in a multi-generational setting. While these are important and contextually specific issues to Tongan faikava, we do not focus on them in this chapter because they primarily involve hetero-monogamy and church-state sanctioned marriage. And although we include comments from older and married men in this chapter, we recall their experiences as young unmarried persons and underscore their observations of youth participants today.

In faikava, Tongan protocols are regularly followed, such as the value of faka'apa'apa (respect), which often upholds gendered divisions between men and women's spaces. As a result, faka'apa'apa generally restricts the presence of brother-sister relations at the same faikava circle. For this reason, combined with the Christianization of Tonga in the mid-nineteenth century and the subsequent rise of conservative religious norms, Tongan kava groups have been dominated by men in recent history. Still, ancient records indicate the existence of faikava groups for women, and today women have begun to revitalize their faikava circles.[5] Moreover, younger generations and university students increasingly apply liberal interpretations of faka'apa'apa while also becoming more multi-ethnic and gender diverse in their kava gatherings. We represent the transition into this new generation of faikava in the diaspora.

In this chapter, we focus on the most common practices we have observed of faikava and our research interests in the north island of

Aotearoa and in Utah of the United States. In this regard, we emphasize Tongan faikava by predominantly cisgender men. We also use the term *Moana* to refer to Oceanic Indigeneity and the broader Oceanic group from which Tongans genealogically align. We likewise acknowledge how related pan-ethnic identities similarly generate visibility in the diaspora, as with "Pacific Islander" and "Pasifika." Yet as People of Color (POC) in settler-colonial nations such as New Zealand and the United States, Tongans and Moana youth experience racialized visibility as nonwhite "others." As POC in the diaspora, they must therefore navigate being racially visible yet culturally unknown. This process allows them to connect with other "others," on the one hand, and yet become further marginalized as Moana people within the larger POC group, on the other. So while POC and white communities might laud and admonish young Tongan men for their perceived stereotypes of athleticism and criminality, respectively, very few would acknowledge their ha'a or kāinga (ancestral and family clans). For these reasons, we merge both POC and Moana realities to demonstrate how youth practice faikava as "spots to kick it and belong" in cities that recognize them as "races" but disavow them as distinct cultures.[6]

To begin, we contextualize the diaspora locations for kava in Aotearoa and Utah. By diaspora, we mean a spatial displacement from one's ancestral homeland and a temporal dislocation from one's ancestral knowledge. In these ways, the Tongan youth of diaspora settings often encompass dismembered identities that suffer from material and ontological violence. We thus examine how they use kava to negotiate their urban realities, musical traditions, and position as POC. Hip Hop and reggae, for instance, have long been integrated into Tongan communities. We intentionally capitalize "Hip Hop" to signal its cultural, philosophical, and spiritual significance for the young Tongans involved in our study. Similarly, in chapter 6, Jessica A. Schwartz shows how the Marshallese youth have turned to Hip Hop to acknowledge their mothers, forge identities, and protest in local festivals and geopolitical arenas against US violence. As this volume demonstrates, Tongan and Moana youth have adopted African American musical traditions in their efforts to respond to colonial oppression in the Native cities of Oceania and the wider diaspora.

Describing cities in comparable terms, the historian Kyle Mays explains that "much cultural exchange takes place within those spaces. Many Native people thrive in cities, and it allows them to expand their cultural repertoire."[7] Emphasizing the relevance of Hip Hop, Mays argues that it is "one of the most important things about the urban culture."[8] Today, Hip Hop and reggae are integral parts of many Tongans' lives whether in their ancestral homes or abroad. Like other Moana people, Tongans have learned from African American diaspora experiences and have often adopted their global expressions.[9] The problematic exploitative appropriation of African American culture and music by colonial capitalist projects can be reinforced by non-Black POC at local levels, albeit without the same power as the entertainment industry. However, many Tongan and other Moana youth connect with these musical cultures because they speak about ancestral connections, anti-colonial and anti-racist struggles, island environments, and spirituality.[10] Following this legacy, we draw from the African American rapper Tupac Amaru Shakur's "Thugz Mansion," a song filled with concepts that are readily available, relevant, and accessible to Tongan youth in urban spaces.[11] In the song, Shakur expresses that he is tired of the police chasing, shooting, and arresting the African American community and describes needing a home where he could kick it with his friends and family without the fear of being intimidated, harmed, or killed by the police. Moreover, his larger body of work, Shakurian thought, speaks to our experiences as urban men of color.[12] Mark Anthony Neal referred to Tupac as both a walking contradiction and as someone who made being an intellectual more possible for everyday people, arguing that he was what the theorist Antonio Gramsci termed an "organic intellectual."[13] We likewise respect Moana intellectuals and their publicly shared ideas that are found in their Hip Hop and reggae lyrics, which include thoughtful observations about their communities and society.[14] We also examine how faikava groups and kalapu (kava clubs) expand the traditional use of kava by opening up spaces to reveal truths that can remedy fragmented identities in the diaspora. As Fehoko has argued, faikava can be understood as a "cultural classroom" where identity is reclaimed and reinforced by way of lea (language) and ʻulungaanga fakatonga (Tongan culture).

As we show in this chapter, faikava spaces can help young Tongan men face their vulnerabilities. By engaging their fonua (heritage, land, culture) in faikava and by openly sharing experience-based ideas, reinforcing their cultural identity, they can then collapse time, space, and diaspora, binding themselves to their ancestors and ancestral homelands. Faikava, we argue, can therefore play a significant philosophical and spiritual role in the healing, mental health, and overall well-being of young Tongan men in the diaspora.[15]

DIASPORA CONTEXTS

Since the 1950s, Tongans have increasingly moved from Tonga to Aotearoa and the United States.[16] Throughout the 1960s and 1970s, these migrations yielded more established Moana communities overseas.[17] Over one-quarter of all Tongans worldwide (approximately 215,000) reside in Aotearoa, constituting the third largest Pacific ethnic group in the country.[18] Utah now houses over 43,000 Moana people, of which more than 10,000 are Tongan.[19] Tongans in these "new" nations (United States, New Zealand) now experience explicit forms of settler-colonialism premised on dominant norms of whiteness, racism, and the displacement of Indigenous peoples.[20] They thus become subjected to the governance of settlers, rather than that of local Indigenous authorities, which is reinforced by socialization in institutions such as churches and schools.[21] Additionally, they are often disciplined by the settler-colonial nation-state through incarceration, another vital topic that is explored by Kepa ʻŌkusitino Maumau, Moana ʻUluʻave-Hafoka, and Lea Lani Kinikini in chapter 2 of this volume. In this process, these "new" nations simply construct and criminalize Tongans as "dark-skinned" immigrants and minorities while simultaneously erasing their ancestral identities.

Why did Tongans travel to these settler-colonial nations in the first place? Moana Hafoka, Moana F. ʻUluʻave, and ʻInoke Hafoka suggest that Tongans migrated "primarily for educational and employment opportunities."[22] Many families emphasized education, frequently interpreted as modern Western schooling, and material security as major forces behind such migration. These experiences often lead to privileging the English language and Eurocentric systems in order to survive in them. However, many who sought a "better life" in "promised lands" often confronted inadequate access to health care, education, and employment. They also suffered from the psychological stress of assimilating to the dominant norms of an imagined whiteness. Domestic and sexual violence, suicide, and harmful drug abuse are now unfortunately common in the Kingdom of Tonga and the Tongan diaspora.[23]

According to Melenaite Taumoefolau, alienation, loneliness, and rejection increasingly inform the diasporic identities of island-born migrants and their children. In response to their oppression, Taumoefolau suggests that youth frequently "turn to the abuse of alcohol and other substances in their search for consolation."[24] For overseas Tongan youth, cultural insecurity and a loss of belonging come from multiple angles when they are not accepted by their traditional community or the dominant Western societies of settler nations. This reality is a uniform experience for the Tongan diasporic communities we have lived within and visited, although each place has its own unique nuances. As Morton argues, diasporic Tongans have begun to create their own identities in this process and within these new urban realities.[25] In their search for belonging, many Tongan youth question their spatial and temporal dislocations.

QUESTIONING THE FORCES OF DISLOCATION

Although Western education was one of the core causes of emigration, paradoxically, schooling is responsible for perpetuating the anxiety, disillusionment, and loneliness among youth.[26] There is no coincidence in the correlation between discipline, violence, schools, church, and state. From the first church-based schools in Tonga up until today, children are removed from their kaliloa (mother's arms), a form of home-based communal learning, and placed instead within the walls of a school to receive disciplined instruction.[27] The sentiments of dislocation are expressed in Shakur's music wherein he imagines the pain of poverty, depicts an education system that views African Americans as criminals, tearfully expresses suicidal ideations, and prays for improved living conditions for his dawgs and the wider African American community. Comparably, many young Tongans have shared with us that much of their Indigenous identities and knowledges are devalued in the pursuit of a "better life" through schooling.[28] However, some of these youth frequent the "cultural classroom" of faikava where relevant knowledge production takes place.

On a winter evening, during a multi-ethnic kava gathering, one such diaspora experience was discussed between a Fijian, Mayan, Sāmoan, and Tongan in the west side of the Salt Lake Valley in Utah. Sitting around a table sharing a single ipu/bilo (coconut shell) to drink our kava, which was prepared and served out of a plastic basin, Tongan millennial 'Inoke Hafoka reflected on his youth, school, and life in the Salt Lake Valley. With the reggae music of Bob Marley playing in the background, he explained the diaspora phenomenon as follows:

> What gave our parents that idea of leaving their home to go to another place? They don't understand the language, they're going to be coming in as immigrants to work the jobs that nobody else wants to work . . . they're trying to figure out, "Why is my kid not receiving the same advantages or

the same lifestyle that was promised . . . while living in this land?" My question now is, "What is considered a better life? Weren't you already living a better life in Tonga? You had a sustainable living, by living off the land, you got a nice beach, you got the ocean right there, not having to have a boss, you're your own boss."[29]

Hafoka commented further that Indigenous traditions in the diaspora have been devalued because they do not fit the pace and "convenience" of Western and capitalist values.

White, Christian, and cisgender norms similarly affect how Tongans measure their humanity.[30] Take, for instance, the matter of discipline. Helen Kavapalu explained that before Christianization, although Tongans physically punished adults, "it cannot be assumed that it was a feature of child socialization."[31] With the continued arrival of Europeans after the late 1700s, Morton Lee argued that chiefly acts of violence that asserted their power over other adults transformed into parental violence over children. Kavapalu even revealed that Christian missionaries brought corporal punishment to Tonga, imparting the idea that it was necessary and proper for the youth. Early missionaries then urged "parents to be vigilant in correcting the willful and unruly nature of children."[32] Invoking the Bible, the missionaries advised parents to use "the rod of correction" when children persistently "misbehaved," instructing parents to "beat them again until they ceased crying."[33] Many Tongan families now practice early missionary-led forms of discipline and violence.

Sāmoan Hip Hop artist Leyo Lazer critically engages these issues by rapping an intergenerational monologue within his song "Love Me." Leyo Lazer has roots in Tāmaki Makaurau, Aotearoa, and is currently based in Brisbane, Australia. This song also went "viral," meaning that Tongans and Moana people widely shared the track in online social media platforms. Many online commenters mentioned how the song rang true to the "Pasifika diaspora experience." Pitched as a monologue, the following verses describe part of a conversation between a son and his father:

FATHER: We fly across the sea to a better destination, give your
brothers and sisters a better education. But you come over here
and you do something else, why? . . . why you fight, why you do
not listen to the teachers? Why you not come to church to help
sing his praise, only bring disgrace, make me shame to show
my face, that's why I hit you, it's the only way you listen . . . You

only good at excuses and listening to that stupid music . . . I told
you, only make friends with the white kids, the kids from the
islands is only make the violence.

SON: I know what you went through, and I know where you came
from, 'cause all my life you've been singing that same song. I
don't want to sit in the can or run with a gang . . . because I give
a damn. But you just don't understand . . . I was looking for
fam, they looked at me as a man, you and mom don't agree, but
that is what I am, but you take that away callin' me all types of
names, leave me scars on my legs, and up and down my face,
then when I'm at school how can I not feel out of place . . . not
everyone is built for a life of submission, not everyone can
persevere through this sort of adversity . . . picking apart my
character isn't helping me. And the church, man, that's the last
place I wanna be, with a bunch of hypocrites in glass houses
judging me . . . you can beat me at church and no one bats an
eyelid. Have you ever thought you brought that with you from
the islands?[34]

As illustrated in the last line, newly adopted systems of punishment and
control are enforced by the infrastructures that maintain colonial and capitalist logics (e.g., church, school) in order to "civilize" the "wild," the "natural," and the "Indigenous."[35] Internalized forms of racism also exist in the
diaspora, as in the father's command, "only make friends with the white
kids, the kids from the islands is only make the violence." These conflicts
and tensions are perpetuated physically and ontologically through the
socialization of each generation in the Tongan and Moana diasporas. These
processes dislocate the youth from their ancestral roots by placing them in
a time and space of racist colonial discipline through violence. This is why
faikava groups can be important "spots to kick it and belong" for Tongan
youth. Through kava, they can merge urban experiences with Indigenous
traditions, reconnect with their lands and ancestors, and momentarily collapse the diaspora paradigms that restrict these conversations altogether.

CREATING URBAN RELATIONSHIPS AND "SPOTS TO KICK IT"

In his composition "Blood Past, Mind Present," the Aotearoa-born Sāmoan
poet Solomon Esera raps about how some Moana diasporic youth have forgotten their traditions. As a result, he calls on young people to navigate

their futures with determination, love, and urgency.[36] Across the cities of Aotearoa and the United States, Tongan youth take up this task by fusing faikava with expressions that prove relevant to them. In their faikava groups, they construct responses to Tupac Shakur's conceptualization of a "Thugz Mansion." As Shakur explains in his song, a "Thugz Mansion" is a home where his homies and family, both alive and dead, could reside in peace. Conceptualizing a world in which Black life matters, he envisions a place where his community and relations could live without fear of the police. For Tongan youth who need spots to kick it, faikava is thus reimagined to fit its context and becomes "cultural classrooms," sites of healing, and "Thugz Mansions." Faikava is transported to new urban homelands as a way to maintain or renew one's connection to ancestral fonua (land, culture) and Indigenous knowledge. As for "Thugz Mansion," this concept incorporates the alienation and racist stereotyping that Tongan youth experience in diaspora (e.g., criminal, deviant, thug). Through faikava and Hip Hop cultures, many youth actively create places of safety, wellness, and spirituality. They also collapse time and space by including the "dead homies" or ancestors who are present. Additionally, family as a core Tongan value and communal organization expands to include "homies" and other relationships made in the diaspora. The idea of a mansion also alludes to the material inequalities and struggles in settler-colonial nations. Although the historical conditions of working-class Black and Brown folks differ, they can nonetheless unite in faikava circles. That is to say, these different struggles are mediated through relationships in the neutralized space of faikava, which is known as "noa" in Tongan. Time then slows down because one becomes mindfully present of the ancestral and place-based relationships of those in attendance.[37] As a noa space, faikava allows for the acknowledgment of struggle and the cultivation of belonging through the active imagining of a "Thugz Mansion."

Take, for example, the reggae band Natural Roots of Utah, whose members come from Aotearoa and Utah. Their kava group is called House of Roots, which is like their "Thugz Mansion," their place of peace, where they mix and drink kava root and make roots music. Lead singer JanWillem van der Beek, who is Sāmoan and Dutch and originally from Aotearoa, writes their music.[38] The lyrics of the song named after their group includes, "plenty a things they won't let us do," referring to diasporic society. Additionally, this song, "House of Roots," says, "come on Mr. Music been waitin' all day for you to set me free . . . I and I go break down all the walls." In another one of their songs about kava, one of its lyrics inspired by Bob Marley states, "when it [kava] hits you, you feel no pain, just like a new song." With their invocation of reggae, Natural Roots has made a spot to kick it in their home, House of Roots, and in their musical audiences. As with Hip Hop, reggae stems from Indigenous (African and Amerindian) music traditions. With its songs of anti-colonial struggle, Tongan and other Moana youth find reggae relatable as ocean-based music. Clough writes that Bob Marley's music arrived in the shadow of "old trade routes to the Oceanic realm—where the family was waiting. In this sense reggae was not imported, it was expected."[39] As a kava club, Natural Roots has brought together reggae and urban diaspora experience to expand roots culture and music.

Tongan and pan-Moana kava groups increasingly appear wherever these communities have arrived. Aotearoa and Utah have thriving kava clubs where faikava gatherings are utilized as spaces to provide refuge for young people. A young man of Tongan ancestry from one of these groups shared that he found belonging in faikava, saying, "I was looking for my culture and kava is where I found it." Many kalapu faikava have also become alternatives for Tongan youth who avoid joining gangs.[40] In various conversations across Aotearoa and Utah, members and leaders of various kalapu in these locations have even observed decreased gang participation by oppressed urban youth. One Tongan elder expressed, "you don't see as many gangs anymore," attributing this change to an increase in youth kalapu formations and the growing number of youth participation in faikava generally. Another millennial Moana kava participant noted that kava has been used to resolve conflicts between clans in the past. Today, the person observed that "some of the OG's [Original Gangstas] have got the youngsters together around a bowl to squash beef [conflict] . . . [where] a lot of them found out how they were related to each other." The camaraderie and community that is often sought out through gang affiliation is offered instead for these youths through faikava.

HEALING WITH LAND AND STORY

Place is central to Indigenous identities as the source of life, culture, and language. Urban kava gatherings collapse the distance created by diaspora because they are physical manifestations of ancestral place. Kava is mana (potency, authority) because as a metonym of fonua (land), it is the actual land itself and therefore contains the power of place. Fonua is a complex concept of land and ocean, which means placenta, people, ancestors, and traditions. Kaimiaina Bourne is a millennial Tongan/Kanaka ʻŌiwi. He is also a member of Dox Brothers, a faikava multi-generational group that is also frequented by youth, in Kirikiriroa, Aotearoa. Sitting in a garage during a faikava one evening, Kaimiaina revealed that his kava community helps "really connect more on an intimate level with our ancestors, and I really enjoy that spiritual connection."[41] In his song "Thugz Mansion," Shakur calls upon his deceased relations to remember him while awaiting his place among them. Similarly, Tongan youth maintain connections to the lands and seas of their ancestry despite where they were born or raised, as they transport place and tradition to new spaces and times through faikava. Located in what is affectionately called Kava Lake City (Salt Lake City, Utah), Uilisoni Angilau shared that "there is a lot of oral history, had I not have been in the faikava circle, I would've never learned."[42] The Tongan language, stories, and songs learned and practiced in faikava are later performed at life events (e.g., funerals), providing participants with relevant community knowledge.

Jennifer Cattermole explains that in Fiji, as in Tonga, the "people are the lewe ni vanua (the flesh/members of the land); the human manifestation of the physical environment. The land belongs to the people, and the people belong to the land."[43] Silvia Solis also calls us to "invoke the places and lands [we] experienced through [our] youth" in order to "return to the places we call home," referring to our own bodies and our mothers as our first lands.[44] Solis speaks with a sense of urgency to heal from the violence of modern life. Indeed, going home takes on many meanings in the sharing of kava in Fiji, Tonga, and elsewhere. Imagining one's transportation to another place and time is one of the most common reasons to faikava. In this manner, when one performs what the ancestors did by singing songs about them and telling their stories in one's own ways, time is collapsed, and the past is present. One can likewise spiritually ingest manifestations of the land in the social ritual of faikava and begin to feel home in one's own body wherever one may be. By bringing the past into the present in faikava, Tongan youth adapt to urban challenges and heal through kava.

Faikava is often a site where dialogues flourish. In faikava circles, various elements of the event facilitate open and critical discussion after entering a state of noa. Talanoa is a pedagogical tool of the "cultural classroom" of faikava, which is fueled by the realities and knowledge of its participants. The Tongan "relationally mindful critical oratory" of talanoa is central in these kava settings. Talanoa is a compound word comprised of tala (to story/tell/relate) and noa (neutralized, liminal). As a process, talanoa mediates mana (power, authority, honor, potency) and tapu (sacredness, restriction, set apart). Talanoa renders that which is tapu, noa, where a balance between mana and tapu takes place; in turn, a potency intensifies through the collective alignment of people's energies (e.g., positive vibes). In order for people to enter into mindful and critical dialogue, their mana must be mediated. Without this calibration of unique energies, different standpoints, and social statuses, faikava will have limited forms of openness and understanding. Talanoa, a common component of faikava, facilitates the observing of rhythm in space and the nurturing of relationships.[45]

Tauhi vā (nurturing relational space) mediates the points between people and places and cultivates the development of skills such as social and environmental spatial awareness. For example, many young people in kava circles learn to bow and say "tulou" (excuse me) as they pass in front of someone or move in between spaces in the gathering. We suggest that tauhi vā is also expressed when people deeply reflect upon the points in between geographical spaces and ancestral times. As we have noted, the Tongan diaspora experiences in Aotearoa and the United States have restricted the youth from fully engaging with their ancestral knowledge and identity. Kava, as a transportable fonua, thereby links young people to their ancestral lands and seas, which contain the mana to heal the cultural and temporal dislocations created by diaspora. Māhina explains that Tongans perform tala-e-fonua in this manner, which is to say, through place-based connection, they speak the poetics of the land and the sea.[46]

As Moana people begin to reside in "new" lands, ancestral relationships to place are re-created in diaspora experiences. Tongans negotiate their identities in these spaces by engaging with Black and Brown Indigenous music and having a racial consciousness as POC. Rose Park–based (Utah) Tongan Hip Hop artist and a member of the H.O.G. Farm Kalapu, KIS. B shared,

> Kava just kind of takes away all of those type of labels that can separate people, I think that's another great thing about roots, mixing [faikava] . . . as far as drinking [alcohol] and smoking and stuff you know, we partied with a lot of people, but people could be really clickish, so people are always like, this is Tongan, you know, this is Sāmoans, or Mexicans are all over here . . . when you faikava, it's a peaceful feeling that brings people together, and in our kava kalapu we have Hungarian, Mexican, Asian, Tongan and Sāmoan people all together.[47]

Tongans also relate with the Indigenous people of the lands on which they now reside. For example, in several kava settings we have observed direct relationship-making with local Indigenous people in Aotearoa. For example, Māori increasingly participate in faikava, and their ancient genealogies are reconnected in talanoa, while new genealogies are also formed through intermarriages. S. Apo Aporosa and Jacinta Forde have demonstrated that despite Aotearoa's climate not being favorable for growing kava, Māori have been utilizing kava to form relationships with other Moana peoples such as Tongans and Fijians.[48] We have also observed and participated in acknowledgments given to local Māori tribes in several kava settings, further illustrating how faikava often seeks to foster harmonious relations to a place. In Utah, some youth also acknowledge the local tribes of North America in their events. And some multi-ethnic Tongans that we have had faikava with also belong to Indigenous tribes in the United States as well (e.g., Lakota, Kiowa). In the next section, we will explore Tongan masculinities and how they are negotiated and healed in faikava circles.

REPAIRING MASCULINITIES

Today, Moana masculinities are influenced by their global visibility in the arenas of rugby, American football, urban gangster life, and tourist exoticism.[49] Western imaginations construct Moana men as "naturally" physical, violent, and exotic. Yet the material and ontological struggles experienced by migrant Pacific diasporic peoples are often overlooked in these narrow and oversimplified masculine narratives.[50] Leyo Lazer raps about the accepted practice by some of these harmful Moana masculinities in his song "Love Me": "instead of seeking help for your anger we'll see it out, 'cause God forbid feelings are something you speak about." Many of our observations from our lived experiences and ethnographic research echo a narrative that Moana men do not talk openly in public, remain stoic and distant, or seldom discuss personal matters. These experiences for Tongan men in urban spaces are collapsed in many kava events. When faikava participants have a strong relational bond that is nurtured through service to one another in times of need, a willingness to share openly emerges and is facilitated through the drinking of kava. Kava has anti-anxiety properties and is a mild relaxer, which does not negatively alter mental cognition; thus, kava foregrounds cultural protocols and fosters healthy social relationships.[51]

Many younger and older men have shared that in a kava session with trusted community one can be more open and share struggle, worry, sorrow, hope, and other emotions. Kava reveals these truths by creating the potential to resolve struggles through the healing power of songs, stories, and relationships. A continual calibration of balance is always necessary, especially so as many Tongan youth continue to struggle in the diaspora. With faikava, even tapu or very sensitive subjects can be discussed if noa is established. When utilized in this way, faikava facilitates forgiveness, reconciliation, and positive well-being. This openness strengthens bonds and relationships and also creates teaching moments between generations. For example, one Fijian father shared, "Here I can talk about sex education with my boys, they usually get uncomfortable, but because I do it in the mix [faikava], we are able to talk about it." This sentiment was echoed by others in Aotearoa, including a Tongan youth who said, "My dad opens up in faikava, and I get to see the other sides of him."

Faikava settings can also neutralize social, religious, and political hierarchies so that youth can speak more directly to a minister, chief, professor, or father. In turn, their elders can also speak more openly and personally. Indeed, the homosocial aspects of faikava allow men to talk to other men about their private issues. As the Aotearoa-based Tongan Hip Hop artist Rizván explained, faikava "is like men's therapy session."[52] Rizván also shared appreciation for the growing participation of women in his kava experiences. In one occasion, an older Tongan woman in Aotearoa cautioned that although excessive participation throughout a week can be problematic for older people who are married, it is much less an issue for young single people. She also reminded us that it's important to recognize that Tongans still have different gender roles and relationships. Another Tongan millennial woman from Utah who sometimes joins faikava circles shared that "women don't have to be in every space all the time; that's a deficit view of where we are absent, which re-centers male conversation." "Instead," she continued, "we should recognize differences in power and fix that; we should be supporting where women are already at and what they are already doing." In our experiences, we found that there is a growing visibility of women's groups that are akin to the men's groups, yet youth kava groups are more diverse along gender lines than those of the older generations, with some exceptions. Additionally, and as a topic for future research, the growing participation of women and LGBTQ people in youth kava settings broadens the possibilities of gender formation and performance.

Kava circles often facilitate spaces where men speak openly and reveal themselves to one another in ways generally not found in more public spaces, where there is greater pressure to perform dominant constructs of masculinity. The power of "spots to kick it and belong" is made evident in an example of a man from Aotearoa who stated that "kava saved my life and gave me positive father figures that I was searching for." He added that "the older brothers [and father figures] made me more responsible, like challenged me to make goals, and I never had that in my life before." Unlike the racial discourses of Aotearoa and the United States that often represent young Tongan men as an "at-risk," "naturally physical," and "troubled" "race," faikava—and by extension the Black and Moana songs that accompany them—welcome Tongan values, perspectives, and identities. In this way, the youth make themselves vulnerable and, in doing so, openly talk about their traumas, reconnect with their ancestors, and strengthen their social bonds and relationships. Faikava spaces thus allow men to re-imagine themselves and their masculinities.

CONCLUSION

The struggles of Tongan and Moana diasporic youth are linked to systems of power that cannot be isolated to individual issues alone. These struggles include material poverty and dislocated identities in time and space, which increase a necessity for autonomous youth spaces. In our philosophy of faikava, Hip Hop, and diasporic youth, we have demonstrated that faikava circles can nurture Tongan youth identities in the cities of Aotearoa and the United States. For many youth, the "cultural classrooms" of faikava manifest as Tupac Amaru Shakur's conceptualization of "Thugz Mansion." They are spaces for belonging, meaningful relationships, stress release, communal cohesion, reverence, and healing. As Shakur theorized, "Thugz Mansion" is a physical and metaphysical place where we live with the people we cherish, including those who have passed away. In this manner, youth identify material, Indigenous, and racial struggles in the diaspora and imagine and create possibilities elsewhere and otherwise. Faikava that are rich in talanoa especially have the potential to heal and re-imagine dominant masculinities in the diaspora. Faikava collapses time, space, and diaspora as spots where young Tongans and their "homies" can "kick it," learn, heal, and begin to create autonomous futures.

NOTES

We thank Keith L. Camacho, Albert Refiti, Kirsten Zemke, Nitasha Sharma, Demiliza Saramosing, Heather Louise Hernandez, and Ata Siulua for their critical readings and editing of this chapter.

1   Vincent Lebot, Mark Merlin, and Lamont Lindstrom, *Kava: The Pacific Elixir: The Definitive Guide to Its Ethnobotany, History, and Chemistry* (Rochester, VT: Healing Arts Press, 1997).

2   Arcia Tecun, 'Inoke Hafoka, Lavinia 'Ulu'ave, and Moana 'Ulu'ave-Hafoka, "Talanoa: Tongan Epistemology and Indigenous Research Method," *AlterNative: An International Journal of Indigenous Peoples* 14, no. 2 (2018): 156–63. We also define talanoa as the co-production of knowledge between interlocutors. Such knowledge can be referenced in academic literature, as with interviews. But because talanoa requires its participants to meditate about ancestral prestige, people, and places in their sharing of gifts, food, and kava, talanoa does not follow the conventional forms of ethnographic research.

3   Refer to Adrian Viliami Bell and Daniel Hernandez, "Cooperative Learning Groups and the Evolution of Human Adaptability: (Another Reason) Why Hermits Are Rare in Tonga and Elsewhere," *Human Nature* 28, no. 1 (2017): 1–15; Edmond S. Fehoko, "Pukepuke Fonua: An Exploratory Study on the Faikava as an Identity Marker for New Zealand–Born Tongan Males in Auckland, New Zealand" (master's thesis, Auckland University of Technology, 2014); and Arcia Tecun (Daniel Hernandez), "Tongan Kava: Performance, Adaptation, and Identity in Diaspora," *Performance of the Real E-journal* 1, no. 1 (2017): 52–64.

4   Afu Taufa, "Her Side of the Story: Exploring the Effects of Heavy Kava Use Based on the Perspective of Tongan Women Residing in Auckland, New Zealand" (master's thesis, University of Auckland, 2014), 159.

5   Daniel Hernandez, "Rootz Vaka Transits: Traversing Seas of Urban Diasporic Indigeneity by Collapsing Time and Space with the Songs and Stories of the Kava Canoe" (PhD diss., University of Auckland, 2019).

6   2Pac (Tupac Shakur), "Thugz Mansion," disc 2, track 2, on *Better Dayz*, Amaru, 2002, compact disc.

7   Kyle T. Mays, *Hip Hop Beats, Indigenous Rhymes: Modernity and Hip Hop in Indigenous North America* (New York: State University of New York Press, 2018), 3.

8   Mays, *Hip Hop Beats*, 3.

9   Kirsten Zemke-White, "Nesian Styles (Re)present R'n'B: The Appropriation, Transformation and Realization of Contemporary R'n'B with Hip Hop by Urban Pasifika Groups in Aotearoa," *Sites: A Journal of Social Anthropology and Cultural Studies* 2, no. 1 (2005): 94–123.

10 Robbie Shilliam, *The Black Pacific: Anti-colonial Struggles and Oceanic Connections* (London: Bloomsbury Publishing, 2015).

11 Isidoro Guzman and Rob Unzueta II, "2Pac and the Role His Work Played in the Critical Development of Men of Color Activist Scholars in Their Efforts to

Create 'Thug Mansion'" (paper presented at the Tupac Amaru Shakur
Collection Conference: Hip Hop Education and Expanding the Archival
Imagination, Atlanta, GA, September 2012), https://radar.auctr.edu/islandora
/object/auc.169%3A0020.

12 Michael Eric Dyson, *Holler If You Hear Me: Searching for Tupac Shakur* (New
York: Basic Civitas Books, 2001).

13 Ken Gewertz, "Symposium Analyzes, Celebrates 'Thug': Legendary Tupac
Shakur Looked at as Cultural Artifact, Force," *Harvard Gazette*, April 24,
2003, https://news.harvard.edu/gazette/story/2003/04/symposium-analyzes
-celebrates-thug.

14 Ibram Kendi, "Dr. Ibram Kendi Commencement Speech," YouTube video,
15:32, posted by "University of Florida," August 22, 2017, www.youtube.com
/watch?v=bTIho5SFDu8.

15 Derek M. Griffith, Katie Gunter, and Daphne C. Watkins, "Measuring
Masculinity in Research on Men of Color: Findings and Future Directions,"
American Journal of Public Health 102, no. S2 (2012): S187–S194.

16 Cathy A. Small, *Voyages: From Tongan Villages to American Suburbs*, 2nd ed.
(Ithaca, NY: Cornell University Press, 2011).

17 Sean Mallon, Kolokesa Māhina-Tuai, and Damon Salesa, eds., *Tangata o le
Moana: New Zealand and the People of the Pacific* (Wellington: Te Papa
Tongarewa, Museum of New Zealand, 2012).

18 New Zealand Census, "2013 Census Ethnic Group Profiles: Tongan," *Stats NZ:
Tatauranga Aotearoa*, 2013, accessed June 9, 2020, http://archive.stats.govt.nz
/Census/2013-census/profile-and-summary-reports/ethnic-profiles.aspx
?request_value=24711&tabname=Populationandgeography#gsc.tab=0; and
"Tongans—Migrations," *Te Ara: The Encyclopedia of New Zealand*, accessed
June 28, 2018, https://teara.govt.nz/en/tongans/page-1.

19 US Census Bureau, "2016 Population Estimates: Utah," https://data.census.gov
/cedsci/all?q=utah&g=0400000US49; and Carol Edison, "South Sea Islanders
in Utah," *Utah History Encyclopedia*, accessed June 9, 2020, www.uen.org/utah
_history_encyclopedia/s/SOUTH_SEA_ISLANDERS_IN_UTAH.shtml.

20 Dolores Calderón, "Moving from Damage-Centered Research through
Unsettling Reflexivity," *Anthropology and Education Quarterly* 47, no. 1 (2016):
5–24.

21 Kehaulani Vaughn, "Sovereign Embodiment: Native Hawaiian Expressions of
Kuleana in the Diaspora" (PhD diss., University of California, Riverside,
2017).

22 Moana Hafoka, Moana F. 'Uluʻave, and 'Inoke Hafoka, "Double Bind: The
Duality of Tongan American Identity," in *Transnational Pacific Islander
Americans and Social Work: Dancing to the Beat of a Different Drum*, ed.
Halaevalu F. O. Vakalahi and Meripa Taiai Godinet (Washington, DC: NASW
Press, 2014), 127–38.

23 Kalafi Moala, "Sexual Assault Crimes on the Rise in Tonga," *Taimi o Tonga*,
March 21, 2016, http://taimiotonga.net/sexual-assault-crimes-on-the-rise-in
-tonga; Helen Morton Lee, *Becoming Tongan: An Ethnography of Childhood*

(Honolulu: University of Hawai'i Press, 1996); Helen Morton Lee, *Tongans Overseas: Between Two Shores* (Honolulu: University of Hawai'i Press, 2003); Veanna Pau'u, Line Tukuafu, and Rugby Latu, "Tapu, Giving a Voice to a Culture of Silence," *Tapu* podcast, May 18, 2018, https://anchor.fm/tapu/episodes/Welcome-to-Tapu-e1gcfo; Jemaima Tiatia-Seath, Roy Lay-Yee, and Martin Von Randow, "Morbidity from Intentional Self-Harm among Pacific Peoples in New Zealand, 1996–2015," *New Zealand Medical Journal* 130, no. 1467 (2017): 23–31; and Katherine Irwin and Karen Umemoto, *Jacked Up and Unjust: Pacific Islander Teens Confront Violent Legacies* (Oakland: University of California Press, 2016).

24 Melenaite Taumoefolau, "Respect, Solidarity, and Resilience in Pacific Worldviews: A Counseling Perspective," in *Pacific Identities and Well-Being: Cross-Cultural Perspectives*, ed. Margaret Nelson Agee, Tracey McIntosh, Philip Culbertson, and Cabrini 'Ofa Makasiale (New York: Routledge, 2013), 115–29, 116.

25 Helen Morton, "Creating Their Own Culture: Diasporic Tongans," *Contemporary Pacific* 10, no. 1 (1998): 1–30.

26 *Schooling the World: The White Man's Last Burden*, directed by Carol L. Black (United States: Lost People Films, 2010), https://schoolingtheworld.org/viewfilm/.

27 Refer to Tevita Fale, talanoa with Daniel Hernandez, Nuku'alofa, Tonga, July 4, 2015; and Sione Lātūkefu, *Church and State in Tonga: The Wesleyan Methodist Missionaries and Political Development, 1822–1875* (1974; Brisbane: University of Queensland Press, 2014).

28 Anita Juárez and Clayton Pierce, "Educational Enclosure and the Existential Commons: Settler Colonialism, Racial Capitalism, and the Problem of the Human," in *Educational Commons in Theory and Practice: Global Pedagogy and Politics*, ed. Alexander J. Means, Derek R. Ford, and Graham B. Slater (New York: Palgrave Macmillan, 2017), 145–66.

29 'Inoke Hafoka, talanoa faikava, Salt Lake City, UT, United States, December 2015.

30 Sylvia Wynter, "Unsettling the Coloniality of Being/Power/Truth/Freedom: Towards the Human, After Man, Its Overrepresentation—An Argument," *CR: The New Centennial Review* 3, no. 3 (2003): 257–337.

31 Helen Kavapalu, "Becoming Tongan: An Ethnography of Childhood in the Kingdom of Tonga" (PhD diss., Australian National University, 1991), 208.

32 Kavapalu, "Becoming Tongan," 209.

33 Kavapalu, "Becoming Tongan," 210.

34 "Leyo Lazer—Love Me," YouTube video, 7:31, posted by "Leyo Lazer," September 21, 2016, www.youtube.com/watch?v=onUufOW1teU.

35 Jodi A. Byrd, *The Transit of Empire: Indigenous Critiques of Colonialism* (Minneapolis: University of Minnesota Press, 2011).

36 "Blood Past, Mind Present—Victoria University of Wellington," YouTube video, 3:49, posted by "Victoria University of Wellington," December 3, 2014, www.youtube.com/watch?v=z2R4yV8hYlk.

37 Tēvita O. Ka'ili, *Marking Indigeneity: The Tongan Art of Sociospatial Relations* (Tucson: University of Arizona Press, 2017).

38 Jan van der Beek, email correspondence with Daniel Hernandez, February 2017.

39 Brent Clough, "Oceanic Reggae," in *Global Reggae*, ed. Carolyn Cooper (Kingston: Canoe Press, 2012), 266.

40 Edmond S. Fehoko, "Social Space and Cultural Identity: The Faikava as a Supplementary Site for Maintaining Tongan Identity in New Zealand," *New Zealand Sociology* 30, no. 1 (2015): 131–39.

41 Kaimana Bourne, talanoa with Daniel Hernandez, Kirikiriroa, Aotearoa, September 2016.

42 Uilisoni Angilau, talanoa with Daniel Hernandez, Kava Lake City, UT, United States, December 2015.

43 Jennifer Cattermole, "Fijian Sigidrigi and the Sonic Representation and Construction of Place," *Transforming Cultures eJournal* 4, no. 1 (2009): 149–171, 157.

44 Silvia Patricia Solís, "Letter to My Children from a Place Called Land," *Global Studies of Childhood* 7, no. 2 (2017): 196–206, 196–97.

45 Refer to Tēvita O. Ka'ili, "Tauhi vā: Nurturing Tongan Sociospatial Ties in Maui and Beyond," *Contemporary Pacific* 17, no. 1 (2005): 83–114; 'Okusitino Māhina, "Tā, vā, and Moana: Temporality, Spatiality, and Indigeneity," *Pacific Studies* 33, nos. 2/3 (2010): 168–202; Konai Helu Thaman, "Nurturing Relationships and Honouring Responsibilities: A Pacific Perspective," *International Review of Education* 54, nos. 3/4 (2008): 459–73; and Moana 'Ulu'ave, "Tauhi va: Nourishing the Space Between—A Collection of Essays" (honors thesis, Brigham Young University, 2012).

46 'Okusitino Māhina, "The Poetics of Tongan Traditional History, 'Tala-ē-fonua': An Ecology-Centred Concept of Culture and History," *Journal of Pacific History* 28, no. 1 (1993): 109–21.

47 KIS. B, talanoa with Daniel Hernandez, Rose Park, UT, United States, December 2015.

48 S. Apo Aporosa and Jacinta Forde, "Māori and Kava: New Drug Fashion or Re-engagement with 'Kawa'?," *Pacific Dynamics: Journal of Interdisciplinary Research* 3, no. 1 (2019): 72–85.

49 Refer to Hokulani K. Aikau, *A Chosen People, A Promised Land: Mormonism and Race in Hawai'i* (Minneapolis: University of Minnesota Press, 2012); Vicente M. Diaz, "Tackling Pacific Hegemonic Formations on the American Gridiron," *Amerasia Journal* 37, no. 3 (2011): 90–113; Gina L. Hawkes, "Indigenous Masculinity in Sport: The Power and Pitfalls of Rugby League for Australia's Pacific Island Diaspora," *Leisure Studies* 37, no. 3 (2018): 318–30; Ty P. Kāwika Tengan and Jesse Makani Markham, "Performing Polynesian Masculinities in American Football: From 'Rainbows to Warriors,'" *International Journal of the History of Sport* 26, no. 16 (2009): 2412–31; and Fa'anofo Lisaclaire Uperesa, "Fabled Futures: Migration and Mobility for Samoans in American Football," *Contemporary Pacific* 26, no. 2 (2014): 281–301.

50 Brendan Hokowhitu, "Tackling Māori Masculinity: A Colonial Genealogy of Savagery and Sport," *Contemporary Pacific* 16, no. 2 (2004): 259–84.

51 S. Apo Aporosa, "Understanding Cognitive Functions Related to Driving Following Kava (*Piper methysticum*) Use at Traditional Consumption Volumes," supplement, *Journal of Psychopharmacology Conference* 31, no. 8 (2017): A84.

52 Rizván Tuʻitahi, talanoa with Daniel Hernandez, Tāmaki Makaurau, Aotearoa, August 2016.

CHAPTER 10

THE "YOUNG KINGS OF KALIHI"

Boys and Bikes in Hawai'i's Urban Ahupua'a

DEMILIZA SARAMOSING

WALKING TOWARD THE ENTRANCE OF THE KALIHI VALLEY Instructional Bicycle Exchange (KVIBE) nonprofit organization, I passed rows of bikes ranging in colors and sizes. As I entered, boys in their middle school uniforms formed clusters within the facility, giggling with one another while sharing a couple of Spam musubis from the 7-Eleven down the street. Other boys occupied the communal area, bobbing their heads and dancing to the latest rap music by Migos and 21 Savage that reverberated throughout the building and spilled out into the KVIBE parking lot. Another group gathered around a bike, scrubbing off its rust while inserting new brake cables. Kevin Faller, a program manager at KVIBE, walked up to me from out of the office. "Sawp Demz, welcome home," he said, giving me a hug.

Soon after, he broke away and shouted, "Eh boys! It's time fo' circle awp!" Boys ranging from eight to sixteen years old unstacked mini-stools and placed them in a circle inside KVIBE's communal space. Once they organized their chairs, everyone, including myself, congregated to the space and plopped themselves onto the stools. The youth and staff then shared their names and identified their homes, as with Chuuk, the Marshall Islands, the Philippines, Sāmoa, Haiti, Hawai'i, Kam IV (the Kalihi Valley homes) and KPT (the Towers of Kuhio Park) federal housing, and KVIBE. Their elders included mothers, fathers, siblings, and grandparents as well as Nelson Mandela, Papa Mau Piailug, and Malcolm X. By honor-ing their ancestors, KVIBE urged the youth to embody Nakem. In the Ilo-kano language, Nakem means the embodiment of "soul-consciousness."

Given that a Nakem pedagogy guided KVIBE's programming, a praxis first developed by instructor Dr. Jeffrey Acido, I explore in this chapter how Nakem allowed the youth to center their cultural backgrounds and experience collective healing in the urban space of Kalihi, Oʻahu.[1] As Acido argues, Nakem encouraged the youth to challenge colonial narra-tives as well as foreground stories that highlight their experiences and value their ancestors' knowledge and wisdom. By way of bicycling and popular education, KVIBE also helped the youth build community with one another as well as rewrite denigrating narratives about their lan-guages, bodies, and places they call home. Through this realization, I argue that their stories became truths that challenged colonial heteropatri-archy in and (re)mapped their relations with Kalihi.[2]

Drawing from my ethnographic fieldwork in 2017 and 2018, I examine how KVIBE utilized Nakem pedagogy to engage immigrant and Indige-nous worldviews in their attempt to decolonize Kalihi. Following the scholar Roderick N. Labrador's framework in *Building Filipino Hawaiʻi* and his call for increased conversations by and about Filipinos in Hawaiʻi, I demonstrate how KVIBE created the Young Kings of the Kalihi urban ahupuaʻa—a division of land under the Hawaiian political system that extends from the uplands to the sea.[3] In the opening of this chapter, I underscore the multilayered stories of Kalihi to better contextualize the creation of KVIBE. First, I share a genealogy of Kalihi rooted in ʻike Hawaiʻi (Native Hawaiian knowledge), offer a brief overview of the com-munity's demographics, and discuss KVIBE's boys-centered space. I then examine vignettes about KVIBE to demonstrate how the youth learn about and enact everyday empowerment and decolonization in urban Kalihi. These include, first, the everyday experiences of youth at KVIBE; second, their participation in the Annual Kalihi Ahupuaʻa Bike Ride; and third, their engagement with the Kalihi Bike Advocacy Committee. In order to protect their identities, I am also using pseudonyms, composite backgrounds, and public photos of other KVIBE youth not featured in this chapter.

My investment with KVIBE is also personal. As a Bisaya settler raised by working-class parents, I grew up as a latchkey kid in Kalihi. After school, I spent the majority of time with my friends and sisters on the streets of Kalihi, around the tables of fast food establishments, and in the rooms of nonprofit organizations. A decade later, these experiences allowed me to connect with the KVIBE staff and youth in an intimate way that might not have been available to other researchers. At the same time, I am a woman of color feminist in a predominantly male space of storytellers. In this regard, I am an outsider ethnographer to a heterosexual and patriarchal world of boys and men. As with Moses Ma'alo Faleolo's critique of Sāmoan grief and gangs in chapter 8, colonial heteropatriarchy similarly affects Pacific Islander youth in Auckland.

KALIHI: A MULTISTORIED PLACE AND
THE EMERGENCE OF KVIBE

In the Kumulipo (Hawaiian creation story), Wākea, the sky father, and Haumea, the Earth mother, left the border of Kahiki to become the parents of the Kānaka Maoli and the Hawaiian Islands. Haumea was a woman who bore many names, such as Papa, Kamaha'ikana, and Laumiha. In their human form, they lived on the misty hill of Kilohana, which stood high up in the valley of Kalihilihi 'O Laumiha (Eyelashes of Laumiha or Kalihi), upland on the northeast side, on the cliff that rises west of the coral beds of He'eia.[4] Wākea and Haumea favored Kalihi ahupua'a because of its abundant crops and seafood. One day, guardsmen of the ali'i (chief) Kumuhonua detained Wākea for his frequent picking of wild bananas that were not only important food for sustenance but also for offerings to the nā akua (gods) Kāne and Kanaloa. Haumea saw this hewa (wrong) of the ali'i for overstepping his kuleana (responsibility) in claiming the food of the forest meant for all people to gather. She notes this hewa while recognizing that the ali'i claimed these bananas although he himself had not labored for them. She then followed them to the place where her kāne (man) was to be burned to death.[5] Haumea then approached the teary-eyed Wākea to honi him goodbye (sharing breath through the nose) but instead struck the breadfruit tree that he was bound to and made a thundering sound that shook the earth. The tree then opened up like the mouth of a large cave, and the two disappeared inside of it, thereby escaping the men of the ali'i and rescuing Wākea. This mo'olelo or story of abundance, mana wāhine (powerful women), and pono (balance) constitutes the primary Native Hawaiian genealogy of Kalihi.

Today, Kalihi or Kalihi Valley, also known as "the edge" in the Hawaiian language, is a neighborhood located five miles west from downtown Honolulu and the hot spot tourist destination of Waikīkī on the island of

O'ahu. The place consists of a dense population of 55,000 residents and includes 'Ālewa Heights, 'Iwilei, Kalihi Kai, Kalihi Uka, Kalihi Valley, Kalihi Waena, Kamehameha Heights, Kapālama, and Pālama.[6] It is a gateway community for many immigrant arrivals. In general, the community mirrors the working-class families of its students at Governor Wallace Rider Farrington High School, which is predominately comprised of Filipinos (59.1 percent), Micronesians (11.8 percent), Sāmoans (9.7 percent), and Native Hawaiians (9.6 percent).[7] Kalihi also houses the most federal housing projects.[8] The per-capita annual income is $14,634, ranking the community in the lowest quartile in the state.[9] Kalihi residents have higher rates of unemployment, frequent usage of welfare and food stamp assistance, and lower levels of home ownership than all other residents.

Across social media platforms, Kalihi is locally known to be "the city with no pity." With over 2,370 students, Governor Wallace Rider Farrington High School enrolls one of the largest populations in the state and serves low-income and minority/non-haole (nonwhite) students.[10] Students who identify as immigrants and who require instruction in English as a second language make up a large proportion of the population (about 13.8 percent).[11] Over 50 percent of students receive free or reduced-cost lunches.[12] Furthermore, 64.3 percent of adolescents living in the Farrington area have reported living in unsafe neighborhoods; according to a statewide survey, they highlighted much community disorganization (fighting), low family attachment, and poor family supervision.[13]

In light of these issues, the Kokua Kalihi Valley Comprehensive Health Center (KKV) formed in 1972 to provide holistic health services for the people of Kalihi, such as behavioral health support, elderly care, environmental preservation, food production, and youth mentorship programs.[14] In 2003, KKV mainly addressed a historically neglected public health issue in Kalihi Valley, that is, the physical infrastructure and built environment of communities that influence their physical activity. As Kalihi Valley is the first home for many new Asian and Pacific Islander immigrants coming to the United States, the state soon found that the physical infrastructure of its streets, sidewalks, schools, parks, and other public services could not adequately support this growing population. In other words, since Kalihi Valley did not have a built environment that was activity friendly, community members' health became deeply impacted. For instance, health data at KKV showed how a patient population in Kalihi Valley increasingly suffered from exercise-related chronic conditions such as diabetes, cardiovascular disease, and obesity.[15]

In their exploration of these concerns, KKV used an active living by design (ALbD) partnership model to develop two projects with community members over the course of five years: (1) Hoʻoulu ʻĀina ("to grow because of the land"), a hundred-acre upland Kalihi Valley Nature Preserve and (2) the Kalihi Valley Instructional Bicycle Exchange. As the Kanaka Maoli scholar Mary Tuti Baker has shown, Hoʻoulu ʻĀina and KKV allowed both Kānaka Maoli and guests of Kalihi to "work in healthy sustainable relations with ʻāina and each other."[16] Moreover, Hoʻoulu ʻĀina facilitated this process of Indigenous resurgence and decolonization by privileging the place-based praxis of aloha ʻāina (love for that which feeds). By transforming the resources of state agencies, charitable foundations, and individuals through the praxis of aloha ʻāina, Baker demonstrated how Hoʻoulu ʻĀina and KKV could pave decolonial pathways for humans, plants, animals, weather, dirt, and rock. KVIBE, the sibling organization of Hoʻoulu ʻĀina, likewise stressed aloha ʻāina in the urban core of Kalihi, Hawaiʻi. In 2005, KVIBE opened its doors to encourage physical exercise through bicycling, mentor mainly young boys, and create a safe space for youth after school.

KVIBE: A COMMUNITY RESPONSE TO COLONIAL HETEROPATRIARCHY IN HAWAIʻI

Over the last three years, the KVIBE staff included Jeffrey Acido (Kuya Jeff), Kevin Faller (Kuya Kevin), Gracieuse Seven Jean-Pierre (Ate Grace), Brock Corby (Kuya Bo), Mackson Phillips (Kuya Max), and Justin Jay Vinoya (Kuya Justin). Given their emphasis on building relationships by way of Nakem pedagogy, they used the Tagalog kinship terms *ate* and *kuya*—to respect "older sisters" and "older brothers."[17] Their team also consisted of individuals from Chuukese, Filipino (Ilokano and Tagalog), Haitian, and haole (white) backgrounds. Together, the organization has implemented other kinds of programming such as intern movie nights and monthly community dinners. These activities built close relationships and trust amongst KVIBE staff and youth as well as with other members in the Kalihi community. The staff were also motivated by different reasons to work with KVIBE youth. For example, Kuya Kevin went out of his way to bring barbers from Ewa Beach and Nānākuli to Kalihi. The barbers then offered free haircuts that normally cost $50 each to the KVIBE youth. As he expressed, "Demz, this is beautiful. Seeing all these people together. I didn't have this kind of support growing up. Now we've become resources to the community."

The organization now mobilizes around bicycling, popular education, and immigrant and Indigenous worldviews as a response to what Katherine Irwin and Karen Umemoto term "colonial patriarchy."[18] As they demonstrate, colonial patriarchy variously oppressed Kānaka Maoli, Filipino, Sāmoan, and other economically marginalized youth in the schools of Hawai'i. Following Irwin and Umemoto, I also want to stress the heterosexism of colonialism and patriarchy, hence my analysis of "colonial heteropatriarchy" as a nationalist ideology that attempts to uphold white heteronormative superiority and undermine Indigenous and people of color epistemologies in Hawai'i.

Beyond the realm of schooling, colonial heteropatriarchy permeates other identities and institutions across Hawai'i. "Local identity," for instance, promotes Hawai'i as a multicultural paradise while erasing settler colonial violence against Kānaka Maoli and eliding anti-immigrant racism.[19] Yet the media, popular culture, and schools often represent the young, working-class, and Brown men of Kalihi as dangerous and inferior. Because a majority of KVIBE youth are Chuukese and Filipinos, they face pressures to "localize" their identities as part of a multicultural paradise. Labrador calls this process "racial hazing," or the ways in which immigrants experience denigrating initiation-type activities (e.g., the target of ethnic joking), disidentify with their cultural heritages and histories, and uphold a "local" identity that disavows interracial conflict and settler violence.[20] As an immigrant community, Filipinos have witnessed racial hazing as early as 1906 when they arrived in Hawai'i as laborers for the sugar and pineapple plantations. Under the Immigration and Naturalization Act of 1965, a smaller group of Filipino professionals and additional workers for the agricultural and tourism industries later entered Hawai'i.

Although "Filipino" is a fraught coalitional identity, all Filipinos are still impacted by the anti-Filipino racism of the government, the economy, and everyday life in Hawai'i. For these reasons, many Filipinos have not achieved upward mobility like their Chinese and Japanese counterparts. Instead, they continue to be stereotyped as dog-eaters, "FOBs" (fresh off the boat), and low-wage workers, among other things. Since the late 1980s, Chuukese and other Micronesian immigrants have become the new subjects of vitriolic racial hazing discourse in all spheres of society.[21] This racial prejudice against Micronesians in Hawai'i is historically rooted in the unfulfilled and racially charged imperial policies between the United States and the different nations of the Micronesian region: the Federated States of Micronesia, the Republic of the Marshall Islands, and the Republic of Palau. In an interview, the late Chuukese educator Joakim Peter explained how the post–World War II United States initiated the 1986 Compact of Free Association (COFA) with these nations for US exclusive use and military strategic positioning in the Pacific. In exchange, these nations negotiated an open immigration policy, funding for education, health care, infrastructure, and other services—all of which were never fulfilled.[22] In 1996, US Congress passed both the Personal Responsibility and Work Opportunity Reconciliation Act (PRWORA) and the Illegal Immigration Reform and Immigrant Responsibility Act (IIRAIRA) that led to the termination of COFA communities' federal benefits, including Medicaid, even when many COFA migrants suffer from chronic diseases that stem from US nuclear testing in Micronesia.

After these landmark policy decisions undercut nationwide social services, Governor Linda Lingle then scapegoated Micronesian residents for consuming social services and burdening taxpayers in Hawai'i. As a result, COFA communities, including the Chuukese youth of KVIBE, have become the targets of individual and institutional race-based violence. The dehumanization is widespread, with some people even likening them to "cockroaches." Since its inception, KVIBE has sought to address these fraught interethnic relationships by cultivating an urban Oceanic space where the youth can reconnect with Indigenous and immigrant values that allow them to aloha themselves, one another, their ancestral lands, and all places they call home. In cultivating these sensibilities, the youth engage in Hawaiian movements for life, land, and sovereignty.

NEGOTIATING AND NAVIGATING THE "RIGHT WAY" TO BE A MAN IN URBAN KALIHI

By design, KVIBE has become a site that foregrounds the lived experiences and healing for boys within the community impacted by colonial heteropatriarchy. It is a fluid space where the majority of boys identify as Chuukese, Kānaka Maoli, Ilokano, and Marshallese. A few also hold mixed-race/ethnic backgrounds such as Black and Sāmoan and Kānaka Maoli and Chuukese. When I asked, "Why boys?" Kuya Kevin and Kuya Jeff explained that there aren't enough healing and educational spaces for boys as there are for girls. While I agree that there must be spaces for young men in Kalihi, program manager Ate Grace and I also believed there have yet to be more spaces for girls. They could then discuss, challenge, and heal from their unique interlocking experiences of navigating classism, racism, misogyny, and sexism. For example, when Chuukese, Filipino, and Sāmoan girls entered the KVIBE facility, they privately revealed their insecurities about their dark skin or their inability to often go outside due to their fathers' perceptions that they were "too young." For this reason, Ate Grace and I took mentorship roles outside of KVIBE programming to create empowerment spaces for the girls, as with our collective Visions of Women with Abundance (figure 10.1).

Throughout my time with KVIBE in 2017 and 2018, the staff members and youth did engage in difficult conversations that addressed the harming and silencing of girls and women. This helped ease some of my own discomfort in working alongside the staff and informally mentoring KVIBE youth on the importance of centering girls, women, and queer, trans, and nonbinary youth. However, this harm sometimes went unchecked with Ate Grace's labor as a Black woman staff member, as with her creating of programs about toxic masculinity and safe healing spaces for girls. In this manner, KVIBE, a boy-oriented organization, can better acknowledge its perpetuation of gender oppression in Kalihi. Unlearning colonial heteropatriarchy can allow us to uproot it in our programming

FIGURE 10.1. Visions of Women with Abundance's "Calling All Women: Safe Space, Dream-Building, Talk Story" and strategy meeting, 2018. (Photo credit: Demiliza Saramosing)

efforts and protect our youth who experience everyday and institutional violence at the intersections of race, ethnicity, indigeneity, class, gender, and sexuality.

As I found in my interviews with the KVIBE youth, they faced the brunt of racism while negotiating their understanding of what it means to "be a man" in Hawai'i. They often grappled with their understandings of hegemonic gender binaries: women versus men, feminine versus masculine, weak versus strong, and so on. Moreover, heteropatriarchal societies uphold hegemonic masculinity practices that legitimize men's dominant position in colonial society and justify the subordination of women, subaltern masculinities, and the distancing from femininity, weakness, passivity, and vulnerability.[23] Haunani-Kay Trask also stated, "Because American culture, like western civilization generally is patriarchal, that is, structured and justified by values that emphasize male dominance over women and nature, American institutions reward men and male-dominant behaviors with positions of power."[24] For example, since the men in Kalihi have been structurally feminized and racialized through colonial heteropatriarchy in Hawai'i, I observed how the male leadership at KVIBE sometimes asserted their masculinity in toxic ways by exercising outright power, voice, and control over women.

But as Kanaka Maoli scholar Ty P. Kāwika Tengan reminds us, we cannot view KVIBE's practicing of a subaltern masculinity as separate from hegemonic masculinity. In *Native Men Remade*, Tengan states that creating these fine distinct boundaries "would be to replicate the debilitating dichotomies upon which colonial hegemonies and authority rest as well as to miss the complexities of what actually takes place on the ground. Hegemonies are always incomplete, allowing interplay between structure and agency—an interplay that involves and transforms ideologies of gender and power."[25]

Although KVIBE attempted to decolonize hegemonic masculinity, they did so while drawing on specific settler hegemonic beliefs and practices (i.e., heteronormativity, politics of respectability, productive citizenship, etc.) for male youth survival in a US state that punishes and criminalizes their deviance as working-class "brown boys" in Kalihi.[26] As I observed, KVIBE staff members sometimes replicated heteropatriarchal norms by redefining the "right" way for a man to do well in school, stay out of trouble, and be a productive contributor to settler norms (i.e., collaborating on projects with the City and County of Honolulu and the Honolulu Police Department). Yet KVIBE staff members contrasted this idealized notion of manhood with a feminized, "weak" man who unproductively "parties and drinks on the weekends" and seems to be living out the stereotypes that society has assigned to him. For these reasons, I ask, How can we value the lives of all youth, even those who are rendered morally unworthy by the state? What does it mean to build the "Young Kings of Kalihi" in an urban ahupuaʻa? And how did KVIBE decolonize dominant gender constructs for "contradictory and even subversive purposes"?[27] In the following sections, I share vignettes about KVIBE's everyday interactions, their reading of poetry, their bike ride through Kalihi, and their urban planning with the city. My goal is to demonstrate how these vignettes speak to KVIBE's everyday struggle to fight back against the denigrated, racialized narratives placed on them and their communities. At KVIBE, the youth center their stories and experiences in order to aloha themselves and others in and beyond the US settler state.

THE KVIBE YOUTH AND THEIR DAY-TO-DAY

In this section, I examine the everyday experiences of the youth at KVIBE, briefly focusing on their repairing of bicycles and their writing of poetry. With regard to the former, the staff members and the youth celebrated those who frequently have shown progress in the work they've done in the community as well as in the maintenance of their bikes. For those who have put in extra work around the shop, the staff members acknowledged them in the workspace and encouraged them to assert what they know. Take, for instance, the story of Lil' TJ. One day, program manager Kuya Kevin queried, "We just got new bike lights! Who wants them?" Hearing this, Lil' TJ turned around with his long, light brown curly hair swaying and quickly said, "I do!" Kuya Kevin questioned, "Do you deserve this?" Standing at three feet tall, Lil' TJ looked up at Kuya Kevin's five-foot, six-inch frame and responded, "Yes I do. I take care of my bike and I've kept my bike longer than the older boys." Kuya Kevin then rewarded him with the bicycle lights. By knowing what he earned, Lil' TJ implored Kuya Kevin and everyone else who was listening to recognize how responsible he had been with his bicycle. Moreover, eight-year-old Lil' TJ showed us that he was not afraid to say what he deserved due to his positive track record of taking care of his own bike. Given that our heteropatriarchal society does not value youth voices the same way as it does adult voices, Lil' TJ challenged and debunked the notions that the youth cannot assert their opinions and defend what they believe is right.[28]

When the youth were not repairing their bicycles, KVIBE facilitated daily Nakem circles with the youth (e.g., stating their names, homes, and ancestors). One day, program manager Ate Grace and I organized a "Where I'm from" poetry activity to gain a deeper understanding of the boys' social biographies. After thirty to forty minutes of poetry writing, eighteen boys shared their pieces. One youth, a ten-year-old Chuukese boy, talked about how others perceived him and his community versus how his community saw itself:

> I am from Chuuk where it is silent at night because of ghosts. I am from
> the place that they bombed. I am from where people are poor. I am
> from getting teased for being Chuukese. I am from where there is gangs, a
> place where there is a lot of fight. . . . I am an immigrant. I am a person
> who loves my life. I am a person who loves my family and my friends.
> I am a person who got to be a junior intern at KVIBE by working hard
> and earning things I want to have and love to live because of all my
> homes. I am from where people love their life even though they are poor.

This KVIBE member demonstrated how aware he was of the US nuclear bomb tests that took place in the Marshall Islands, an area located near Chuuk in Micronesia, which started the exodus of migrants from this region to Hawai'i. Now in Kalihi, the haunting lingered as the boys encountered racism, gang violence, and socioeconomic struggle. Framing his life through abundance, the Chuukese boy talked about how he loved his life as an immigrant because of his own relationships to Chuuk, Kalihi, and KVIBE. Overall, he shared how KVIBE transformed him into a leader who became empowered by the connections he made with various peoples and places.

In another poem, a fifteen-year-old Ilokano youth illustrated his struggles with finances and other dynamics within the household:

> Where I'm from, alcohol is an escape. An escape to feel safe. We fake that
> we safe 'cuz the world is insane. My mom still in pain. Where I'm from we
> can only daydream because we stuck in this mainstream of having picket
> fence day dreams. Where I'm from, home is just a memory, a place where
> my ancestors once lived. Where I'm from, money is the incentive. They
> say money is the root of all evil but where I'm from money is the root of
> all people. Where I'm from, it's hard to listen. Everyone is killin' and
> makin' a living. "Where I'm from" is what they want me to say. "Where

I'm at" is what I'm trying to say. "What I am? What am I?" I'm a brown
Ilokano boy who is just trying to find his way back home.

In this passage, the youth discussed the American Dream that never came
to his family. But by engaging Nakem pedagogy and embracing his identity as a "brown Ilokano boy," his firm stance and performance indicated
to me that money served as the source of oppression in his household. The
Ilokano poet even yearned to return to Ilocos Norte, Philippines, where
his "ancestors once lived."

Throughout the poetry reading, many of the youth sobbed loudly into
their shirts. The older teenagers then wrapped their arms around the
younger boys as a sign of support as they wept. With tears streaming down
my own face, I also embraced the boys sitting closest to me. Although Ate
Grace did not write a poem, she stood from her seat and shared an
impromptu poem:

I am from Kalihi. New immigrant on the block. I am Haitian. I am from a
group of boys that are men. That are wise. That are hard. That are
angry. That are sad. That are depressed. That are happy. That are extraordinary. That are rare. Diamonds in the rough. I am from where pressure
makes diamonds. I am from crying. That is the only way to express my
healing. I am from where I see grown men crying, and I rejoice. I am
from where I was ashamed, "You poor Haitian. Because your mom can't
read or write in English." I am from all of you. I am from your red eyes,
your sniffling noses, your lifted heads, your high hopes, your big dreams,
your big smile. I am from your sister line. I am from your mother's line.
When I look at myself, I am from you and you are from me.

As the daughter of two political refugees who fled to the United States
from persecution in Haiti in the early 1990s, Ate Grace connected her
diaspora Caribbean experiences to the youth and aligned herself with
their matrilineal line. In other interviews, she told me that her home city
of Atlanta, Georgia, was Kalihi to her and that she saw her stories and the
boys' stories as one in the same.

THE 2017 KALIHI AHUPUAʻA BIKE RIDE

Outside of the KVIBE facility, the youth took to the streets for a variety
of reasons. In this section, I explore how KVIBE organized the Kalihi

Ahupuaʻa Bike Ride (KAR) as an educational bike ride from the mauka (mountain) to the makai (ocean) areas of the Kalihi ahupuaʻa. In 2018, I participated in the eight-mile downhill trek of five "story stops" where the youth learned about the Kānaka Maoli significance of each site and their roles in transforming the public face of Kalihi.[29] Here I discuss one such "story stop." Since 2017, KAR has been designed and led by the young Kings of Kalihi Valley to offer information about the health resources and cultural knowledge of Kalihi and to instill a sense of community pride for Kalihi.

In the inaugural KAR in 2017, 130 multigenerational riders from different ethnic, cultural backgrounds and gender identities attended the event. They met at the first story stop at Hoʻoulu ʻĀina, the peak of Kokua Kalihi Valley's hundred-acre park. As the sister nonprofit organization of KVIBE, the staff of Hoʻoulu ʻĀina invited the people of Kalihi and beyond to malama ʻāina (care for the land). Such tasks included the breaking down of cassava branches to grow more cassava plants, the planting of sugar cane and ʻawa (kava root), and the clearing of weeds around native plants. Grounded in Kānaka Maoli ways of knowing and being, they wholeheartedly believed in the proverb, "If we don't have healthy land, we can't have healthy people." Over the years, KVIBE followed this principle by developing a stronger relationship with Hoʻoulu ʻĀina. For instance, the KVIBE staff members consistently brought the youth every third Saturday of each month to Hoʻoulu ʻĀina for community workdays. Kanoa O'Connor, a Kanaka Maoli and Hoʻoulu ʻĀina farmer, subsequently developed a closer relationship with the KVIBE youth. I witnessed this closeness in action as four of the boys latched onto his arms and legs as they walked over to their designated workstation on one workday. It is this kind of intimacy that enabled an event like KAR to blossom. This strong relationship led to Kanoa's narration of the first story stop at Hoʻoulu ʻĀina for the 130 riders.

They started KAR by doing their "aloha circles," or genealogical introductions that resembled the Nakem culture circles of KVIBE. When I interviewed Kanoa, he told me, "The kids become the best example of how to begin a circle, respect everyone, and how to be proud of who you are, where you come from, and who you come from." Before the riders departed the nature park, riders joined hands as Kanoa shared some of the moʻolelo of Kalihi:

Does anyone know what the word *Kalihi* means? The really, really old name of this ahupuaʻa, of this valley, is actually Kalihilihi ʻO Laumiha.

That translates to "the Eyelashes of Laumiha." And this valley was famous for gods and strong beings (like) Laumiha. Her name means "Intense-Silence."[30] See the ridgelines coming down into the valley and forming smaller valleys? Our kūpuna [elders] had names for all of these smaller valleys contained within the larger valley. For generations, the old timers called the land that we are standing on right now 'Ōuaua. If you break that down into smaller words, it's 'ō-ua-ua, and in Hawaiian, *ua* means "rain." This place is called "o-rainy-rain," and it rains up here almost every day. Taken together, the word *'ōuaua* also means to have tough or thick skin, and we like to say the people of old must have named this place 'Ōuaua because they had to have tough skin to deal with the rain here. We like to think that it speaks to greater Kalihi as well. People that come from here have that tough, thick skin; it's a calling card of the Kalihi people.[31]

At this story stop, Kanoa drew special attention to the Kānaka Maoli names of Kalihi's land and rain as well as acknowledged the ancestral and present-day folks living in Kalihi. Although I did not attend the first KAR, I was present at the 2018 KAR where I saw riders leaning in attentively while nodding their heads to the moʻolelo of Kalihi at the Hoʻoulu ʻĀina story stop. Kanoa highlighted the sacredness of Kalihi as he told the story of Laumiha, the female akua (god) who represents both land and being in this place. Due to high levels of rain in Kalihi or 'Ōuaua, we can assume that the Kānaka Maoli ancestors who lived there had to have thick skin to withstand the rain. In other words, Kanoa's interpretation of 'ōuaua resonates with the people of Kalihi. In my interview with him, he clarified what he meant and offered an expansive concept of "we":

Kalihi, for a lot of our community, it's the contact point. The frontline for our communities being pushed out of our Native lands because of colonization, where they can't call the places they come from home anymore. Kalihi is a space that is inviting, a piece of land with open arms for all the refugees of colonization. We have the most public housing in state. Most of our brothers and sisters from the Pacific that are in the housing, their homelands, not gonna be similar to housing situations [in Kalihi]. In terms of colonization, Kalihi is a place where people can come and are coming. That's where Hoʻoulu ʻĀina is coming from. We need a space more like home for all of our Native people. A space where they're doing things they could be doing back home like farming or accessing forest. Reminds a lot of people of home.

Although many of the residents in Kalihi today are not native to Hawai'i, Kanoa recognized how their Indigenous identities connected to other places in the Pacific.[32] According to Kanoa, the thick, tough skin of Kalihi residents stemmed from a large number of them being "refugees of colonization." This perspective welcomed the KVIBE boys to live and be in Kalihi and to call the place home (figure 10.2). Moreover, this viewpoint reflected a conversation I had with Ty P. Kāwika Tengan. As he expressed, "It seems to me that the boys at KVIBE are not claiming Kalihi Valley. Rather, it's about how the valley is claiming them." As "refugees of colonization," Kalihi Valley and KVIBE indeed became what Kanoa called a "kīpuka," or "a little piece of forest that survives the lava flow that takes down the forest." In Kanoa's closing remarks at the first story stop, he captured the significance of these stories of Kalihi as the riders descended the summit of Kalihi Valley. From there, they flowed from the deep, wet, and green hills, traversing streets, homes, and shops to the drier and lower area of the valley.

Many of the youth enjoyed being able to freely reclaim and occupy Kamehameha IV Road as working-class Brown boys of Kalihi. Kamehameha IV Road lies right outside where most of them live, so they could

FIGURE 10.2. KVIBE youth on their bikes and smiling at the camera, 2012. (Photo credit: KVIBE)

bike freely down to the makai (sea) side of the Kalihi ahupuaʻa. One of the Ilokano boys stated, "It felt like we're the Kings of Kalihi because the cops shut down the road for us, and we had complete freedom to ride throughout the streets of Kalihi." This freedom is vital to Brown boys who are oftentimes racially targeted and stunted by the state. The youth appreciated being able to ride with a large group of community members who came to the event and took pride in their leadership in executing a safe and educational ride. There were impatient drivers and curious passersby as well, some of whom paused to witness KAR's communal takeover of Kalihi streets. While KAR is led by boys, one of the Chuukese youth in KVIBE respected the feminine power of Laumiha in Kalihi. Referring to this akua of the area, he noted how she welcomed "present kings and queens, kids, families, friends of all ages . . . to shelter, and teach to become the best versions of themselves."[33] His sentiment exemplified how KVIBE encouraged the youth to appreciate the people and place of Kalihi, decolonize hegemonic masculinities, and respect women. Moreover, the Chuukese boy shared his thoughts about healing, stating, "As we voyage and navigate the bikes through the city, the adversity and the ʻohana (family) builds up together, stopping and acknowledging the different environments of nature, the glimpse of Kalihi and its wonderful stories of healing it has to offer."[34] By organizing events like KAR every year that connect youth with their urban bikes to the land, KVIBE cultivated and expanded aloha ʻāina (love of the land) in and kuleana (responsibility) for Kalihi.

THE KALIHI BIKE ADVOCACY COMMITTEE

Indeed, KVIBE's support of and participation in KAR demonstrated its commitment to the youth as community members learned about the Kānaka Maoli place names throughout the Kalihi ahupuaʻa. While KVIBE members strove to anchor themselves in Kānaka Maoli knowledge of Kalihi, they also grappled with pragmatic issues within the city, namely, the attainment of better and safer streets in the community. In this section, I examine KVIBE youths' joint partnership with the Hawaiʻi Bicycle League (HBL) and their civic engagement with the settler city of greater Honolulu. KVIBE and HBL have had a long-term partnership that includes organizing collective bike meets and participating in each other's community dinners. In recent years, they have been discussing plans to create new bike lanes and safer streets throughout the Kalihi community.[35] After both organizations successfully worked with policy-makers to repave Kamehameha IV Road, City and County of Honolulu officials asked the organizations to weigh in on the conversation of "complete streets" in the city, an initiative to ensure that streets are safely shared and accessible to pedestrians, especially those with disabilities, bus users, motorists, and bicyclists.[36]

While HBL consisted of adults, KVIBE mainly worked with youth.[37] As the younger group, KVIBE contributed to a discussion that would impact the structure and culture of the Kalihi community. In fact, Ilokano KVIBE member Dwayne, who first joined KVIBE when he was eleven years old, organized and successfully executed the transformation of Kamehameha IV Road right outside of the KVIBE facility into a complete streets model. Even though a police station lies on Kamehameha IV Road, which used to be a four-lane road, there were constant speeding issues, risking the safety of the youth attending schools and playing in the nearby district park. As a result, the crosswalks for pedestrians were dangerous. Even with KVIBE's doors open to the public since 2005, there were no safe places to bike on the streets. In 2012, the complete streets city ordinance passed with support from HBL, KVIBE, Kokua Kalihi Valley, Kaewai Elementary and Dole Middle Schools, and the Kalihi Valley Neighborhood Board. The Caldwell administration then executed the plan to transform Kamehameha IV Road from the two lanes in each direction to one lane in each direction, a center turn lane, and bicycle lanes. Pertaining to bicycle lanes, the city implemented a "right sizing" approach to make room for cyclists, which has led to an average 29 percent reduction in injuries. According to the HBL website, the change received mostly very positive responses, such as "I can't believe how much easier it is to cross the road now! People actually stop when you step out in the crosswalk!"[38] Due to their successful partnership, HBL and KVIBE formed the Kalihi Bike Advocacy Committee to fight for more complete streets in Kalihi (figure 10.3).

One Tuesday night in April 2018, an HBL member came to the KVIBE facility to discuss with the boys' action plans for the committee. He passed out a map of the Honolulu area with blue, green, and red lines. The green lines represented routes that were already approved and repaved for the complete streets initiative. The HBL member noticed that Kamehameha IV Road was still in blue, which meant that the route was still pending approval. He told everyone that it is now coded green due to the 2012 complete streets ordinance efforts of Dwayne, who was seventeen at the time of this meeting, and thanked him from across the table. Everyone clapped to

FIGURE 10.3. Advocacy for complete streets on Kamehameha IV Road, 2016. (Photo credit: KVIBE)

acknowledge Dwayne's past efforts. Dwayne then explained his task in monitoring the speed of cars along Kamehameha IV Road and his activism in attaining complete streets for it. Later, he shared how this work empowered him to continue being a member of KVIBE. Afterward, the HBL representative interjected and asked the group, "So now we're looking to see where we want more complete streets running through Kalihi. What do you all think?"

RJ, one of the Ilokano boys, quickly responded with his own experiences bicycling on Gulick Avenue. When he rode his bike on that road, many of the people driving cars beeped and yelled at him to get off the road. He explained that even when Gulick Avenue has enough room to share with bicyclists, most of the time the drivers did not like to share the roads. For this reason, he did not feel safe bicycling home and anywhere near the streets leading toward Saint Anthony Church, the Oʻahu Community Correctional Center, and the H1 freeway. Many of the boys nodded in agreement and voiced their own experiences. A Sāmoan youth, Ashton, informed everyone that School Street, in front of KVIBE, as well as North King Street should be repaved for students walking to their

schools. By repaving these roads, Ashton imagined a more seamless transport for students going to the high school, especially those who want to
ride their bicycles. Marvin, a Chuukese youth, proposed a re-pavement
plan for the complete streets initiative on Dillingham Boulevard in order
to allow more bicyclists in the busiest area of Kalihi; he also wanted to
honor Eki Cyclery, the neighborhood's first bike shop.

In this Kalihi Bike Advocacy Committee, the boys shared their rich
"street knowledge" with the HBL representative. They knew the community streets on an intimate level as bicyclists who frequented the landscapes
of Kalihi. Bicycling enabled them to see their struggles with other cars and
buses. They also connected more vividly with pedestrians crossing the
streets. More vitally, bikes linked riders with the community on a more
grounded level. Thus, it is fitting for KVIBE boys to be central advocates in
a movement for more complete streets in the ahupuaʻa of Kalihi.

CONCLUSION: HOʻOMANAʻO

Throughout this chapter, I explored the reciprocal relationships between
KVIBE's young Kings of Kalihi and Kalihi's urban ahupuaʻa through three
sites of study: the KVIBE youths' everyday experiences, poetry, and interactions within the bike facility; the Annual Kalihi Ahupuaʻa Bike Ride;
and KVIBE's civic engagement participation with the Kalihi Bike Advocacy Committee. These young Kings are built here in Kalihi. Though they
are recipients of colonial heteropatriarchal legacies in Kalihi, they are also
decolonial agents of change. They are fostering alternative masculinities in
the remapping of their relations, their ancestors and ancestral lands, and
all places they call home.

Yet as these boys navigate the challenges of colonial heteropatriarchy,
they could reinforce the hegemonic binaries that violently impact marginalized racial, class, gender, and sexual identities that are not deemed
respectable to settler societal norms in occupied Hawaiʻi. Indeed, as
KVIBE worked alongside the state, City and County of Honolulu, and the
Honolulu Police Department, the youth began to improve their everyday
struggles in Kalihi. They are not simply building bikes. They are creating
urban infrastructure in Kalihi, a place they are learning to aloha, rooted in
Indigenous and immigrant values.

In July 2018, twenty KVIBE youth leaders led more than 150 bicyclists
on the second annual KAR. They stopped at Puea Cemetery to pay respect
to Kalihi-based Kanaka Maoli Joseph "Uncle Joe" Kahahawai Jr. In 1932, a

group of haole (white) US Navy vigilantes led by Thalia Massie's husband, Thomas Massie, and her mother, Grace Fortescue, kidnapped and killed Uncle Joe, who was one of five local boys racially charged and accused of beating and raping Thalia Massie. Although there were political pressures to exonerate Kahahawai's killers, the territorial governor commuted their manslaughter sentences, and soon after they were free to leave the islands. For the 2018 KAR, the youth leaders wore T-shirts with the image of Uncle Joe on their chests as a way to connect his story to their lived experiences. Six sixteen-year-old KVIBE boys from Filipino, Micronesian, and Native Hawaiian backgrounds took turns memorializing Uncle Joe's story in relation to their own experiences of being racialized and criminalized as dangerous working-class "brown boys." Uncle Joe's death offered the boys a connection to the injustices that also took the lives of José Rizal, Emmet Till, Trayvon Martin, and others who were criminalized by colonial heteropatriarchal systems. They closed the remembrance with Hoʻomanaʻo—*To remember*.

As the youth recalled, Uncle Joe "was a brown boy (from Kalihi), just like us." Through their engagement with moʻolelo, Nakem pedagogy, and the power of Hoʻomanaʻo, they clearly found value in the story of Uncle Joe. That is to say, they gained a critical consciousness to better resist a society that punishes their racialized deviance. By being equipped with these critical tools, a praxis that stemmed from their involvement with KVIBE, they began to understand how the colonial heteropatriarchal systems that led to Uncle Joe's death—US imperialism, colonialism, and militarism—are the same systems they collectively fight today. This collective critical consciousness is necessary for the decolonization of Kalihi and other Native cities across Oceania.

In one of my conversations with KVIBE Chuukese staff member and US military veteran Kuya Max, he shared with me a Chuukese elder's thoughts about islander solidarity with the Kānaka Maoli. Paraphrasing him, Kuya Max said, "When we got here to Hawaiʻi, all we saw were American dollars. We became American, and we strived for the American Dream. All we see are American dollars, buildings, structures, etc. [The elder] says that we need to meet other islanders not as Americans, but as islanders. Islander to islander." Just like how the KVIBE youth saw their experiences in Uncle Joe, it is important to continue recognizing these Indigenous encounters while refusing recognition from the US settler state.[39] By sharing our appreciation for Kalihi, we can create a society not based on colonial heteropatriarchy. And like Haumea, we can strike the feet of what is not pono (balance) in the urban ahupuaʻa of Kalihi, unsettle the colonial city, and ride the "wheels of liberation" provided by KVIBE.

NOTES

1 Jeffrey Tangonan Acido, "Nakem Pedagogy (Soul Consciousness) and Constitutive Elements of Nakem Praxis" (PhD diss., University of Hawaiʻi at Manoa, 2014).

2 I borrow Mishuana Goeman's (re)map concept to talk about how KVIBE (re) maps heteropatriarchal settler urban space in Oʻahu. See Mishuana Goeman, *Mark My Words: Native Women Mapping Our Nations* (Minneapolis: University of Minnesota Press, 2013), 3–4.

3 Roderick N. Labrador, *Building Filipino Hawaiʻi* (Urbana: University of Illinois Press, 2015).

4 Noenoe K. Silva, *The Power of the Steel-Tipped Pen: Reconstructing Native Hawaiian Intellectual History* (Durham, NC: Duke University Press, 2017), 197–200.

5 Silva, *Power of the Steel-Tipped Pen*, 197–200.

6 Center on the Family, College of Tropical Agricultural and Human Resources, University of Hawaiʻi at Mānoa, "Farrington Area Community Profile," 2003, accessed July 3, 2020, https://uhfamily.hawaii.edu/sites/uhfamily.hawaii.edu /files/publications/CommunityProfileSeries_2018.pdf.

7 Wallace Rider Farrington High School, "School Status and Improvement Report: School Year 2016–2017," November 2017, http://arch.k12.hi.us/PDFs /ssir/2017/Honolulu/106SSIR-1.pdf.

8 Hawaii Public Housing Authority, "Information for Communities," accessed February 22, 2019, www.hpha.hawaii.gov/infoforcommunities/index.htm.

9 Stella M. Gran-O'Donnell, "Being, Belonging, and Connecting: Filipino Youths' Narratives of Place(s) and Wellbeing in Hawaiʻi" (PhD thesis, University of Washington, 2016), 44.

10 Wallace Rider Farrington High School, "School Status."

11 Wallace Rider Farrington High School, "School Status."

12 Wallace Rider Farrington High School, "School Status."

13 Wallace Rider Farrington High School, "School Status."

14 "Kōkua Kalihi Valley—About Us: History," accessed July 3, 2020, www.kkv .net/history.

15 Mark H. Hamamoto, David D. Derauf, and Sheryl R. Yoshimura, "Building the Base: Two Active Living Projects That Inspired Community Participation," *American Journal of Preventive Medicine* 37, no. 6 (2009): S345–51.

16 Mary Tuti Baker, "Hoʻoulu ʻĀina: Embodied Aloha ʻĀina Enacting ʻOiwi Futurities" (PhD diss., University of Hawaiʻi at Mānoa, 2018), 133.

17 The youth called me "Ate Demi" during my time with them, an effort that reinforced the hegemony of Tagalog over the multiple languages spoken at KVIBE.

18 Katherine Irwin and Karen Umemoto, *Jacked Up and Unjust: Pacific Islander Teens Confront Violent Legacies* (Oakland: University of California Press, 2016), 18.

19 Candace Fujikane and Jonathan Y. Okamura, eds., *Asian Settler Colonialism: From Local Governance to the Habits of Everyday Life in Hawaii* (Honolulu: University of Hawai'i Press, 2009).

20 Roderick N. Labrador, "'I no eat dog, k': Humor, Hazing, and Multicultural Settler Colonialism," in *Beyond Ethnicity: New Politics of Race in Hawai'i*, ed. Camilla Fojas, Rudy P. Guevarra, and Nitasha Sharma (Honolulu: University of Hawai'i Press, 2018), 67.

21 Joakim Peter, Wayne Chung Tanaka, and Aiko Yamashiro, "Reconnecting Our Roots: Navigating the Turbulent Waters of Health-Care Policy for Micronesians in Hawai'i," in Fojas, Guevarra, and Sharma, *Beyond Ethnicity*, 193–210.

22 Paul Lyons and Ty P. Kāwika Tengan, "COFA Complex: A Conversation with Joakim 'Jojo' Peter," *American Quarterly* 67, no. 3 (2015): 663–79.

23 Irwin and Umemoto, *Jacked Up and Unjust*.

24 Haunani-Kay Trask, *From a Native Daughter: Colonialism and Sovereignty in Hawai'i* (Honolulu: University of Hawai'i Press, 1999), 92.

25 Ty P. Kāwika Tengan, *Native Men Remade: Gender and Nation in Contemporary Hawai'i* (Durham, NC: Duke University Press, 2008), 15.

26 Anita Hofschneider, "#BeingMicronesian in Hawaii Means Lots of Online Hate," *Honolulu Civil Beat*, September 19, 2018, www.civilbeat.org/2018/09/beingmicronesian-in-hawaii-means-lots-of-online-hate.

27 Tengan, *Native Men Remade*, 15.

28 Irwin and Umemoto, *Jacked Up and Unjust*.

29 Radiant Cordero, "History and Resilience Experienced through Kalihi Ahupua'a Bike Ride," *Summit*, accessed July 23, 2020, https://static1.squarespace.com/static/5a99ee147c9327a2ff73fe81/t/5dfd53ad0e6154726670d58b/1576883133546/Summit+Magazine_Kalihi+Ahupua'a+Bike+Ride.pdf.

30 In an interview I conducted with Kanoa, he told me that silence is a form of reverence. During ceremonies that were performed at certain parts of the Lunar calendar, Kānaka Maoli were expected to keep completely silent. Noises were kapu (forbidden), and not adhering to this kapu could mean losing your life. Laumiha, too, he said, has this connotation of being "very, very sacred—something that should be revered."

31 Cordero, "History and Resilience."

32 Kanoa's viewpoint is rooted in KKV's community-engaged research on promoting Indigenous health and well-being for all Kalihi residents. Refer to research in Sharon Ka'iulani Odom, Puni Jackson, David Derauf, Megan Kiyomi Inada, and Andrew H. Aoki, "Pilinahā: An Indigenous Framework for Health," *Current Developments in Nutrition* 3, Supplement 2 (2019): 32–38.

33 "KVIBE Kalihi Ahupua'a Ride 2018," YouTube video, posted by "KVIBE KVIBE," February 7, 2019, www.youtube.com/watch?v=Coe-_om_d4k.

34 "KVIBE Kalihi Ahupuaʻa Ride 2018."

35 Hawaii Bicycling League, "Advocacy Resources," accessed April 27, 2018, www .hbl.org/advocacy/advocacy-resources-and-updates.

36 City and County of Honolulu, "Complete Streets," accessed April 19, 2018, www.honolulu.gov/completestreets.

37 City and County of Honolulu, "Kalihi," accessed April 27, 2018, www .honolulu.gov/completestreets/kalihi.

38 Hawaii Bicycling League, "Kamehameha IV Rd Complete Streets Celebration 4/28," accessed April 19, 2018, www.hbl.org/kalihicelebration.

39 Audra Simpson, *Mohawk Interruptus: Political Life across the Borders of Settler States* (Durham, NC: Duke University Press, 2014), 22.

CONTRIBUTORS

STELLA BLACK is of Ngāi Tūhoe and Ngāti Whakaue. She is a Māori researcher and PhD candidate at the Auckland University of Technology. Stella has a particular passion in working with Māori youth in a range of fields including mental health, addictions, and community-based co-design interventions.

ALIKA BOURGETTE (Kanaka ʻŌiwi) is a PhD student in the Department of History at the University of Washington where he investigates Native space-making, community kinship, and gender formations in Kakaʻako, Honolulu, in the late nineteenth and early twentieth centuries. He also explores the ways Native Hawaiian communities navigate landscapes of colonial violence through complex, multifarious relations beyond the enclosed family.

KEITH L. CAMACHO is a professor in the Asian American Studies Department and a faculty affiliate in the Critical Race Studies Program at the University of California, Los Angeles. He is the author of *Sacred Men: Law, Torture, and Retribution in Guam* (Duke University Press, 2019), co-editor of *Militarized Currents: Toward a Decolonized Future in Asia and the Pacific* (University of Minnesota Press, 2010), and former senior editor of *Amerasia Journal*.

THOMAS DICK is co-founder of Further Arts, a cultural organization based in Vanuatu, where he lived for almost a decade. Living and working with communities in Vanuatu, Tom produced several festivals, CDs, and films, including the Vanuatu Women's Water Music.

SARAH DOYLE is a development practitioner and photographer based in the Pacific with a focus on capacity building, advocacy, evaluation, and research. Over the past eight years in Vanuatu, Sarah has facilitated creative and cultural development through community-driven projects in arts, media, and education aimed at amplifying local voices.

MOSES MA'ALO FALEOLO is the undergraduate program leader for the School of Social Work and the Associate Dean Pacific for the College of Health, Massey University of New Zealand, Auckland campus. He is also the primary investigator of a Marsden Fast Start award. Over the course of three years, the Marsden will fund his research project, *Toward a Pacific Criminological Theory: Life Histories of Sāmoan Young People's Involvement in Gangs in Oceania*.

EDMOND FEHOKO grew up in Auckland in Aotearoa and is an active leader in the Tongan community. Edmond is from the Ha'apai islands of Kotu, Nomuka, Mo'unga'one, and Ma'ufanga in Tongatapu. He completed a master's thesis on kava and Tongan males and is currently completing a doctorate at the Auckland University of Technology on problem gambling in the Tongan community in New Zealand.

MARY K. GOOD is assistant professor of cultural anthropology at Wake Forest University in North Carolina, United States. Her research with youth on the island of 'Eua in Tonga focuses on the ways global modernity, including digital media and changing ideas of employment, affect youths' understandings of morality, sentiment, and competing responsibilities.

'INOKE HAFOKA grew up in Utah and has been an active member in the Tongan community. 'Inoke descends from Faleloa and 'Uiha in the Ha'apai islands and Ha'akio and Taoa in Vava'u. He is currently a doctoral candidate at the University of California, Los Angeles, doing research on education and Tongan mobility in the airlines.

JACQUIE KIDD is from the Ngāpuhi iwi in the North of Aotearoa and is associate professor at the Auckland University of Technology. Jacquie's research focuses on community-centered solutions to Māori health inequities and whānau ora (family well-being).

LEA LANI KINIKINI is the daughter of Taniela Vaiokema Kinikini of 'Uiha, Ha'apai and Mayone Woodbury of Ogden, Utah. She spent her early career teaching Pacific studies at the Oceania Centre, University of the

South Pacific, and currently serves as chief diversity officer at Salt Lake Community College in Utah.

KEPA ʻŌKUSITINO MAUMAU is the second son of Ailini Finau from Fuaʻamotu, Tongatapu, and Kepa Fangalua Maumau from Kolonga and Tatakamotonga, Tongatapu. A gifted student from an early age, Kepa has served as a tutor, is an illustrator, and continues to pursue liberatory education and community work.

VAOIVA PONTON completed her doctorate in education at the University of Melbourne, where she investigated the impediments against and motivations for learning among Sāmoan students in Melbourne, Australia. Spending the last twenty years as an educator, she is interested in strategies to enhance student success in the transition from school to the tertiary sector. Her experience of utilizing Pacific methodologies with the Melbourne Sāmoan community is highlighted along with data collated from the research undertaken.

DEMILIZA SARAMOSING is a diasporic Boholanon and Mindanawon Bisaya feminist born and raised in Kalihi, Hawaiʻi. She completed her master's in Asian American studies at the University of California, Los Angeles, and is currently a PhD student in American studies at the University of Minnesota, Twin Cities. Her scholar-activisms reside at the intersections of Oceanic ethnic studies, critical youth studies, Native and Women of Color feminisms, performance studies, and urban studies. As an active member of her community, she hopes to continue centering the decolonial possibilities of Oceanic urbanism through the lens of Kalihi.

JESSICA A. SCHWARTZ, associate professor of musicology at the University of California, Los Angeles, explores DIY research methodologies and the sonics of (dis)identification in anti-colonial context. She is the author of *Radiation Sounds: Marshallese Music and Nuclear Silences* (Duke University Press, 2021) and *Misfit Musicology* (in progress). She has published articles in the journals *Punk & Post-Punk*, *Music & Politics*, *American Quarterly*, and *Women and Music*; helped co-found the Marshallese Educational Initiative (501c3); and hosts the *Punkast Series*, a podcast experience that detours the political through punk.

DANIEL HERNANDEZ publishes under the name Arcia Tecun. He grew up in Utah where he was introduced to kava in the Moana communities. He is of Mayan descent (K'iche', Tz'utujil, Mam, Kaqchikel) with European, Afro, and Judeo-Arabic roots as well. He has completed a doctorate at the University of Auckland in anthropology/ethnomusicology. His research is on kava songs, stories, and urban Indigenous identities.

KATEY THOM is of Pākehā (New Zealand European) descent and is senior lecturer at the Auckland University of Technology. Katey is a social justice researcher in mental health, addictions, and law.

MOANA 'ULU'AVE-HAFOKA was born on the west side of Salt Lake City, Utah, to 'Alama and Losaline 'Ulu'ave, both of Niuafo'ou, Tongatapu. A graduate of Brigham Young University and the Harvard Graduate School of Education, Moana has a career in public policy and higher education.

INDEX